MARVEL MASTERWORKS

PRESENTS

the AMAZING SPIDER-MAN

VOLUME 1

COLLECTING

THE AMAZING SPIDER-MAN NOS. 1-10

& AMAZING FANTASY NO. 15

STAN LEE • STEVE DITKO

MARVEL MASTERWORKS

CREDITS

THE
AMAZING SPIDER-MAN Nos. 1-10
& AMAZING FANTASY No. 15

Writer: **Stan Lee**

Artist: **Steve Ditko**

Penciler: Jack Kirby (No. 8)

Letterers: Art Simek (*Amazing Fantasy No. 15*, Nos. 2, 6-9)
John D'Agostino (No. 1)
John Duffy (Nos. 1-3)
Sam Rosen (Nos. 4, 5, 8, 10)

Color Reconstruction: Transparency Digital

Art Reconstruction: Pond Scum

Special Thanks: Tom Brevoort, Michael Goldman & Ralph Macchio

MARVEL MASTERWORKS: THE AMAZING SPIDER-MAN VOL. 1 — BARNES & NOBLE EDITION. Contains material originally published in magazine form as AMAZING FANTASY #15 and AMAZING SPIDER-MAN (Vol. 1) #1-10. Second printing 2003. ISBN# 0-7607-3793-2. Published by MARVEL COMICS, a division of MARVEL ENTERTAINMENT GROUP, INC. OFFICE OF PUBLICATION: 10 East 40th Street, New York, NY 10016. $12.95 per copy in the U.S. and $20.75 in Canada (GST #R127032852); Canadian Agreement #40668537. **Printed in Italy.** STAN LEE, Chairman Emeritus. For information regarding advertising in Marvel Comics or on Marvel.com, please contact Russell Brown, Executive Vice President, Consumer Products, Promotions and Media Sales at 212-576-8561 or rbrown@marvel.com

10 9 8 7 6 5 4 3 2

MARVEL MASTERWORKS
CONTENTS

INTRODUCTION
BY STAN LEE

Poor Spidey. He was almost never born! Now if that doesn't catch your interest, I'll never write another intro!

It's hard to remember all the arguments that were used to convince me not to feature our friendly neighborhood wall-crawler in his own series. But, just to give you an idea, here are some of them...

You can't name a hero "Spider-Man" because people hate spiders!

You can't feature a teenager as a super hero. Teenagers can only be sidekicks. (Spidey was a teenager when the series started.)

You can't give a hero so many problems. Readers won't think he's heroic enough.

You can't have a hero who isn't big and glamorous and handsome. (Peter was just your average nerdy type of student in those days.)

You can't have a hero whose Aunt May is always wet-nursing him. It's not macho enough.

Well, I guess that gives you the idea. Sort of reminds me of the bumblebee. You know they say the bumblebee can't possible fly because he's designed all wrong aerodynamically. The only thing is, never tell that to a bee! Hey, maybe I should have called him "Bumblebee-Man"? Nah! I figure shooting webs is more exciting than making honey! (See how these big, momentous decisions are made?)

Anyway, Steve Ditko and I chose not to listen to the voices of doom, and we just went right along and turned Spidey loose in a comic book called *Amazing Fantasy*, an issue that was dated August 1962—which means it probably went on sale sometime in the spring of '62 for reasons too convoluted for anyone to understand.

Of course, even that wasn't easy. You see, by the end of '62 the powers-that-be still hadn't okayed my creating a series based on Spider-Man. But, I had an out. We were about to discontinue our *Amazing Fantasy* series. That meant nobody would care what stories I put into it, because it would be the last issue anyway. I can see the light coming on in your eyes! You guessed it! It was a perfect opportunity to make sure the world would be Spideyless no longer, and if the pundits were right and the strip failed, so what? It was the mag's last issue anyway.

Well, not only did ol' Web-head not fail, but the final issue of *Amazing Fantasy*, with Spidey on the cover, proved to be our biggest seller of the year! Naturally, as soon as we saw the sales figures, he was given his own magazine.

The rest is history.

The world's favorite wall-crawler, who violated every rule in comic-book publishing history, became the most popular super hero in all of comicbookdom! And the more unique and more offbeat we made him, the more his popularity grew—which ought to tell us something!

But, up till now, I've been extremely derelict in granting Steve Ditko but a single mention. However, it's only because I was saving the best for last!

Without the amazing artistry and superb story sense of Sturdy Stevey, Spidey would be like a hamburger without ketchup, or Rambo without a snarl. If ever there was a perfect artist and co-plotter for our amazing arachnid, it had to be dazzling Mr. D! His layouts and drawings set the unique illustrative style for the strip, a style that would last for many years to come, a style that made Spidey utterly distinctive among comic strip creations. His sense of pacing, his flair for action scenes, and his ability to make the most outlandish situations look totally believable after he had drawn them gave the early Spider-Man stories an impetus that helped keep them rolling until this very day.

Y'know, even though Spidey is over a quarter-century old, it seems that his career is still beginning. Even now, as I write these wondrous words, a feature film of his exploits is being prepped in Hollywood, his internationally syndicated comic strip is appearing in more than five hundred newspapers throughout the world, and there are presently four best-selling comic books that feature his exploits each and every month, not to mention the countless guest appearances he makes in almost every title Marvel publishes. Not bad for a guy named after an insect that everyone hates!

Well, I could go on and on, and it probably seems to you as if I will, but I think we could both spend our time to better advantage reading the yarns that are waiting for you up front. We've a whole passel of delicious damsels, vile villains and sensational supporting actors ready to thrill and delight you!

So keep thy webs untangled, O True Believer, and never forget—with great power there must also come great responsibility!

EXCELSIOR!

Stan Lee

1987

AMAZING
MC
COMICS CODE AUTHORITY
12¢
FANTASY
15 AUG
INTRODUCING
SPIDER MAN
THOUGH THE WORLD MAY MOCK PETER PARKER, THE TIMID TEEN AGER...
...IT WILL SOON MARVEL AT THE AWESOME MIGHT OF SPIDER-MAN!
ALSO IN THIS ISSUE:
AN IMPORTANT MESSAGE TO YOU, FROM THE EDITOR--ABOUT THE NEW AMAZING!

SPIDER-MAN!

LIKE COSTUMED HEROES? CONFIDENTIALLY, WE IN THE COMIC MAG BUSINESS REFER TO THEM AS "LONG UNDERWEAR CHARACTERS"! AND, AS YOU KNOW, THEY'RE A DIME A DOZEN! BUT, WE THINK YOU MAY FIND OUR SPIDERMAN JUST A BIT... DIFFERENT!
SAY, GANG, WE NEED ONE MORE GUY FOR THE DANCE! HOW ABOUT PETER PARKER OVER THERE?
ARE YOU KIDDIN'? THAT BOOKWORM WOULDN'T KNOW A CHA-CHA FROM A WALTZ!
PETER PARKER? HE'S MIDTOWN HIGH'S ONLY PROFESSIONAL WALLFLOWER!
Stan Lee & S. DITKO
1

AS YOU MAY HAVE GATHERED, PETER PARKER WAS FAR FROM BEING THE BIGGEST MAN ON CAMPUS! BUT, HIS UNCLE BEN THOUGHT HE WAS A PRETTY SPECIAL LAD...
YOU'RE NOT FOOLIN' ME, PETEY! I KNOW YOU'RE AWAKE -- AND IT'S TIME FOR SCHOOL!
GOSH, UNCLE BEN--YOU'RE WORSE THAN A ROOM FULL OF ALARM CLOCKS!

AS FOR PETE'S AUNT MAY, SHE THOUGHT THE SUN ROSE AND SET UPON HER NEPHEW!
I COOKED YOUR FAVORITE BREAKFAST, PETEY--WHEATCAKES!
DON'T FATTEN HIM UP TOO MUCH, DEAR! I CAN HARDLY OUT-WRESTLE HIM NOW!

THE FACULTY AT MIDTOWN HIGH WAS ALSO FOND OF THE CLEAN-CUT, HARD-WORKING HONOR STUDENT!
KEEP UP THE GOOD WORK, PARKER, AND YOU'RE SURE TO RATE A SCHOLARSHIP WHEN YOU GRADUATE!
I'LL DO MY BEST, SIR!

BUT ALAS, OTHER TEENAGERS CAN SOMETIMES, UNWITTINGLY, BE SO VERY CRUEL TO A SHY YOUNG MAN...
SALLY, I, EH, WAS WONDERING IF YOU'RE BUSY TONIGHT...?
PETER, FOR THE UMPTEENTH TIME, YOU'RE JUST NOT MY TYPE...

...NOT WHEN DREAM BOATS LIKE FLASH THOMPSON ARE AROUND!
I ADMIRE YOUR GOOD TASTE, DOLL! GET LOST, BOOKWORM!

LOOK, THERE'S A GREAT NEW EXHIBIT AT THE SCIENCE HALL TONIGHT! WOULD ANY OF YOU LIKE TO GO WITH ME?
SCIENCE HALL! HAH!
YOU STICK TO SCIENCE, SON! WE'LL TAKE THE CHICKS!

YES, FOR SOME, BEING A TEEN-AGER HAS MANY HEART-BREAKING MOMENTS!
SEE YOU AROUND, BOOKWORM!
GIVE OUR REGARDS TO THE ATOM-SMASHERS, PETER!

SOME DAY I'LL SHOW THEM! -SOB- SOME DAY THEY'LL BE SORRY! --SORRY THAT THEY LAUGHED AT ME!
SCIENCE EXHIBIT
EXPERIMENTS IN RADIOACTIVITY
OPEN TO THE PUBLIC
ROOM 30
2

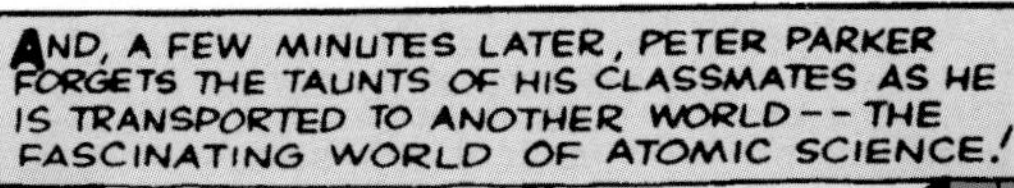

AND, A FEW MINUTES LATER, PETER PARKER FORGETS THE TAUNTS OF HIS CLASSMATES AS HE IS TRANSPORTED TO ANOTHER WORLD -- THE FASCINATING WORLD OF ATOMIC SCIENCE!

AND NOW FOR A DEMONSTRATION OF HOW WE CAN CONTROL RADIOACTIVE RAYS HERE IN THE LABORATORY...

BUT, AS THE EXPERIMENT BEGINS, NO ONE NOTICES A TINY SPIDER, DESCENDING FROM THE CEILING ON AN ALMOST INVISIBLE STRAND OF WEB...

A SPIDER WHOM FATE HAS GIVEN A STARRING, IF BRIEF, ROLE TO PLAY IN THE DRAMA WE CALL LIFE!

ACCIDENTALLY ABSORBING A FANTASTIC AMOUNT OF RADIOACTIVITY, THE DYING INSECT, IN SUDDEN SHOCK, BITES THE NEAREST LIVING THING, AT THE SPLIT SECOND BEFORE LIFE EBBS FROM ITS RADIOACTIVE BODY!
OW!

A-A SPIDER! IT BIT ME! BUT, WHY IS IT BURNING SO? WHY IS IT **GLOWING** THAT WAY??

MY HEAD-- IT FEELS STRANGE! I-I NEED SOME AIR!
LOOKS AS THOUGH OUR EXPERIMENT UNNERVED YOUNG PARKER!
TOO BAD! HE MUST HAVE A WEAK STOMACH!

WHAT'S **HAPPENING** TO ME? I FEEL-- DIFFERENT! AS THOUGH MY ENTIRE BODY IS CHARGED WITH SOME SORT OF FANTASTIC ENERGY!
HONK! HONK!

WRAPPED IN HIS THOUGHTS, PETER DOESN'T HEAR THE AUTO WHICH NARROWLY MISSES HIM, UNTIL THE LAST INSTANT! AND THEN, UNNOTICED BY THE RIDERS, HE UNTHINKINGLY LEAPS TO SAFETY-- BUT WHAT A LEAP IT IS!
THAT WAS **ONE** EGGHEAD WHO WON'T DAYDREAM ANY MORE WHEN HE CROSSES A STREET!
YOU CAN SAY **THAT** AGAIN!
3

WHAT'S COME OVER ME! I-I'M SCALING THIS WALL JUST AS EASILY AS I CAN WALK!

MOMMY! LOOK AT THE MAN WALKING UP THE SIDE OF A BUILDING!
THAT'S THE LAST HORROR MOVIE I TAKE YOU TO, YOUNG MAN!

IT'S INCREDIBLE! I REACHED THE ROOF IN JUST A FEW SECONDS!
WHAT'S THIS?? I CRUSHED THIS STEEL PIPE AS THOUGH IT WERE PAPER!

IT'S THE SPIDER! IT HAS TO BE! SOMEHOW--IN SOME MIRACULOUS WAY, HIS BITE HAS TRANSFERRED HIS OWN POWER--TO ME!

I CAN WALK DOWN THIS CABLE AS EFFORTLESSLY AS THE SPIDER ITSELF CAN GLIDE ALONG ITS WEB!

I-I'VE GOT TO HAVE TIME TO THINK! I'VE GOT TO PLAN WHAT TO DO WITH THIS UNBELIEVABLE ABILITY WHICH FATE HAS GIVEN ME!

A FEW MINUTES LATER...
HMMM... THIS WILL BE A GOOD CHANCE TO TEST MY POWER AGAIN!
$100 TO THE MAN WHO CAN STAY IN THE RING THREE MINUTES WITH CRUSHER HOGAN

FILLED WITH EXCITEMENT, PETE RACES BACK HOME, AND...
I'LL PUT ON SOME OLD CLOTHES, AND LEAVE MY GLASSES HERE! BUT--WHAT IF I FAIL? I DON'T WANT TO BE A LAUGHING STOCK! I-I'LL FIND SOME WAY TO DISGUISE MYSELF!
4

A FEW MINUTES LATER...
I'LL TRY FOR THAT HUNDRED DOLLARS, CRUSHER!
WELL, WELL! IF IT AIN'T A LITTLE MASKED MARVEL! STEP UP, SUCKER!

NOW JUST RELAX, SHORTY! I'LL TRY TO MAKE THIS AS PAINLESS AS POSSIBLE!

IT WORKS! I HAVE THE SPEED, THE AGILITY, THE VERY STRENGTH OF A GIGANTIC SPIDER!
HEY!

PUT ME DOWN! YOU WIN! YOU WIN!

YOU--YOU'RE NOT HUMAN! NOBODY CAN DO THAT!
WANNA BET?

GREATEST ACT I'VE EVER SEEN!
HMMM, THAT MASKED CHARACTER MAY BE JUST WHAT I'VE BEEN LOOKING FOR!
SENSATIONAL! FANTASTIC! AND THAT MASK GIMMICK GIVES HIM JUST THE RIGHT TOUCH OF MYSTERY! HE WAS TERRIFIC!
5

LISTEN, FRIEND, I'M A TV PRODUCER! WITH THAT ACT OF YOURS I CAN MAKE YOU A FORTUNE! AND KEEP THE MASK ANGLE -- IT'S GREAT SHOWMANSHIP! HERE'S MY CARD! CALL ME! YOU'D BE A SMASH ON ED SULLIVAN'S SHOW!
THANKS...

LATER, AT HOME AGAIN...
SHOWMANSHIP?? HE HASN'T SEEN ANYTHING YET! SINCE I HAVE THE POWERS OF A SPIDER, I'LL DESIGN MYSELF A SPIDER COSTUME! AND... OH, HI, AUNT MAY!
YOU LOOKED A LITTLE TIRED, PETEY, SO WE BROUGHT YOU SOME CRACKERS AND MILK!

CRACKERS AND MILK! BLESS 'EM-- IF THEY ONLY KNEW!
NOW LET'S SEE-- A SPIDER NEEDS A WEB! THIS LITTLE DEVICE SHOULD JUST DO THE TRICK!

I'LL FASTEN ONE TO EACH ARM-- IT'LL OPERATE BY THE SLIGHTEST PRESSURE OF ANY FINGER!

I'LL NEED A NAME --WELL, GUESS SPIDERMAN IS AS GOOD AS ANY! LOOKS PRETTY GOOD, IF I DO SAY SO MYSELF!

SO, THEY LAUGHED AT ME FOR BEING A BOOKWORM, EH? WELL, ONLY A SCIENCE MAJOR COULD HAVE CREATED A DEVICE LIKE THIS!

WITH SOME STRONG LIQUID CEMENT AT THE END, I CAN PULL MYSELF UP ANYWHERE WITH MY LITTLE WEB!
AND MY COSTUME IS THIN ENOUGH TO WEAR, UNSEEN, UNDER MY STREET CLOTHES!

OKAY, WORLD-- BETTER HANG ONTO YOUR HAT! HERE COMES THE SPIDER-MAN!
6

PART 2
NOW ANYBODY WITH THE INTELLIGENCE OF A SEVEN YEAR OLD KNOWS THAT IF A MAN APPEARED ON TV WHO SEEMED TO BE MORE SPIDER THAN HUMAN, HE'D BE AN OVERNIGHT SENSATION! ESPECIALLY WHEN HIS FEATS WERE PERFORMED WITHOUT THE HELP OF TRICK PHOTOGRAPHY! WELL, YOU CAN JUST IMAGINE HOW THE PUBLIC REACTED TO SPIDERMAN!
I'M SEEIN' IT WITH MY OWN EYES, AND I STILL DON'T BELIEVE IT!
TV

SURE THEY LOOK AMAZED, INCREDULOUS, AWESTRICKEN! WOULDN'T YOU???

AFTER ALL, WHEN WAS THE LAST TIME YOU SAW A MAN WITH HIS OWN FANTASTIC SPIDER WEB???

OKAY, SPIDER-MAN --CUT! THAT'S ENOUGH! DON'T SHOW 'EM TOO MUCH! LEAVE 'EM BEGGIN' FOR MORE!
7

AS HIS FIRST TV SPECTACULAR ENDS, PETER PARKER BREATHES THE FIRST SWEET SCENT OF FAME AND SUCCESS!
I'M FROM LIFE! WE'LL PAY ANY PRICE FOR A PICTURE SPREAD!
SIGN WITH ME! I'LL PUT YOU IN THE MOVIES!
WAIT! WE WANT AN INTERVIEW!
SEE MY AGENT, BOYS! I'M BUSY!

WHEW! RID OF 'EM AT LAST!
HEY! WHAT'S GOIN' ON??
STOP! THIEF! STOP HIM! IF HE MAKES IT TO THE ELEVATOR, HE'LL GET AWAY!

MADE IT!

I'M SAFE NOW! THAT COP CAN NEVER GET DOWN TO THE LOBBY AS FAST AS I CAN IN THIS HIGH-SPEED EXPRESS ELEVATOR! LUCKY THAT GOON IN A COSTUME DIDN'T STOP ME!

WHAT'S WITH YOU, MISTER?? ALL YOU HADDA DO WAS TRIP HIM, OR HOLD HIM JUST FOR A MINUTE!
SORRY, PAL! THAT'S YOUR JOB! I'M THRU BEING PUSHED AROUND --BY ANYONE! FROM NOW ON I JUST LOOK OUT FOR NUMBER ONE --THAT MEANS--ME!

I OUGHTTA RUN YOU IN--
SAVE YOUR BREATH, BUDDY! I'VE GOT THINGS TO DO!

AND, A FEW HOURS LATER...
PETER, YOU KNOW THAT MICROSCOPE YOU'VE ALWAYS WANTED? YOUR UNCLE AND I BOUGHT IT FOR YOU THIS AFTERNOON!
GOSH, THAT'S TERRIFIC!

YOU'RE THE GREATEST FAMILY ANY FELLA EVER HAD!
THEY'RE THE ONLY ONES WHO'VE EVER BEEN KIND TO ME! I'LL SEE TO IT THAT THEY'RE ALWAYS HAPPY, BUT THE REST OF THE WORLD CAN GO HANG FOR ALL I CARE!
8

IN THE DAYS THAT FOLLOW, THE SPIDERMAN BECOMES THE SENSATION OF THE NATION!
SPIDERMAN SLATED FOR NEW TV SERIES!
Daily Chronicle
SPIDERMAN WINS SHOWBIZ AWARD!
The VIEWER 10¢
SPIDERMAN PLAYS TO PACKED HOUSE!
Daily Voice
WHO IS THE SPIDERMAN?

AND, ONE EVENING AS PETER PARKER RETURNS HOME FROM A PERSONAL APPEARANCE...
A POLICE CAR! IN FRONT OF OUR HOUSE! WHAT CAN BE WRONG??

BAD NEWS, SON--YOUR UNCLE HAS BEEN SHOT--MURDERED!
UNCLE BEN --DEAD! NO! NO, IT CAN'T BE!

WHO DID IT?? WHO SHOT HIM??
IT WAS A BURGLAR-- YOUR UNCLE SURPRISED HIM! BUT DON'T WORRY, LAD! WE'VE GOT HIM TRAPPED! HE'S IN THE OLD ACME WAREHOUSE AT THE WATERFRONT! WE'LL GET HIM!

YOUR AUNT IS NEXT DOOR-- THE NEIGHBORS ARE LOOKING AFTER HER! WAIT--
I'VE GOT TO GO! I'VE GOT TO GET HIM!

I KNOW THE OLD ACME WAREHOUSE! IT'S BEEN DE-SERTED FOR YEARS! A KILLER COULD HOLD OFF AN ARMY IN THAT GLOOMY, OLD PLACE!

BUT HE WON'T HOLD OFF-- SPIDERMAN!
9

THE WAREHOUSE IS AT THE OTHER SIDE OF TOWN...

...BUT I'LL BE THERE IN NO TIME!

MEANWHILE...
HE'S IN THERE SOMEWHERE, BUT HE'LL PICK US OFF LIKE FLIES IF WE CHARGE HIM!

ALL I GOTTA DO IS HOLD 'EM OFF TILL THE MOON GOES DOWN, THEN I OUGHTTA BE ABLE TO SLIP AWAY IN THE DARK!
YOU'LL NEVER ESCAPE AGAIN, MURDERER!

HUH?? WHAT THE-- ???
SURPRISED TO SEE ME?

NOT HALF SO SURPRISED AS YOU'RE GOING TO BE!

GOTTA GET AWAY! GOTTA HIDE! I MUST BE SEEIN' THINGS!
10

THERE'S NO PLACE ON EARTH WHERE YOU CAN HIDE FROM ME!

FIRST, MY WEB WILL RELIEVE YOU OF YOUR GUN!
WHIZZZZT!

AND THEN MY FISTS WILL DO THE REST!

THAT-- THAT FACE! IT'S-- OH NO, IT CAN'T BE!
IT'S THE FUGITIVE WHO RAN PAST ME! THE ONE I DIDN'T STOP WHEN I HAD THE CHANCE!

I HATE TO DO IT, BUT WE'LL HAVE TO RUSH HIM NOW! CAN'T TAKE A CHANCE OF HIM SLIPPING BY IN THE DARK!
CAPTAIN-- LOOK!!

IT'S HIM!
ON A-- SPIDER'S WEB!

AND, A SHORT DISTANCE AWAY...
MY FAULT-- ALL MY FAULT! IF ONLY I HAD STOPPED HIM WHEN I COULD HAVE! BUT I DIDN'T-- AND NOW --UNCLE BEN-- IS DEAD...

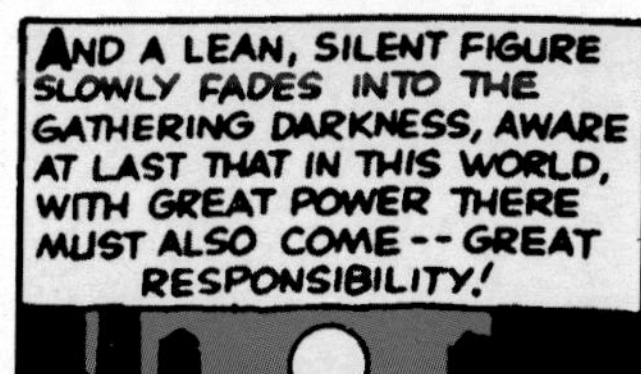

AND A LEAN, SILENT FIGURE SLOWLY FADES INTO THE GATHERING DARKNESS, AWARE AT LAST THAT IN THIS WORLD, WITH GREAT POWER THERE MUST ALSO COME -- GREAT RESPONSIBILITY!

AND SO A LEGEND IS BORN AND A NEW NAME IS ADDED TO THE ROSTER OF THOSE WHO MAKE THE WORLD OF FANTASY THE MOST EXCITING REALM OF ALL!

BE SURE TO SEE THE NEXT ISSUE OF AMAZING FANTASY --- FOR THE FURTHER AMAZING EXPLOITS OF AMERICA'S MOST DIFFERENT NEW TEEN-AGE IDOL -- SPIDERMAN!

the End

INC.
12¢
the AMAZING SPIDER-MAN
MC
APPROVED BY THE COMICS CODE AUTHORITY
1 MAR.
2 GREAT FEATURE-LENGTH SPIDER-MAN THRILLERS!
THE FANTASTIC FOUR THINK I'M TRAPPED! BUT THEY DON'T SUSPECT MY REAL POWER!
EXTRA ADDED ATTRACTION: SPIDER-MAN MEETS THE FANTASTIC FOUR, AS
"the CHAMELEON STRIKES!"

SPIDER-MAN
SCRIPT: STAN LEE • ART: STEVE DITKO • LETTERING: JOHNNY DEE
NOTE: SPIDER-MAN FIRST APPEARED AS A FEATURE IN AMAZING FANTASY#15 AUG.! SO GREAT WAS YOUR RESPONSE VIA LETTERS AND POSTCARDS, THAT IT WAS DECIDED TO GIVE HIM HIS OWN MAGAZINE! A BRIEF SUMMARY FOLLOWS...
FREAK!
PUBLIC MENACE!
SURE, YOU'VE READ MANY STORIES ABOUT MANY DIFFERENT MAGAZINE HEROES! BUT THERE'S NEVER BEEN A STORY LIKE THIS ONE-- BECAUSE THERE'S NEVER BEEN A HERO LIKE---
SPIDER-MAN!
V-816
1

OUR SCENE IS THE BEDROOM OF PETER PARKER, THE TEEN-AGE STUDENT WHOM MANY CONSIDER TO BE A SHY BOOKWORM... BUT, OH, IF THEY ONLY KNEW!
UNCLE BEN IS DEAD! AND ALL BECAUSE I WAS TOO LATE TO SAVE HIM!
MY SPIDER-MAN COSTUME! I WISH THERE WERE NO SUCH THING!

IT ALL STARTED WHEN I WAS BITTEN BY A RADIO-ACTIVE SPIDER...
AND I FOUND MYSELF POSSESSED OF A SPIDER'S POWERS! SO I DESIGNED A COSTUME TO GO INTO SHOW BUSINESS AND CASH IN!
OUCH!

"BUT WHILE I WAS BUSY SHOWING OFF, AN ARMED BURGLAR FIRED ONE FATAL SHOT AT UNCLE BEN WHEN HE WAS SURPRISED ROBBING OUR HOUSE!"
"AS SOON AS I LEARNED WHAT HAD HAPPENED, I SPED THRU THE CITY VIA MY SPIDER'S WEB, LUSTING FOR VENGEANCE!"
HE WON'T ESCAPE SPIDERMAN!
"AND I SOON CAUGHT THE KILLER, AND TURNED HIM OVER TO THE POLICE!"
GOT YOU!
Y-YOU AINT HUMAN!

AND NOW, UNCLE BEN IS GONE, AND AUNT MAY AND I ARE ALONE!

AND WHAT'S WORSE, WITHOUT UNCLE BEN, WE'VE NO MONEY TO PAY OUR BILLS!
PLEASE GIVE ME A LITTLE MORE TIME! I'LL PAY THE RENT NEXT WEEK, IF YOU'LL ONLY WAIT!
2

AND SO...
AUNT MAY, THERE'S ONLY ONE THING TO DO! I'VE GOT TO QUIT SCHOOL AND GET A JOB!
NO, PETER, YOU MUSTN'T! YOUR UNCLE ALWAYS DREAMED OF YOU BEING A SCIENTIST SOME DAY! YOU MUST CONTINUE YOUR STUDIES!

BUT I'VE GOT TO HELP AUNT MAY SOMEHOW! WAIT! WITH MY POWERS AS SPIDER-MAN, I CAN DO ANYTHING!

"I CAN GO ANYWHERE! NO ONE, NOTHING CAN STOP ME!"
"ANY AMOUNT OF MONEY COULD BE MINE--JUST FOR THE TAKING!"

"BUT NO! WHAT AM I THINKING OF??! I'M NO CRIMINAL! I'M NOT A THIEF! BESIDES, IF I WERE EVER ARRESTED AND IMPRISONED, IT WOULD BREAK AUNT MAY'S HEART!"
NO! THERE'S ONLY ONE OTHER WAY! I'VE GOT TO PERFORM AGAIN! I'VE GOT TO BRING MY SPIDER-MAN ACT BEFORE THE PUBLIC ONCE MORE! I'LL CALL A BOOKING AGENT TONIGHT!

A FEW DAYS LATER ... AT SCHOOL...
HEY, GANG! LOOK! SPIDER-MAN'S GONNA PUT ON A SHOW AT THE TOWN HALL TONIGHT!
AND THE ADMISSION IS ONLY A DOLLAR!
LET'S ALL GO!
COUNT ME OUT, KIDS! I CAN'T MAKE IT!

WE MIGHT HAVE KNOWN! HE'D RATHER STUDY!
AW, WHO NEEDS THAT WALKIN' BOOKWORM ANYWAY!
IT'LL BE MORE FUN WITHOUT HIM!
3

THAT NIGHT, AS THE AUDIENCE IS AMAZED BY SPIDER-MAN'S PROWESS, NONE SUSPECT THE REAL REASON THAT PETER PARKER COULDN'T BE IN THE AUDIENCE ...
I COULDN'T VERY WELL BE DOING THIS ACT AND SITTING IN THE AUDIENCE ALSO!

FINALLY, AFTER THE SHOW...
IT'S TIME TO PAY YOU, SPIDER-MAN, BUT I CAN'T GIVE YOU CASH! I'VE GOT TO GIVE YOU A CHECK, SO THERE'S A RECORD FOR TAXES! WHAT NAME SHOULD I WRITE THE CHECK OUT TO?
NAME?? I CAN'T TELL YOU MY REAL NAME! NO ONE MUST KNOW MY IDENTITY!

JUST MAKE OUT THE CHECK TO SPIDER-MAN!
OKAY, YOU'RE THE BOSS! BUT YOU'LL HAVE A MIGHTY TOUGH TIME CASHING IT!

A TOUGH TIME CASHING IT, EH? WELL, WE'LL JUST SEE ABOUT THAT!

I'D LIKE TO CASH THIS CHECK!
I'LL HAVE TO SEE SOME IDENTIFICATION!
WHAT ABOUT MY COSTUME?
DON'T BE SILLY! ANYONE CAN WEAR A COSTUME! DO YOU HAVE A SOCIAL SECURITY CARD, OR A DRIVER'S LICENSE IN THE NAME OF SPIDER-MAN??
N-NO-- I DON'T!

BUT, AS SPIDER-MAN FINDS THAT HE CANNOT CASH HIS DESPERATELY-NEEDED CHECK, JUST ACROSS TOWN, A MAN AT A TYPEWRITER IS MAKING STILL MORE TROUBLE FOR HIM!
WHEN I'M THRU WITH THIS ARTICLE, SPIDER-MAN WILL BE RUN OUT OF TOWN!

AND, THE NEXT NIGHT...
MIGHT AS WELL GO ON BACK WHERE YOU CAME FROM, SPIDER-MAN! THERE'LL BE NO SHOW TONIGHT--OR ANY NIGHT!
WHAT? WHY? WHAT HAPPENED?
4

THIS HAPPENED! LOOK AT THIS EDITORIAL! THE PAPER HAS EVERYONE SO STEAMED UP, THEY'LL PROBABLY TOSS YOU IN JAIL IF YOU SHOW YOUR FACE!
BUT WHY? WHAT HAVE THEY GOT AGAINST ME? WHAT HAVE I DONE?
SPIDER-MAN MENACE

BUT, NOT SATISFIED WITH MERELY WRITING EDITORIALS, J. JONAH JAMESON, PUBLISHER OF THE POWERFUL "DAILY BUGLE" DELIVERS LECTURES ALL OVER TOWN...
WE CANNOT ALLOW THAT MASKED MENACE TO TAKE THE LAW INTO HIS OWN HANDS! HE IS A BAD INFLUENCE ON OUR YOUNGSTERS!

CHILDREN MAY TRY TO IMITATE HIS FANTASTIC FEATS!

THINK WHAT WOULD HAPPEN IF THEY MAKE A HERO OUT OF THIS LAWLESS, INHUMAN MONSTER! WE MUST NOT PERMIT IT!

"I SAY THAT SPIDER-MAN MUST BE OUTLAWED! THERE IS NO PLACE FOR SUCH A DANGEROUS CREATURE IN OUR FAIR CITY!"

THE YOUTH OF THIS NATION MUST LEARN TO RESPECT REAL HEROES -- MEN SUCH AS MY SON, JOHN JAMESON, THE TEST PILOT! NOT SELFISH FREAKS SUCH AS SPIDER-MAN -- A MASKED MENACE WHO REFUSES TO EVEN LET US KNOW HIS TRUE IDENTITY!

I DON'T GET IT! HOW DO OTHER SUPERHUMAN GUYS, LIKE THE FANTASTIC FOUR AND THE ANT MAN, GET AWAY WITH IT ?? NOBODY BOTHERS THEM! AND THEY ALWAYS SEEM TO MAKE ENOUGH DOUGH!
BAH! I DON'T EVEN BELIEVE THAT THERE IS A SPIDER-MAN! IT'S ALL A PUBLICITY STUNT!
DAILY BUGLE
SPIDER-MAN MENACE
SPIDER-MAN MENACE
SPIDER-MAN MENACE
5

WELL, IF I CAN'T MAKE A LIVING AS SPIDER-MAN, THE ONLY **OTHER** THING TO DO IS FIND A PART-TIME JOB! I'LL TAKE A LOOK THRU THE WANT ADS...

BUT AGAIN PETER PARKER MEETS WITH FRUSTRATION...
SORRY, SONNY! I AIN'T LOOKIN' FOR A SCHOOL KID! THE JOB I ADVERTISED IS FOR A **MAN!**
BUT...
EXTRA! JOHN JAMESON ABOUT TO ORBIT EARTH IN ROCKET...
DAILY BUGLE

SAY--THAT LOOKS LIKE--IT **IS!** IT'S AUNT MAY! I WONDER WHERE SHE'S GOING?

OH, **NO!** SHE'S PAWNING HER JEWELRY!
SHE MUST BE **DESPERATE** FOR MONEY! BUT SHE DOESN'T WANT ME TO KNOW! SHE DOESN'T WANT TO WORRY ME!

FOR ME! SHE'S DOING IT ALL FOR ME! AND THERE'S NO WAY I CAN REPAY HER! NO WAY I CAN HELP HER! I CAN'T EVEN FIND A **JOB!**

EXTRA! JOHN JAMESON, SON OF THE PUBLISHER OF THE "DAILY BUGLE" ABOUT TO ORBIT EARTH! **EXTRA!**
IT'S ALL **HIS** FAULT! BECAUSE OF **HIM**, I CAN'T PERFORM IN PUBLIC AS THE SPIDER-MAN!

BUT I CAN'T GIVE UP! I'VE GOT TO EARN SOME MONEY--SOMEHOW!
I CAN'T LET AUNT MAY DOWN! EVEN IF IT MEANS THE SPIDER-MAN WILL AGAIN STALK THE CITY BY NIGHT!
6

SPIDER-MAN
PART 2
NEXT DAY, HAVING NOTHING BETTER TO DO, PETER PARKER FINDS HIMSELF AMONG THE SPECTATORS ANXIOUSLY AWAITING THE ORBIT FLIGHT OF JOHN JAMESON!
IT SURE MUST TAKE A LOT OF COURAGE TO GO UP IN ONE OF THOSE BABIES!
I'LL BET EVEN SPIDER-MAN WOULD THINK TWICE BEFORE VOLUNTEERING FOR THIS RIDE, HUH?
I SUPPOSE SO...
FIFTEEN MINUTES TO BLAST-OFF! ALL UNAUTHORIZED PERSONNEL CLEAR THE FIELD!

THIS IS IT, JOHN! MAKE YOUR COUNTRY PROUD OF YOU, SON-- AS PROUD AS I, YOUR FATHER, AM TODAY!
I'LL DO MY BEST, DAD-- I PROMISE!
GOOD LUCK TO YOU, BOY!

MINUTES LATER, THE CAPSULE, WITH JOHN JAMESON INSIDE, IS SET IN ORBIT BY A PERFECT LAUNCH...
7

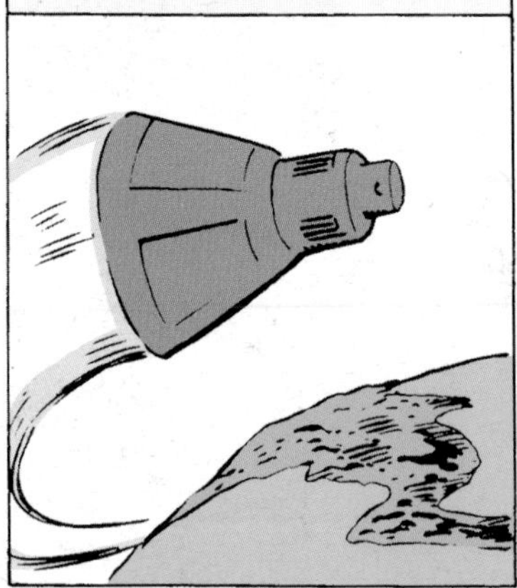
BUT THEN, DISASTER STRIKES! A SMALL SECTION OF THE FORWARD GUIDANCE PACKAGE BREAKS LOOSE FROM THE CAPSULE, AND FALLS INTO SPACE...

WITHOUT THIS ESSENTIAL GUIDANCE UNIT, THE CAPSULE GOES INTO AN ERRATIC ORBIT, COMPLETELY OUT OF CONTROL!
SOMETHING'S WRONG! I CAN'T CONTROL HER!

THIS FLASHING RED LIGHT! IT CAN MEAN ONLY ONE THING! I'VE LOST THE HEART OF THE GUIDANCE DEVICE! THERE IS NO WAY TO DIRECT THE CAPSULE NOW!

MEANWHILE, MILES AWAY...
WHAT IS IT? WHAT WENT WRONG?
CAPSULE IS OUT OF CONTROL, SIR! COMPONENT 24-3B HAS BROKEN LOOSE! CONDITION RED!

WHAT'S THAT?? WITHOUT THE MISSING PART HE WILL CONTINUE TO GO INTO LOWER AND LOWER ORBIT UNTIL HE CRASHES TO EARTH!
GENTLEMEN, WE HAVEN'T MUCH TIME! WE MUST FIND SOME WAY TO SAVE JOHN JAMESON'S LIFE, EVEN THOUGH THE CAPSULE IS DOOMED!

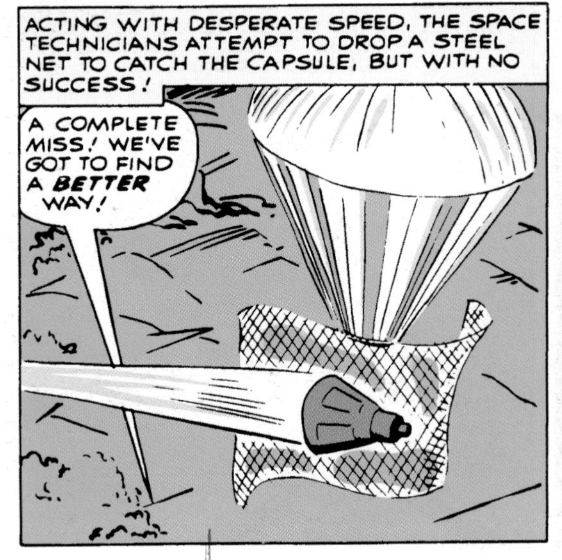
ACTING WITH DESPERATE SPEED, THE SPACE TECHNICIANS ATTEMPT TO DROP A STEEL NET TO CATCH THE CAPSULE, BUT WITH NO SUCCESS!
A COMPLETE MISS! WE'VE GOT TO FIND A BETTER WAY!

WHILE, UNSUSPECTED BY ALL, A BETTER WAY DOES EXIST! IN THE FORM OF PETER PARKER, WHO HAS OBSERVED THE ENTIRE DRAMATIC EVENT...
THERE'S ONLY ONE PERSON WHO CAN SAVE JOHN JAMESON...
8

...AND THAT IS... SPIDER-MAN!

I'VE GOT TO REACH THE MISSILE CONTROL CENTER THE FASTEST WAY--THE WAY THAT ONLY SPIDER-MAN CAN TAKE!

MADE IT! AND NOW...
WE HAVE A SPARE 24-3B GUIDANCE UNIT... BUT THERE IS NO WAY TO GET IT TO JAMESON IN TIME!

YOU'RE WRONG! THERE IS A WAY!
SPIDER-MAN!

LET ME HAVE THE MISSING UNIT! I'LL GET IT TO THE CAPSULE SOMEHOW!
VERY WELL! WE HAVE NOTHING TO LOSE! THERE IS NO WAY WE CAN DO IT!
SPIDER-MAN-- BAH! HE'S JUST A PUBLICITY-SEEKING PHONY! HE'S TRYING TO GRAB A HEADLINE! WHAT CAN HE DO?

INSTEAD OF FLAPPING YOUR LIPS, MISTER--JUST WATCH AND SEE WHAT I CAN DO!
WAIT!
9

THE CAPSULE IS GETTING LOWER EVERY SECOND! I'VE GOT TO REACH A JET FAST!

ARRIVING AT A NEARBY FIELD, SPIDER-MAN'S AMAZING WEB SHOOTS OUT, ENGULFING THE GUARD'S GUN HAND BEFORE THE SENTRY CAN FIRE...
HALT! IDENTIFY YOURSELF!
NO TIME FOR THAT NOW!

WITHIN SECONDS, THE MIGHTY COSTUMED FIGURE HAS COMMANDEERED A PLANE AND A PILOT, AS THEY TAKE TO THE AIR...
I'LL PROBABLY BE GROUNDED FOREVER FOR DOING THIS, SPIDER-MAN, BUT I GOT A HUNCH THAT IF ANYONE CAN SAVE THAT POOR JOKER, YOU'RE THE GUY!

HERE COMES THE CAPSULE NOW! BUT WE COULD NEVER CATCH IT!

WE DON'T HAVE TO CATCH IT!
WAIT! WHAT ARE YOU GONNA DO?

I'VE GOT TO HITCH A RIDE ON THAT THING AS IT PASSES BY!
THIS WILL BE MY FIRST AND LAST CHANCE! IF IT DOESN'T WORK, LOOK OUT BELOW!
10

HERE GOES!
TWNNNNG!

I HIT IT!

MUSTN'T LET GO!

UGH--I'VE GOT TO PULL MYSELF UP--FIGHTING AGAINST ALL THIS WIND RESISTANCE!
EVEN MY STRENGTH CAN JUST BARELY DO IT!

THERE! I REACHED IT! BUT NOW...
THE CAPSULE IS LOSING ALTITUDE DANGEROUSLY! CAN I ATTACH THE MISSING UNIT IN TIME??!
11

SPIDER-MAN
PART 3
WHAT A LUCKY BREAK! IT FIT IN PLACE AS SMOOTH AS SILK!

AND, WITHIN THE CAPSULE...
CAPSULE UNDER MANUAL CONTROL AGAIN! WILL EJECT CHUTE AND LAND IMMEDIATELY!

HE'S SAFE! I DID IT!
12

SPIDER-MAN SUCCEEDED! THE CAPSULE IS ABOUT TO LAND!
MY BOY! HE'S **SAFE!**

THIS IS AS GOOD A TIME AS ANY FOR ME TO GET OFF! I'LL BET I'M THE ONLY LIVING PERSON WHO EVER HAD A RIDE LIKE **THAT** BEFORE!

I'D BETTER MAKE MYSELF SCARCE NOW! I'D JUST BE EMBARRASSED IF EVERYONE WANTS TO CONGRATULATE ME AND MAKE A BIG FUSS ABOUT WHAT I'VE DONE!

ANYWAY, FROM NOW ON I GUESS I SHOULDN'T HAVE ANY TROUBLE ABOUT PERFORMING IN PUBLIC! I'LL BET EVEN MISTER JAMESON HIMSELF WOULD HIRE ME!

BUT, WHEN HE READS THE NEXT EDITION OF THE NEWSPAPER, PETER PARKER IS ASTOUNDED TO SEE...
OH, NO! IT **CAN'T** BE!

IT ISN'T POSSIBLE! WHY? **WHY??**
5¢ DAILY BUGLE 5¢
THIS NEWSPAPER DEMANDS THAT SPIDER-MAN BE ARRESTED AND PROSECUTED!
Editorial by: J. JONAH JAMESON
13

AND, FINALLY--UNDER PRESSURE OF THE ANGRY NEWSPAPERMAN'S CONTINUAL BARRAGE...

AND SO, A LONELY BOY SITS AND BROODS, WITH THE FATE OF SOCIETY AT STAKE! WHAT WILL HIS DECISION BE? WHAT WILL SPIDER-MAN DO NEXT?? ONLY TIME WILL TELL!

The END

SPIDER-MAN
VS. THE CHAMELEON!
HOW CAN YOU DEFEAT A MAN WHO CAN CHANGE HIS IDENTITY BEFORE YOU CAN CATCH HIM?? PERHAPS YOU DON'T KNOW THE ANSWER, BUT THE SPIDER-MAN WAS DETERMINED TO FIND OUT-- NO MATTER WHAT THE COST!
EXTRA BONUS EXTRA!! IN THIS SAME AMAZING TALE YOU WILL MEET AMERICA'S MOST FAMOUS, MOST COLORFUL GROUP OF SUPER-ADVENTURERS THE FANTASTIC FOUR!!
SCRIPT........ STAN LEE
ART........... STEVE DITKO
LETTERING.... JOHN DUFFI
1

WE KNOW HIM AS PETER PARKER ...BUT THE WORLD KNOWS HIM ONLY AS SPIDER-MAN!
SAY! WHY DIDN'T I THINK OF IT BEFORE? THERE'S THE WAY I CAN MAKE SOME MONEY--BY JOINING THE FANTASTIC FOUR!
FANTASTIC FOUR

THEY'LL PROBABLY JUMP AT THE CHANCE TO HAVE A TEEN-AGER WITH SUPER POWERS WORKING WITH THEM! IT'LL BE A NATURAL!

HERE'S THEIR PRIVATE ELEVATOR, BUT THE BLAMED THING ISN'T WORKING!
UH OH-- I FORGOT! IT CAN ONLY BE OPERATED BY ONE OF THE FOUR, USING A SPECIAL ELECTRONIC BEAM!

WELL, THAT WON'T STOP SPIDER-MAN! FORCING A COUPLE OF LOCKED DOORS OPEN IS MERE CHILD'S PLAY FOR-- HECK! I DIDN'T FIGURE THE ELEVATOR WOULD BE ABOVE ME! NO ROOM TO CLIMB PAST IT!

MINUTES LATER, PETER PARKER REACHES THE ROOF OF AN ADJOINING BUILDING...
WELL, THERE'S MORE THAN ONE WAY TO SKIN A CAT! I SHOULD'VE THOUGHT OF THIS RIGHT AWAY!

THEY'LL PROBABLY BE TWICE AS IMPRESSED WHEN THEY SEE HOW EASILY I GET INTO THEIR PRIVATE SKYSCRAPER HEADQUARTERS!

HERE GOES NOTHING!

MEANWHILE, DOWN BELOW...
IT'S THE SPIDER-MAN! WHAT A BONUS I'LL GET FOR THIS SHOT!
HE'S HEAD-ING FOR THE FANTASTIC FOUR'S HEAD-QUARTERS!
HE BALANCES HIMSELF ON THAT STRAND OF WEB LIKE A HUMAN SPIDER!

AT THAT MOMENT, AN ALARM RINGS IN THE READY ROOM OF THE FANTASTIC FOUR...
THE ALARM! SOMEONE IS TRYING TO SNEAK IN!
HE MUST BE SOME KINDA NUT TO THINK HE CAN TAKE US BY SURPRISE!
BRIN-N-NG!

THERE'S HIS PICTURE ON OUR VIEW-PLATE! IT'S SPIDER-MAN!
WHY DIDN'T HE PHONE FOR AN APPOINT-MENT, LIKE ANYONE ELSE?
'CAUSE HE'S A TEEN-AGE CORNBALL SHOW-OFF, JUST LIKE THE TORCH!

HOW OBLIGING OF THEM TO LEAVE A WINDOW OPEN FOR ME! THIS IS A BREEZE!
ACTIVATE DEFENSE MEASURE B, JUST TO BE SAFE!

GREETINGS, GROUP! YOU SHOULDN'T MAKE IT SO EASY FOR PEOPLE TO DROP IN ON YA!

GOT NEWS FOR YOU, LOUD-MOUTH--IT AIN'T THAT EASY!
WHA--? A PLEXI-GLASS CAGE! DROPPED FROM THE CEILING!

THIS GIZMO MAY KEEP OUT THE RIFF-RAFF, GRUESOME, BUT IT'S A JOKE TO ME!
THAT DEVICE COST US THOUSANDS! IF YOU WRECK IT--

DON'T WORRY, RUBBER-FACE! THIS SQUIRT'S GONNA BE TAUGHT SOME MANNERS, RIGHT NOW!
OWW! YA BIG APE--WHO DO YA THINK YOU'RE PUSHIN' AROUND?

DID YA FORGET YOU'RE MESSIN' WITH A GUY WHO HAS THE PROPORTIONATE STRENGTH OF A SPIDER?
FOR CRYIN' OUT--! THAT'S WHAT I GET FOR PULLIN' MY PUNCH ON ACCOUNTA HIS SIZE!

NOW HOLD IT, SON! WE DON'T WANT TO FIGHT WITH ANY STRANGERS--AT LEAST, NOT TILL WE KNOW WHAT WE'RE FIGHTIN' ABOUT!
WHO'S FIGHTIN'? JUST CONSIDER THIS A LITTLE EXHIBITION!

HE CAUGHT MY HAND IN THAT NET OF HIS! HE CERTAINLY DOES LIVE UP TO HIS NAME!
3

WHILE INVISIBLE, I MIGHT BE ABLE TO GET THIS ROPE OVER OUR IMPETUOUS YOUNG FRIEND!
MY SPIDER INSTINCT SENSES DANGER BEHIND ME! HAVE TO MOVE FAST!

WHO TOSSED THAT ROPE? DON'T SEE ANYONE!
WAIT! IT MUST BE THE INVISIBLE GIRL!
WELL, I'LL JUST GIVE 'ER A WHIRL FOR HER MONEY!

THAT'S IT, YOU ANIMATED INSECT! FUN'S OVER! I'LL SETTLE YOU NOW!
FLAME ON!
HE'S GOT ME IN A CIRCLE OF FLAME!

WELL, I'LL JUST JUMP OVER THAT CLOWN'S LITTLE TRAP...
...AND KEEP OUTTA REACH UNTIL HIS FLAME DIES DOWN!
THEN IT'LL BE MY TURN!
HEY! STAY STILL, DARN IT!

OKAY--THAT'S IT! NO MORE FUN AND GAMES, FELLA! SOMEONE MIGHT GET HURT! NOW, SUPPOSE YOU TELL US WHAT YOU'RE HERE FOR!
GET OUTTA THE WAY, KILL-JOY! GIMME ANOTHER CRACK AT 'IM!
IT'S ABOUT TIME SOME-ONE ASKED ME!

I CAME UP HERE TO JOIN UP WITH YOU! I WANNA BE A MEMBER OF THE FANTASTIC FOUR!
SO I THOUGHT I'D GIVE YOU A DEMONSTRATION OF WHAT I CAN DO!
SO NOW, LET'S GET DOWN TO BUSINESS... HOW MUCH DOES THE JOB PAY? I FIGURE I'M WORTH YOUR TOP SALARY!

I KNEW IT! THAT KOOK HAS ROCKS IN HIS HEAD!
AFRAID YOU MADE A MISTAKE, SPIDER-MAN! WE'RE A NON-PROFIT ORGANIZATION!
WE PAY NO SALARIES OR BONUSES! ANY PROFIT WE MAKE GOES INTO SCIENTIFIC RESEARCH!
YOU CAME TO THE WRONG PLACE, PAL! THIS ISN'T GENERAL MOTORS!

WE JUST KEEP ENOUGH MONEY TO PAY OUR EXPENSES! EVERY OTHER CENT GOES INTO DEVELOPING THE MOST EFFECTIVE SUPER-CRIME-FIGHTING APPARATUS WE CAN CREATE!
BESIDES, AREN'T YOU WANTED BY THE POLICE? THIS ISN'T "OUTLAWS ANONYMOUS"!

I MIGHT HAVE KNOWN! YOU'RE JUST LIKE ALL THE REST! READY TO BELIEVE THE WORST OF ANYONE!
OKAY, KEEP ME OUT OF YOUR GROUP! WHO NEEDS YOU? I'LL MAKE YOU GUYS LOOK LIKE PIKERS!
WAIT! COME BACK!

TOO BAD HE LEFT SO SUDDENLY! PERHAPS WE COULD HAVE **HELPED** HIM!
AWW! WE'VE GOT **ENOUGH** PROBLEM KIDS TO WORRY ABOUT NOW!
SOMEHOW, I HAVE A FEELING WE'LL BE HEARING **MORE** FROM THAT YOUNG MAN IN THE FUTURE!

AND NOW OUR SCENE SHIFTS TO A DEFENSE INSTALLATION AT THE EDGE OF TOWN...
WITH MY MULTI-POCKET DISGUISE VEST, IT WILL BE AN EASY MATTER FOR **THE CHAMELEON** TO BECOME **YOU,** FRIEND JANITOR!

MINUTES LATER...
SO FAR SO GOOD! DISGUISED AS THE JANITOR, IT WAS EASY TO GAIN ACCESS TO THIS RESTRICTED AREA!
AND NOW, ANOTHER FAST CHANGE AND I WILL TAKE THE IDENTITY OF PROFESSOR NEWTON!

HAH! NOTHING CAN STOP **THE CHAMELEON!** WITH THE RIGHT DISGUISE, I CAN STEAL ANYTHING FROM ANYWHERE, UNCHALLENGED!

THAT NIGHT AT **THE CHAMELEON'S** HIDEOUT...
THE IRON CURTAIN COUNTRIES WILL PAY A FORTUNE FOR THESE PLANS!
HMM... A T.V. NEWS BULLETIN...
THE ENTIRE CITY IS WONDERING WHY **SPIDER-MAN** VISITED THE **FANTASTIC FOUR** TODAY! "NO COMMENT" SAYS THE **FF!**

RUMORS ARE FLYING ALL OVER NEW YORK! UNOFFICIAL SOURCES CLAIM **SPIDER-MAN** IS BEING CONSIDERED FOR **MEMBERSHIP** IN THE **FF!** "NONSENSE!" CLAIMS THE POLICE COMMISSIONER!
HMM... I THINK **SPIDER-MAN'S** VISIT IS OF INTEREST TO **THE CHAMELEON,** TOO!

YES, INDEED-- **VERY** INTERESTING!
ILY GLOBE
LATEST ON SPIDER-MAN
GRAND JURY REQUESTS IMMEDIATE PROBE
The F.B.I. has been alerted for possible action

THERE IS ONLY **ONE** REASON **SPIDER-MAN** WOULD WANT TO JOIN THE **FANTASTIC FOUR!** BEING SOUGHT BY THE POLICE, THERE IS NO WAY FOR HIM TO EARN A LEGITIMATE LIVING! HE MUST BE DESPERATE FOR MONEY! AND THIS IS WHERE **I** COME IN!

SPIDER-MAN WILL MAKE A PERFECT **FALL GUY--** FOR ME! WHEN I STEAL THE SECOND HALF OF THESE MISSILE DEFENSE PLANS, I'LL HAVE HIM PUT THE POLICE OFF MY TRAIL!
5

SPIDER-MAN HAS THE POWERS AND INSTINCTS OF A SPIDER! SO I WILL SEND HIM A MESSAGE THAT ONLY HIS SPIDER SENSES WILL BE ABLE TO PICK UP!

CALLING SPIDER-MAN! MEET ME ON ROOF OF LARK BUILDING AT TEN TONIGHT! IT WILL BE VERY PROFITABLE FOR YOU!

AND MILES AWAY, AT A NEIGHBOR-HOOD MUSEUM, WHERE PETER PARKER IS STUDYING THE SPIDER EXHIBIT...
SOMEONE IS TRYING TO CONTACT SPIDER-MAN! I CAN SENSE THE FREQUENCY WAVES! BUT WHO--?

WELL, NO MATTER WHO IT IS, I CAN'T AFFORD TO PASS UP A CHANCE FOR PROFIT! I'LL JUST LEAVE MY CLOTHES UP HERE, AND THEN...

A FEW MINUTES BEFORE TEN P.M....
ALMOST TIME FOR ME TO TAKE OVER THE ELEVATOR NIGHT SHIFT!
YES, IT IS TIME! BUT NOT FOR YOU--FOR THE CHAMELEON!

AFTER BINDING AND GAGGING THE REAL ELEVATOR OPERATOR, THE BOGUS ONE BRAZENLY TAKES HIS PLACE!
I'LL RELIEVE YOU NOW!
IT'S ABOUT TIME! I'M BUSHED!

THEN, ONCE INSIDE THE ELEVATOR...
SO FAR, MY TIME-TABLE IS RUNNING RIGHT TO THE SPLIT-SECOND! NOW TO CHANGE TO MY SPIDER-MAN GUISE!

AND FINALLY...
SPIDER-MAN! H-HOW DID YOU GET IN? W-WHAT DO YOU WANT?
THOSE MISSILE DEFENSE PLANS WHICH YOU'RE HOLDING!

I CAN'T BELIEVE IT! YOU -- A TRAITOR! WAIT--
MY WEB WILL KEEP YOU A PRISONER UNTIL I CAN ESCAPE!
THIS ARTIFICIAL WEB ISN'T AS STRONG AS SPIDER-MAN'S REAL ONE, BUT NO ONE'LL NOTICE THE DIFFERENCE!
6

SECONDS LATER...
HELP! POLICE! SPIDER-MAN'S HEADING FOR THE ROOF WITH STOLEN PLANS! HELP!!
HE FINALLY BROKE FREE! GOOD! IT'S ALL GOING ACCORDING TO PLAN!

HERE'S MY SHIP! I CAN'T FAIL NOW!
I'LL BE GONE JUST BEFORE THE REAL SPIDER-MAN GETS HERE!

I'M SORRY I WON'T BE THERE TO HEAR SPIDER-MAN TRY TO TALK HIMSELF OUT OF MY TRAP!
STRANGE -- THAT HELICOPTER MUST HAVE JUST LEFT THE ROOF I'M HEADING FOR!

I WONDER WHO SENT FOR ME? NOBODY IS WAITING ON THE ROOF!

LOOK! THERE HE IS!
FREEZE, SPIDER-MAN! WE WANT THOSE SECRET PLANS YOU STOLE!
PLANS?... STOLE?... I'M BEGINNIN' TO SMELL A RAT!

I DON'T KNOW WHAT THIS IS ALL ABOUT, BUT NOBODY'S FRAMIN' ME FOR ANYTHING!
THAT'LL HOLD YOU TILL I CAN GET AWAY!

WHAT A FOOL I WAS! THE MESSAGE WAS A TRICK TO PIN A CRIME ON ME! AND I FELL FOR IT!

BUT WHO COULD HAVE--? WAIT! THAT HELICOPTER! THE PILOT IS THE ONE THE POLICE REALLY WANT!

IF HE HASN'T FLOWN TOO FAR, I CAN USE MY SPIDER'S SENSES TO "TUNE IN" ON THE SHIP... GET ITS LOCATION!
GOT 'IM! HE'S OUT TOWARDS THE WATERFRONT! I'VE GOT TO STOP HIM!
7

WELL, IF I'M GOING TO CATCH ME A SPEEDING WHIRLEY-BIRD, THERE'S ONLY **ONE** WAY TO DO IT...

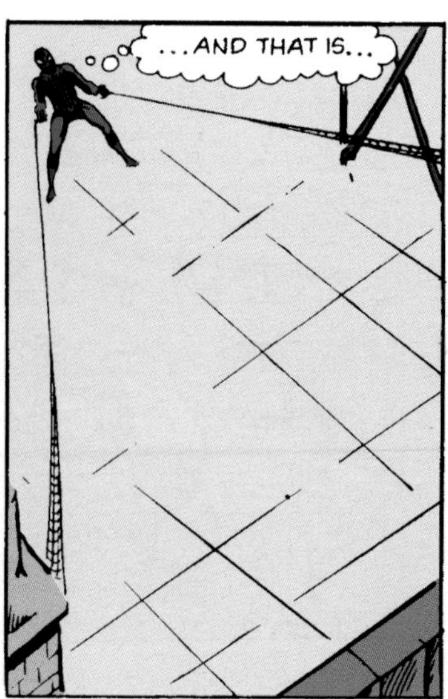
...AND THAT IS...

...TO GET A REAL FAST **START!** LIKE **THIS!**
TWANNNG!

HE'S ALREADY REACHED THE SEA!
BUT I CAN MAKE A PARACHUTE OUT OF MY WEB AND FLOAT DOWN TO THAT MOTORBOAT BELOW! I'M NOT LICKED YET!

MINUTES LATER...
I'M JUST IN TIME! THERE'S THE CHOPPER-- AND THERE'S A RED SUB SURFACING TO MEET IT!

BUT, WITH MY WEB OVER THE CONNING TOWER, THEY WON'T BE ABLE TO OPEN THE HATCH!
OUR HATCH IS JAMMED! IT WON'T OPEN! HOW WILL WE GET THE PLANS, COMRADE?
FORGET THE PLANS! WE'VE BEEN **SEEN!!... SUBMERGE!**

NOW TO FIND OUT WHO FRAMED ME!
SPIDER-MAN! BUT **HOW--?**

I CAN'T SHAKE HIM OFF--NO MATTER **HOW** I MANEUVER!

HE--HE RIPPED OFF THE DOOR WITH HIS BARE HANDS!
END OF THE LINE FOR YOU, COMMIE! HEAD THIS SHIP TOWARDS SHORE--AND I MEAN **NOW!**

AND, BEFORE THE POLICE HAVE LEFT THE LARK BUILDING ROOF...
LOOK!
HERE'S THE GUY YOU'RE LOOKIN' FOR! THE GUY WHO STOLE THOSE PLANS AND IMPERSONATED ME!

BUT IN THE NEXT SPLIT-SECOND, THE WILY CHAMELEON DROPS A TINY SMOKE PELLET, AND BREAKS FREE IN THE CONFUSION...
BEFORE THEY KNOW WHAT HAPPENED, I'LL HAVE TAKEN A NEW DISGUISE, AND BE FREE!

HE CAN'T GET OUT OF THE BUILDING! ALL EXITS ARE GUARDED!... SEARCH EVERY ROOM!

LET THEM SEARCH! I KNEW THIS DISGUISE WOULD COME IN HANDY! WHO WOULD EVER SUSPECT A POLICEMAN?

I'LL LOOK IN HERE, MEN!
I'LL TAKE THIS CORRIDOR!
AND I'LL HEAD FOR THE STREET UNDER YOUR VERY NOSES!

BUT AGAIN THE CHAMELEON HAS RECKONED WITHOUT SPIDER-MAN'S SUPERNATURAL SPIDER'S INSTINCTS...
THAT TINGLE I FEEL! MY QUARRY IS CLOSE-- WITHIN STRIKING DISTANCE!

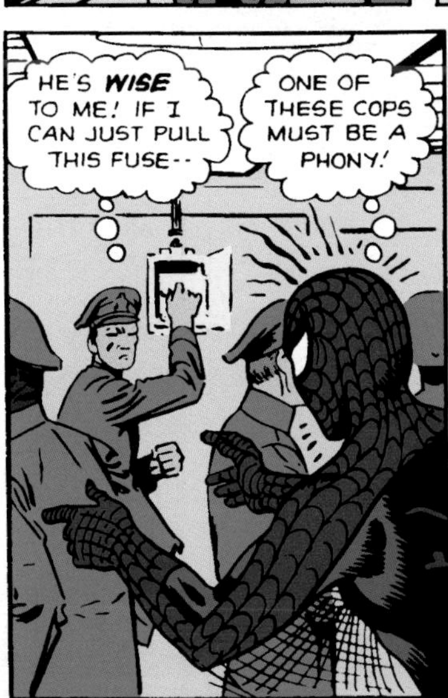
HE'S WISE TO ME! IF I CAN JUST PULL THIS FUSE--
ONE OF THESE COPS MUST BE A PHONY!

HE'S DOUSED THE LIGHTS! BUT THAT WON'T STOP ME! I CAN STILL SENSE HIM IN THE DARK!

I'LL JUST SHOOT MY WEB OVER-- OH, NO!
I'M ALL OUT OF THE SPECIAL FLUID!
9

I' VE GOT TO REACH THAT EXIT BEFORE **HE** DOES! THIS IS THE FASTEST WAY!

THAT FIGURE-- LEAVING THE OTHERS-- IT'S **HIM!**

BUT, AS THE LIGHTS GO ON AGAIN, **THE CHAMELEON** RESORTS TO ONE, LAST, DESPERATE RUSE...
HELP! GRAB HIM! IT'S **THE CHAMELEON,** DISGUISED AS **SPIDER-MAN** AGAIN!
WHA--?

OH, **NO,** YOU DON'T! YOU'RE NOT GONNA FOOL US THAT WAY A **SECOND** TIME!
WAIT!... HE'S **LYING!** **I AM SPIDER-MAN!**
IT **WORKED!** NOW TO SLIP AWAY!

IN A FIT OF WHITE-HOT FURY, THE POWERFUL **SPIDER-MAN** WRENCHES FREE OF THE STARTLED OFFICERS' GRASP, AND...
LOOK AT HIM GO UP THAT WALL! HE **WAS** THE **REAL SPIDER-MAN!**
EVERY TIME I TRY TO HELP, I GET INTO **WORSE** TROUBLE! WELL, THEY CAN CATCH THAT SPY **THEMSELVES** NOW!

AND WITHIN MINUTES, CATCH HIM THEY **DO**...
HERE HE **IS,** CAPTAIN! I SPOTTED HIM BY HIS TORN UNIFORM-- I COULD SEE HIS OTHER DISGUISE BENEATH IT!
BLAST IT! I MUST HAVE RIPPED IT IN MY SCUFFLE WITH **SPIDER-MAN!**

AND, AS **THE CHAMELEON** IS LED AWAY, A LONE FIGURE LOSES HIMSELF IN THE SHADOWS OF THE SILENT NIGHT...
NOTHING TURNS OUT RIGHT... ***SOB*...** I WISH I HAD NEVER **GOTTEN** MY SUPER POWERS!

LATER, AS THE LATE EDITIONS COME OUT, FOUR FAMOUS FIGURES PONDER THE CASE OF THE AMAZING ***SPIDER-MAN!***
REED, HE'S SO POWERFUL, AND SO CONFUSED! WHAT IF **SPIDER-MAN** EVER TURNS HIS SUPER POWERS **AGAINST** THE LAW?
YEAH! IF A **TEEN-AGER** CAN BE SO BLAMED STRONG, HOW STRONG'LL HE BE WHEN HE GETS **OLDER?**
AW, WE WON'T EVER HAFTA WORRY ABOUT **HIM!**
WON'T WE, JOHNNY? I WONDER...

AND THE WHOLE **WORLD** WILL HAVE TO WONDER-- UNTIL OUR NEXT GREAT ISSUE! **DON'T MISS IT!!**

The END

A PERSONAL MESSAGE FROM
SPIDER-MAN
Hi, friends!
Hope you enjoyed this issue of the new AMAZING SPIDER-MAN!
Beginning with our THIRD ISSUE* there'll be a letters page for your knocks and boosts, called THE SPIDER'S WEB! So, send your letters along now to SPIDER-MAN, THIRD FLOOR, 655 MADISON AVE., N.Y. 21, N.Y.!
Don't miss my new and different adventures in issue #2, on sale the beginning of February, 1963. Better ask your dealer to reserve your copy NOW, because judging by advance reports the demand will be greater than the supply!
Yours for thrills and fantasy... Spider-Man
*NOTE:
We can't print your letters till our THIRD issue because our SECOND issue will already be on the presses by the time you read this!

the AMAZING
SPIDER-MAN
APPROVED BY THE COMICS CODE AUTHORITY
IND.
MARVEL COMICS GROUP 12¢
2 MAY
2 GREAT NEW SPIDER-MAN THRILLERS!
2 GREAT NEW SUPER-VILLAINS!
featuring: "The VULTURE!" and...
DITKO

...SPIDER-MAN IS TRAPPED BY "the TERRIBLE TINKERER!"

SPIDER-MAN

"DUEL TO THE DEATH WITH The VULTURE!"

THE MOST COLORFUL SUPER-HERO OF ALL... SPIDER-MAN! HIS NAME MAKES THE UNDER-WORLD TREMBLE! BUT THERE IS ONE WHO DOES NOT TREMBLE! WHAT FANTASTIC POWER CAN THE VULTURE HAVE WHICH MAKES HIM SO SURE HE CAN DEFEAT... SPIDER-MAN?
SCRIPT: STAN LEE
ART: STEVE DITKO
LETTERING: JOHN DUFFY

FOR DAYS, A NEW AND OMINOUS DANGER HAS MENACED THE VAST CITY OF NEW YORK! NO MAN KNOWS WHERE HE'LL STRIKE NEXT! NO ONE CAN COPE WITH THIS NEW, AWESOME THREAT! WITHOUT WARNING, WITHOUT THE SLIGHTEST SOUND, HE STRIKES!

FOR THIS IS -- **THE VULTURE!**
IT'S **THE VULTURE!** HE STOLE MY BRIEFCASE -- WITH A FORTUNE IN BONDS! **HELP!!**

I'VE **READ** ABOUT HIM--BUT NEVER EXPECTED TO **SEE** HIM!
I DIDN'T **BELIEVE** IT! I THOUGHT HE DIDN'T EXIST!
IT'S IMPOSSIBLE! IT CAN'T BE! HOW CAN HE **FLY** -- WITHOUT A SOUND--WITHOUT ANY EFFORT! HE'S MORE LIKE A GIGANTIC BIRD OF PREY THAN A HUMAN!

AND, IN THE EXECUTIVE SUITE OF THE POWERFUL **JAMESON PUBLICATIONS,** MR. J. JONAH JAMESON IS ON HIS USUAL RAMPAGE...
I WANT TO DEVOTE THE NEXT ENTIRE ISSUE OF **NOW MAGAZINE** TO **THE VULTURE!** HE'S BIG NEWS! EVERYONE WANTS TO READ ABOUT HIM!
BUT KEEP PRINTING STORIES ABOUT **SPIDER-MAN** ALSO! I'LL NEVER REST TILL THAT DANGEROUS MENACE IS DESTROYED!
J. JONAH JAMESON PUBLISH
NOW
MAGAZINE

IS **THIS** THE ONLY PHOTO WE HAVE OF **THE VULTURE?** WHAT'S THE MATTER WITH YOU MEN? WHAT AM I **PAYING** YOU FOR? THE PUBLIC WANTS TO **SEE** HIM!

BUT, MR. JAMESON, **NOBODY** CAN GET PICTURES OF HIM! HE'S GONE BEFORE ANY PHOTOGRAPHER CAN GET TO HIM! WE HAVE ONLY AN ARTIST'S DRAWING!

NO MORE EXCUSES! GET ME PICTURES OF **THE VULTURE** -- OR I'LL GET SOME NEW EDITORS!

NOW

MENACE

MEANWHILE, IN A NEARBY HIGH SCHOOL, PETER PARKER OVERHEARS AN INTERESTING DISCUSSION AS THE YOUNG SCIENCE MAJOR PERFORMS AN EXPERIMENT IN THE LAB...

BOY! I'D LIKE TO SEE A CLOSE-UP PHOTO OF **THE VULTURE!!**
A PHOTO OF **THE VULTURE** WOULD BE WORTH A **FORTUNE!** NOBODY CAN GET CLOSE ENOUGH TO HIM TO SNAP ONE!
SAY! THAT'S AN IDEA! I NEVER **THOUGHT** OF IT BEFORE! MAGAZINES PAY BIG MONEY FOR HARD-TO-GET PHOTOS! AND **I** KNOW HOW TO GET THEM!
NOW

AS SOON AS SCHOOL ENDS, THE EXCITED TEEN-AGER RUSHES HOME TO HIS AUNT MAY AND IS DELIGHTED TO LEARN...

AND THEN, IN THE PRIVACY OF HIS ROOM, PETER PARKER CHANGES INTO THE MOST DRAMATIC COSTUMED FIGURE OF ALL--THAT OF ***SPIDER-MAN!...***

MEANWHILE, IN A CAREFULLY-PREPARED HIDEOUT ON THE OUTSKIRTS OF THE CITY...

WELL, WELL! SO THE PARK AVENUE JEWELRY EXCHANGE IS MOVING A MILLION DOLLARS WORTH OF DIAMONDS TO THEIR NEW OFFICES ACROSS TOWN, EH? IT SHOULDN'T BE HARD FOR **THE VULTURE** TO GET HIS HANDS ON THOSE GEMS!

AFTER MAKING CERTAIN HE IS NOT OBSERVED, **THE VULTURE** DARTS FROM HIS HIDING PLACE ATOP AN ABANDONED SILO IN STATEN ISLAND, JUST A FEW SECONDS FROM THE HEART OF MANHATTEN...

NOW FOR THE FIRST PART OF MY INGENIOUS PLAN!

SECONDS LATER, ATOP AN APARTMENT HOUSE WHERE HE HAD BEEN CHECKING HIS CAMERA, **SPIDER-MAN'S** AMAZING SPIDER SENSES PICK UP A STRANGE SENSATION...

SOMETHING COMING THROUGH THE AIR--BUT MAKING NO SOUND!... CAN'T BE A PLANE...

NOT NOTICING THE POWERFUL FIGURE ON THE ROOF TOP, **THE VULTURE** SWEEPS PAST...

THEY'LL **NEVER** FIGURE OUT HOW I'M GOING TO STEAL THOSE DIAMONDS!
I'VE GOT EVERYONE COMPLETELY BAFFLED! NO ONE HAS YET DISCOVERED HOW I MANAGE TO **FLY** WITH THESE ARTIFICIAL WINGS!
WHAT LUCK!... IT'S **THE VULTURE!**

I'LL TOSS SOME MESSAGES WHERE THEY'LL DO THE MOST GOOD!
THE FIRST ONE IS FOR THE **JAMESON PUBLISHING COMPANY** BUILDING!
J. J

MY NEXT MESSAGE IS FOR THE RADIO NETWORK! NOTHING I LIKE BETTER THAN TAUNTING MY ENEMIES!
C RADIO

AND, FINALLY, ONE FOR THE POLICE CHIEF HIMSELF! I'LL BE GONE BEFORE THEY HAVE A CHANCE TO READ THEM!

THE VULTURE HAS NEVER FAILED TO CARRY OUT A THREAT YET!
BUT WE **MUST** GO AHEAD WITH THE TRANSFER OF THE DIAMONDS! WE CAN'T LET THE CITY THINK THAT ONE CRIMINAL CAN MAKE US CHANGE OUR PLANS!
I SHALL STEAL THE DIAMOND SHIPMENT FROM UNDER YOUR NOSES! The Vulture

I DID IT! NOW THAT I'VE WARNED THEM, MY TRIUMPH SHALL BE EVEN GREATER AFTER I'VE SEIZED THE GEM!
IF THESE PHOTOS OF THE VULTURE COME OUT ALL RIGHT, THEY SHOULD BE WORTH A SMALL FORTUNE!

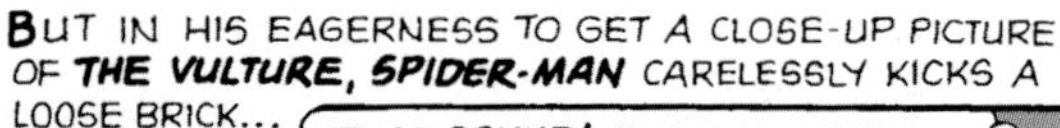
BUT IN HIS EAGERNESS TO GET A CLOSE-UP PICTURE OF THE VULTURE, SPIDER-MAN CARELESSLY KICKS A LOOSE BRICK...

THAT SOUND! THERE'S SOMEONE ON THE ROOF BEHIND ME! I'VE GOT TO MOVE--FAST! AS ONLY A VULTURE CAN!

THERE! I'VE GOT EVERYTHING ADJUSTED PERFECTLY! NOW TO-- HEY!! WHERE'D HE GO?

WELL, WELL! SO SPIDER-MAN HIMSELF IS ON MY TRAIL! GOOD!! IT WILL BE AMUSING TO FINALLY FACE A FOE WORTHY OF MY METTLE!
UGH!

HAVING BEEN MOMENTARILY TAKEN BY SURPRISE, SPIDER-MAN IS STUNNED AND DAZED BY THE VULTURE'S BRUTAL ON-SLAUGHT. AS HIS MERCILESS FOE FLIES TOWARDS A NEAR-BY WATER TOWER...
THIS IS ALMOST TOO EASY!

ONCE I DROP HIM INTO THE WATER BELOW, HE'LL NEVER BOTHER ME AGAIN! WITH SPIDER-MAN OUT OF THE WAY, THE CITY WILL BE MINE!
5

NOW THAT I HAVE DISPOSED OF THAT TEMPORARY INTERRUPTION, I'LL CARRY OUT STEP **TWO** OF MY MASTER PLAN!

MEANWHILE, INSIDE THE TANK, THE SHOCK OF HITTING THE COLD WATER INSTANTLY REVIVES THE POWERFUL **SPIDER-MAN**...
THE VULTURE SOMEHOW TRAPPED ME INSIDE THIS WATER TANK!
WELL, I'VE ONLY MYSELF TO BLAME FOR BEING SO CARELESS!

I'LL JUST SHOOT MY WEB TOWARDS THE TOP AND... **OH, NO!** THE EJECTOR IS EMPTY!
I FORGOT TO REFILL IT SINCE I USED IT LAST! I'VE BEEN SO BUSY WITH THAT CAMERA--! I'VE GOT TO TRY SOMETHING ELSE!

CAN'T CLIMB TO THE TOP--IT'S TOO WET AND SLIMY EVEN FOR **ME** TO GET A TOEHOLD ON!
BUT I SURE AS SHOOTING CAN'T STAY AFLOAT HERE MUCH LONGER!

NOT A PLEASANT CHOICE--I'LL EITHER DROWN OR SUFFOCATE IN HERE!
WAIT A MINUTE! WHAT'S **WRONG** WITH ME? WHY DON'T I USE MY HEAD? I CAN GET OUT OF HERE!

MY MUSCLES ARE FAR STRONGER THAN AN ORDINARY HUMAN'S! THERE'S ONE LITTLE TRICK THAT ONLY THE **SPIDER-MAN** CAN PERFORM!

ALL I'VE GOT TO DO IS REACH THE BOTTOM, SQUAT DOWN, AND PREPARE TO HURL MYSELF UPWARD...

...LIKE **THIS!!**
6

DID IT!!
I MAY NOT BE ABLE TO FLY LIKE THE VULTURE-- BUT MY SPIDER STRENGTH HASN'T LET ME DOWN YET!

MY LUCK'S STILL HOLDING OUT-- HERE'S MY CAMERA!
SURE IS UNBELIEVABLE HOW THE VULTURE MANAGES TO FLY SO SWIFTLY! I'D SURE LIKE TO FIGURE OUT HOW HE DOES IT!

LATER, IN HIS ROOM AGAIN...
THE PICTURES CAME OUT FINE! NOW, WHOM DO I SELL THEM TO? JONAH JAMESON, THE PUBLISHER OF NOW MAGAZINE HATES SPIDER-MAN! I'D GET A KICK OUT OF MAKING HIM PAY GOOD DOUGH FOR MY PICTURES WITHOUT KNOWING I'M THE PHOTOGRAPHER!
NOW
SPIDER-MAN MUST BE CAUGHT!
NOW

ORIGINALLY, I DESIGNED MY SPIDER-MAN COSTUME JUST TO GIVE ME SOME COLOR, SO THAT I COULD MAKE MONEY AS AN ENTERTAINER! BUT, IF...
... I'M REALLY GOING TO BE A SECRET ADVENTURER, I'VE GOT TO MAKE SOME CHANGES! FIRST, I'LL ADD AN EXTRA WEB-FLUID CAPSULE, SO I ALWAYS HAVE ENOUGH SPIDER-WEBBING ON HAND!

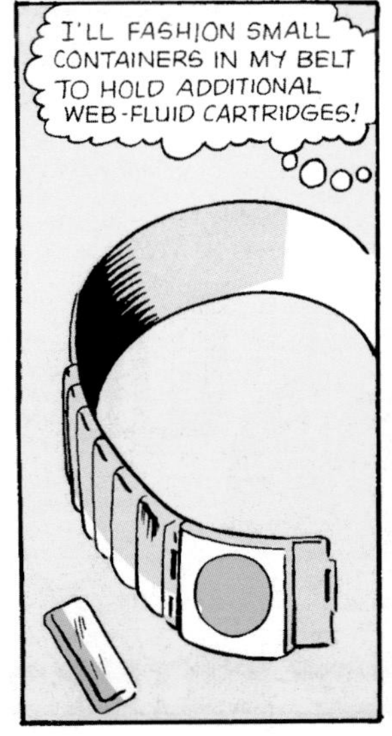
I'LL FASHION SMALL CONTAINERS IN MY BELT TO HOLD ADDITIONAL WEB-FLUID CARTRIDGES!

THEN, WHEN I GET PAID FOR MY PICTURES, I'LL BUY A SPECIAL MINIATURE CAMERA TO SECRETLY ATTACH TO THE BELT BUCKLE!

THERE! THE WHOLE CONTRAPTION FITS UNDER MY SHIRT, WHERE IT'S OUT OF SIGHT, AND DOESN'T INTERFERE WITH MY MOVEMENTS!

AND NOW, I'VE GOT A HUNCH I KNOW THE SECRET OF THE VULTURE'S POWER OF FLIGHT! I'LL JUST WORK ON A LITTLE DEVICE WHICH MAY COME IN HANDY NEXT TIME WE MEET!
7

LONG HOURS LATER...
WHEW! THAT WAS TOUGHER THAN I EXPECTED, BUT IT'S FINISHED NOW!
I WON'T KNOW IF IT'LL WORK TILL I TRY IT-- BUT RIGHT NOW, I'M GONNA GET SOME SHUT-EYE!

THE NEXT DAY, J. JONAH JAMESON RECEIVES AN EXCITING PHONE CALL...
WHAT'S THAT?? YOU'VE GOT SOME EXCLUSIVE PHOTOS OF THE VULTURE THAT YOU WANT TO SELL?? WELL, DON'T WASTE TIME TALKING! GET OVER HERE RIGHT AWAY!
JOE, HAVE THEM STOP THE PRESSES!
J. JONAH J

AND SOON...
SORRY, MR. JAMESON CANNOT SEE ANYBODY RIGHT NOW! HE'S HAVING AN IMPORTANT CONFERENCE!
THESE PICTURES ARE SENSATIONAL-- GREAT! BUT HOW'D A KID LIKE YOU GET THEM?
SORRY, SIR! I'LL SELL THEM TO YOU ON CONDITION THAT YOU NEVER ASK ME THAT QUESTION!

OKAY, OKAY! YOU CAN HAVE YOUR LITTLE SECRET! IT DOESN'T MATTER HOW YOU GOT THEM! THE POINT IS, THESE PICTURES WILL MAKE THE NEXT ISSUE OF NOW A SELL-OUT! I'LL ISSUE A CHECK TO YOU IMMEDIATELY!
AND REMEMBER, MR. JAMESON, I DON'T WANT MY NAME USED! YOU CAN MERELY GIVE CREDIT TO A NOW MAGAZINE STAFF PHOTOGRAPHER!

SURE, MY BOY, SURE! AND IF YOU GET ANY MORE GREAT PICTURES, REMEMBER TO GIVE ME FIRST CRACK AT THEM! WE'RE ALWAYS IN THE MARKET FOR SENSATIONAL PHOTOS! IN FACT...
... IF YOU CAN EVER GET A PICTURE OF THAT PUBLIC MENACE, SPIDER-MAN--
BROTHER, WOULDN'T YOU BE SURPRISED IF YOU KNEW!

THE NEXT DAY, AS SCHOOL LETS OUT...
C'MON, PETER! WE'RE ALL GOING TO WATCH THEM MOVE THE DIAMONDS FROM THE PARK AVENUE JEWELRY EXCHANGE! WE'RE HOPING TO GET A GLIMPSE OF THE VULTURE!
YOU DON'T REALLY THINK THE VULTURE WOULD DARE TRY ANYTHING WITH ALL THE POLICE THERE, DO YOU?
DON'T BE SCARED, BOOKWORM--WE'LL PROTECT YOU!
8

GOSH! THE WHOLE AREA IS CORDONED OFF! AND LOOK-- T.V. CAMERAS, NEWSPAPERMEN, POLICE! IT'S LIKE A CARNIVAL!
THE VULTURE WOULD BE NUTS TO TRY ANYTHING WITH A CROWD LIKE THIS AROUND! THIS IS ONE TIME HE WON'T MAKE GOOD HIS BOAST!

IT IS HARD TO SEE HOW THE VULTURE COULD HAVE A CHANCE AT THE JEWELS UNDER THESE CONDITIONS! THERE ARE POLICE ON EVERY ROOF, AND AN ARMED HELICOPTER FLYING OVERHEAD!

I'D BETTER MAKE MYSELF SCARCE! IF I HAVE TO CHANGE TO SPIDER-MAN, I WON'T BE ABLE TO DO IT IN THE MIDDLE OF THIS MOB!
LOOK, GANG! LITTLE PETEY IS CHICKENING OUT! GUESS THE EXCITEMENT IS TOO MUCH FOR HIS DELICATE LITTLE SELF!

MINUTES LATER, THE VALUABLE JEWELRY SHIPMENT STARTS ITS CROSSTOWN CONVOY, ACCOMPANIED BY PATROL CARS AND THE POLICE WHIRLYBIRD FOLLOWING ABOVE...
POLICE

I WISH THE VULTURE WOULD MAKE A TRY FOR THOSE DIAMONDS, CHUCK! WE'D NAB 'IM FOR SURE!
YEAH, BUT HE WON'T SHOW! HE'S TOO SMART FOR THAT!
POLICE

IT'S ALL CLEAR! START BRINGING THE JEWELS OUT!
NOT A SIGN OF THE VULTURE! HE KNOWS HE WOULDN'T HAVE A CHANCE!

BEFORE THE STARTLED OFFICERS CAN FIRE, THE WILY **VULTURE** PLUMMETS BACK UNDERGROUND, DROPPING THE MANHOLE COVER INTO PLACE ABOVE HIM! THEN...

A SHORT TIME LATER, AT THE OTHER END OF TOWN, A TRIUMPHANT **VULTURE** DECIDES TO LEAVE HIS UNDERGROUND LAIR AS DRAMATICALLY AS POSSIBLE...

MEANWHILE, LEARNING WHAT HAS OCCURRED, PETER PARKER MANAGES TO FIND A DESERTED ALLEY, AND THEN, MOVING WITH BLINDING SPEED...

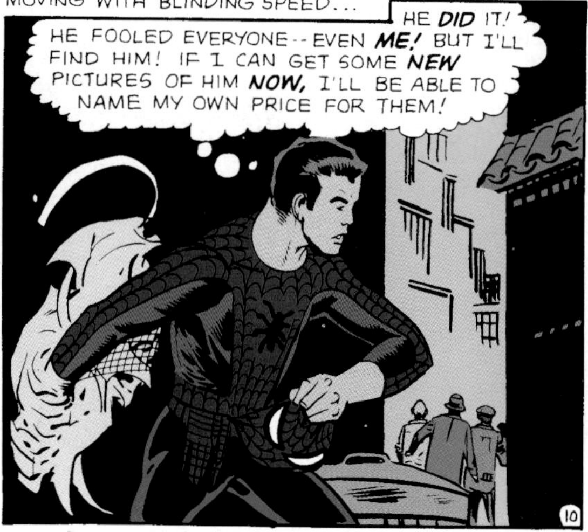

THE THING I LIKE BEST ABOUT BEING THE SPIDER-MAN IS SCALING THESE SHEER WALLS! I DON'T THINK I'LL EVER STOP GETTING A CHARGE OUT OF IT!

NOW, IF THE VULTURE IS ANY-WHERE IN THE AREA, MY SPIDER SENSES WILL DETECT HIM! AHH-- I'M BEGINNING TO GET A TINGLE NOW!

WHAT A BREAK! THERE HE IS NOW! IT'LL BE A CINCH FOR ME TO FOLLOW HIM, USING MY WEB TO SWING FROM BUILDING TO BUILDING!

BUT, AS LUCK WOULD HAVE IT, THE VULTURE CHOOSES TO LOOK BEHIND HIM AT THAT VERY SECOND, AND...
BETTER CHECK TO SEE IF ANY POLICE HELICOPTERS ARE--WHAT THE--! IT'S SPIDER-MAN! HE'S FREE! AND HE'S FOLLOWING ME!

HE'S TOO DANGEROUS! I'VE GOT TO GET RID OF HIM FOR GOOD!
FIRST, I'LL EXECUTE A FAST LOOP-THE-LOOP, WHICH WILL PUT ME BE-HIND HIM!

HOLY SMOKE-- WHERE'D HE GO?!? HE COULDN'T HAVE FLOWN AWAY SO FAST!
11

FOREWARNED BY HIS FABULOUS SPIDER'S SENSE, **SPIDER-MAN** WHEELS ABOUT IN TIME TO AVOID THE FULL IMPACT OF **THE VULTURE'S** SWOOPING DIVE, BUT ONE POWERFUL WING SENDS THE COLORFULLY CLAD FIGURE TOPPLING FROM THE EDGE OF THE ROOF!

NO, YOU DON'T! THIS TIME I'M READY FOR YOU!
WHA--?? HE HIT MY FOOT WITH THAT ACCURSED WEB OF HIS!

PULLING HIMSELF UP HAND OVER HAND, THE MIGHTY **SPIDER-MAN** MANAGES TO GET WITHIN GRABBING DISTANCE OF **THE VULTURE'S** ANKLE, AND THEN...

GOT YOU!

YOU FOOL! HERE IN THE SKY WE'RE IN MY ELEMENT! I'LL SHAKE YOU OFF--AND BE RID OF YOU FOR GOOD!
TALK IS CHEAP, BIRDMAN! THIS TIME I'M STICKING!
AND NOW TO TEST OUT MY LITTLE GADGET! HERE'S HOPIN' IT WORKS!
THAT DID IT! YOU'RE OUT OF CONTROL! I'VE BEATEN YOU!
WHAT DID YOU DO? I CAN'T STAY ALOFT! YOU--YOU'LL KILL US BOTH!
12

SPEAK FOR YOURSELF, MISTER! THE SKY IS MY ELEMENT AS MUCH AS YOURS! JUST WATCH!!

I CAN ALWAYS SAVE MYSELF BY SHOOTING MY WEB AT A NEARBY BUILD-ING--LIKE THIS!

AS FOR THE VULTURE, HE'LL MANAGE TO BREAK HIS FALL BY SPIRALING DOWN, BUT HE'S GONNA HAVE A TOUGH TIME EVER USING THOSE WINGS AGAIN!

HERE COMES THE POLICE HELICOPTER! THEY MUST HAVE SIGHTED US WHEN WE WERE BATTLING! THIS IS MY CHANCE TO GET SOME EXCLUSIVE PIX OF THE CAPTURE OF THE VULTURE!

TAKE 'ER DOWN, CHARLIE! WE WERE RIGHT! IT IS THE VULTURE!
CAN'T GET UP! WIND KNOCKED OUT OF ME! WHAT'LL I DO--??
POLICE

IF THIS DOESN'T TAKE THE CAKE! WHO EVER THOUGHT WE'D BE ABLE TO CAPTURE THE VULTURE SO NICE AND EASY?!! WHAT HAPPENED, FELLA? DID YOU HAVE A TAILSPIN?
PLEASE--NO JOKES!
THESE PICTURES SHOULD BE PRIZE-WINNERS!
13

THAT DOES IT! NOW TO GET THESE SHOTS TO JAMESON AND ASK FOR TOP DOLLAR FOR THEM!
LET'S GO, BIRDMAN! WE'LL GET YOU TO HEADQUARTERS AND FIND OUT ONCE AND FOR ALL HOW YOU MANAGED TO FLY THE WAY YOU DID!

IF THEY ASKED ME, I COULD HAVE TOLD THEM! THE ABSENCE OF NOISE GAVE ME THE CLUE! I SUSPECTED THAT HE HAD DISCOVERED A WAY TO HARNESS MAGNETIC POWER! THAT'S WHY MY GADGET MADE HIM FALL--IT'S AN ANTI-MAGNETIC INVERTER--AND IT WORKED!

THEN, AS THE NEXT DAY DAWNS...
TELL ME, PARKER, ARE YOU A MAGICIAN? HOW DOES A TEEN-AGER LIKE YOU MANAGE TO GET PICTURES THAT OUR BEST STAFF PHOTOGS WOULD GIVE THEIR EYE TEETH FOR?
REMEMBER OUR DEAL, MR. JAMESON? THAT'S MY SECRET! NOW IF YOU DON'T WANT THE PIX--

ARE YOU OUT OF YOUR MIND?! WITH PICTURES LIKE THESE, I CAN ALMOST STAND LIVING IN THE CITY WITH SPIDER-MAN! TAKE A BONUS AND GO OUT AND BUY YOURSELF SOME TWIST RECORDS!
HE THINKS I'M JUST A TYPICAL TEEN-AGE KID! GOOD! THAT'S THE WAY I LIKE IT! AND THIS WAD OF BILLS HE PAID ME IS WHAT I LIKE ALSO!

AND, UPON REACHING HIS HOME...
AUNT MAY, THIS MONEY MEANS YOU'RE NOT GONNA HAVE TO WORRY ABOUT ANY-THING AGAIN! I PAID THE RENT FOR A FULL YEAR, AND TOMORROW I'M BUYING YOU THE NEWEST KITCHEN APPLIANCES YOU EVER DROOLED OVER!
OH, PETER, I'M SO PROUD OF YOU! IT'S JUST LIKE YOUR UNCLE BEN ALWAYS SAID--YOU'RE THE MOST WONDERFUL BOY IN THE WORLD!

WHILE, IN A LONELY CELL, THE VULTURE HAS A SLIGHTLY DIFFERENT OPIN-ION OF OUR HERO...
I WOULDN'T BE HERE IF NOT FOR THAT ACCURSED SPIDER-MAN! BUT SOONER OR LATER, I'LL GET FREE--AND I'LL DEVELOP A FLYING POWER THAT HE CANNOT OVERCOME! AND THEN, SPIDER-MAN, IT WILL BE MY TURN TO GLOAT!
THE END
14

"the UNCANNY THREAT of THE TERRIBLE TINKERER!"
HE LOOKS SO HARMLESS--AND YET THE TINKERER IS ONE OF THE GREATEST MENACES I'VE EVER FACED!
EVERYBODY LOVES A BARGAIN! BUT SOMETIMES IT CAN BE DANGEROUS TO ACCEPT A BARGAIN WHICH IS TOO GOOD TO BE TRUE! ESPECIALLY IF THE BARGAIN IS BEING OFFERED BY SOMEONE LIKE THE TINKERER, WHO-- BUT WAIT! LET'S SEE HOW IT ALL BEGAN--AND HOW IT TOOK SPIDER-MAN TO FINISH IT!
STORY: STAN LEE
ART: STEVE DITKO
LETTERING: ART SIMEK
X-171
1

A STORY HAS TO START SOMEWHERE, SO LET'S BEGIN OURS IN THE SCIENCE LAB OF MIDTOWN HIGH, WHERE WE FIND PETER PARKER HARD AT WORK WHILE...
GOSH, I THOUGHT CLASS WOULD NEVER END TODAY! I COULDN'T BEAR LOOKING AT ONE MORE TEST TUBE OR BUNSEN BURNER!
QUIET! YOU'LL BREAK PETER'S HEART! HE CAN'T BEAR TO BE PARTED FROM THEM!
THERE'S THE BOY I WAS TELLING YOU ABOUT, DOCTOR! HE'S PETER PARKER, OUR TOP SCIENCE STUDENT!

PETER, PROFESSOR COBBWELL HAS ASKED ME TO RECOMMEND A STUDENT WHO COULD HELP HIM WITH SOME RESEARCH OVER THE WEEK-END, AND I WAS WONDERING--?
GOSH! A CHANCE TO WORK WITH THE MOST FAMOUS ELECTRONICS EXPERT IN TOWN? I'D BE DELIGHTED, SIR!
THANK YOU, MY BOY! I HAVE SOME URGENT EXPERIMENTS TO PERFORM, AND WILL APPRECIATE YOUR ASSISTANCE!

HERE IS MY ADDRESS, SON! ON YOUR WAY OVER TOMORROW, PLEASE STOP AT THE RADIO REPAIR SHOP AND PICK UP A SMALL RADIO FOR ME! I HAD SOME NEW TUBES PUT IN IT!
SURE, I'LL BE GLAD TO, DOCTOR COBBWELL!

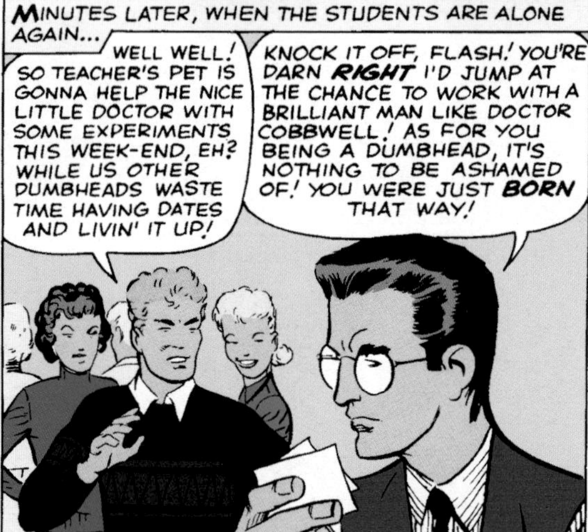
MINUTES LATER, WHEN THE STUDENTS ARE ALONE AGAIN...
WELL WELL! SO TEACHER'S PET IS GONNA HELP THE NICE LITTLE DOCTOR WITH SOME EXPERIMENTS THIS WEEK-END, EH? WHILE US OTHER DUMBHEADS WASTE TIME HAVING DATES AND LIVIN' IT UP!
KNOCK IT OFF, FLASH! YOU'RE DARN RIGHT I'D JUMP AT THE CHANCE TO WORK WITH A BRILLIANT MAN LIKE DOCTOR COBBWELL! AS FOR YOU BEING A DUMBHEAD, IT'S NOTHING TO BE ASHAMED OF! YOU WERE JUST BORN THAT WAY!

THEN, BEFORE THE ANGRY FLASH THOMPSON CAN THINK OF A SUITABLE RETORT, PETER PARKER IS GONE! AND, THE NEXT DAY, AT HOME...
I'D BETTER TAKE MY SPIDER-MAN OUTFIT! NEVER KNOW WHEN I'LL NEED IT! BESIDES, I FEEL ALMOST UNDRESSED WITHOUT IT!

HMMM, HERE'S THE PLACE THE DOC WANTED ME TO PICK UP HIS RADIO!
THE TINKERER REPAIR SHOP--SURE IS AN OFF-BEAT NAME! WONDER WHAT KIND OF KOOKIE CHARACTER RUNS IT?
TINKERER
2

INSIDE THE SHOP...
I'M THE TINKERER! WHAT CAN I DO FOR YOU, MY BOY?
I'M HERE TO PICK UP A RADIO FOR DR. COBBWELL!

OH YES! DOCTOR COBBWELL! JUST A MINUTE -- I'LL GET IT!
BOY, I SURE CALLED IT RIGHT! HE LOOKS LIKE A CHARACTER STRAIGHT OUT OF GRIMM'S FAIRY TALES!

THEN, SUDDENLY...
STRANGE... MY SPIDER SENSE PICKS UP ODD ELECTRIC IMPULSES! MUST BE COMING FROM HIS TESTING EQUIPMENT!
I'VE GOT TO STOP GETTING SO SUSPICIOUS ALL THE TIME! THE TINKERER LOOKS ABOUT AS DANGEROUS AS A SECOND-HAND CREAMPUFF!

MEANWHILE, IN A SOUND-PROOFED BASEMENT WORKROOM, DIRECTLY UNDER THE SHOP...
DR. COBBWELL IS READY FOR HIS RADIO! IT IS ONE OF OUR SPECIAL JOBS!
GOOD! I HAVE JUST FINISHED IT! HE MAY HAVE IT NOW!

I HAVE INSERTED OUR SPECIAL DEVICE! HE WILL NEVER SUSPECT THAT THIS IS NOW MUCH MORE THAN A SIMPLE RADIO!

SO FAR NONE OF OUR "SPECIAL" CUSTOMERS SUSPECTS WHAT WE HAVE DONE TO THEIR RADIOS WHILE WE WERE SUPPOSED TO BE REPAIRING THEM!
NATURALLY! OUR PLAN MUST BE COMPLETELY SECRET, UNTIL WE ARE READY TO STRIKE!
3

AND THEN, AFTER THE LONG CLIMB UPSTAIRS AGAIN...
YOU MEAN YOU ONLY CHARGE A DIME TO FIX RADIOS?? BUT--
TUT TUT, MY BOY! I LIKE TO GIVE BARGAINS! THEY BRING ME IN LOTS OF CUSTOMERS!

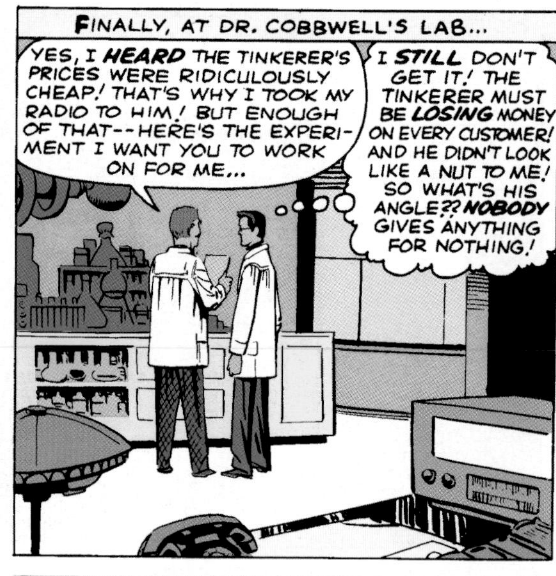
FINALLY, AT DR. COBBWELL'S LAB...
YES, I HEARD THE TINKERER'S PRICES WERE RIDICULOUSLY CHEAP! THAT'S WHY I TOOK MY RADIO TO HIM! BUT ENOUGH OF THAT--HERE'S THE EXPERIMENT I WANT YOU TO WORK ON FOR ME...
I STILL DON'T GET IT! THE TINKERER MUST BE LOSING MONEY ON EVERY CUSTOMER! AND HE DIDN'T LOOK LIKE A NUT TO ME! SO WHAT'S HIS ANGLE?? NOBODY GIVES ANYTHING FOR NOTHING!

THIS IS BATTY! I'VE GOT TO FORGET THE TINKERER AND CONCENTRATE ON WHAT I'M DOING!
BUT SOMETHING ABOUT HIM KEEPS STICKIN' IN MY CRAW!

WAIT! I KNOW! THOSE ELECTRICAL IMPULSES WHICH I SENSED IN HIS SHOP! NOW I SENSE THEM HERE!
THE PART OF ME WHICH IS SPIDER-MAN IS REACTING SUSPICIOUSLY TO THEM! I'VE GOT TO CHECK THIS OUT!

BUT WHERE CAN THE IMPULSES BE COMING FROM? THE RADIO IS SHUT OFF! AND DOCTOR COBBWELL DOESN'T HAVE ANY OTHER ELECTRICAL GADGETS OPERATING NOW!

HE'S PUTTING ON HIS COAT! THIS IS MY CHANCE--AS SOON AS HE LEAVES!
I HAVE TO LECTURE AT THE INSTITUTE NOW, PETER! I'LL BE BACK IN A FEW HOURS!

SLAM!
HE'S GONE! NOW TO SEE WHAT THIS IS ALL ABOUT!
4

HEY, NO ORDINARY RADIO HAS GADGETS LIKE THAT INSIDE OF IT! THERE'S WHERE THE IMPULSES ARE COMING FROM--EVEN WITH THE SET OFF!
THAT DOES IT! NOW I'M THRU KIDDIN' AROUND!

NOW SPIDER-MAN IS GONNA TAKE ANOTHER LOOK-SEE AT THE TINKERER'S SHOP!

THE PLACE IS CLOSED FOR THE DAY! WELL, THAT WON'T STOP ME!

I'M GETTING THOSE SAME STRANGE IMPULSES AGAIN! THEY'RE COMING FROM BELOW!

WOW! NO INNOCENT LITTLE REPAIR SHOP EVER HAD A BASEMENT WORKROOM LIKE THAT BEFORE! IT'S MORE LIKE A CONCRETE-REINFORCED DUNGEON!
LUCKY THE DOOR'S OPEN! GUESS THEY'RE NOT EXPECTIN' VISITORS!

AND, INSIDE THE ISOLATED WORKROOM...
YOU HAVE DONE YOUR WORK WELL, TINKERER! WE ARE ALMOST READY TO STRIKE!
YES! OUR ELECTRONIC SPY DEVICES, HIDDEN IN RADIOS BELONGING TO IMPORTANT EARTHLINGS, HAVE ENABLED US TO LEARN MUCH ABOUT THEIR STRENGTHS AND WEAKNESSES, BEFORE WE ATTACK THIS UNSUSPECTING PLANET!
QUIET! I AM PROCESSING THE LATEST PICTURES RELAYED BACK TO US BY OUR PIN-POINT TV SPY DEVICE WHICH YOU PLANTED IN THE RADIO OF A MILITARY LEADER!
5

HOW CLEARLY WE CAN HEAR AND SEE! MY DEVICES NEVER FAIL!
SILENCE! I MUST RE-MEMBER WHAT THEY SAY!
I SUMMONED YOU, COLONEL, TO DISCUSS OUR PLANS FOR THE DEFENSE OF OUR EASTERN SEABOARD IN CASE OF A SURPRISE ATTACK BY ANY HOSTILE FORCE...

SO THAT'S WHAT IT'S ALL ABOUT! THEY'RE ENEMY ALIENS FROM ANOTHER PLANET, USING SOME SORT OF EERIE SPY DEVICES WHICH THEY PLACE IN OUR RADIOS IN ORDER TO LEARN OUR MILITARY AND SCIENTIFIC SECRETS!
A SPY!
MY SPIDER INSTINCT WARNS ME-- SOMEONE IS BEHIND ME!

WHEW! NOT A SECOND TOO SOON! NOW, NO PLACE TO GO BUT INSIDE!

A COSTUMED EARTH CREATURE! SEIZE HIM!
IT'S NOT GONNA BE THAT EASY, BUDDY-BOY!

SEE WHAT I MEAN??

LOOK! HE CAN CLIMB SHEER WALLS!
HE IS NO ORDINARY EARTHLING! HE IS SPIDER-MAN! GET HIM!

IF HE ESCAPES WITH KNOWLEDGE OF OUR PLANS, WE ARE LOST!
HAH! THAT INVERTER MECHANISM, THROWN AT HIM, LOOSENED HIS GRIP ON THE CEILING! HE'S FALLING!
6

NOW WE HAVE HIM! RENDER HIM HELPLESS!
WE CAN OVERWHELM HIM BY SHEER WEIGHT OF NUMBERS!
I'VE GOT NEWS FOR YOU! IT'S BEEN TRIED BEFORE!

HIS STRENGTH IS GREATER THAN WE SUSPECTED!
HE SHOOK US ALL OFF! A WEAPON! WE NEED A WEAPON!

WE HAVE A WEAPON! THE TINKERER IS NEVER UNPREPARED! THIS WILL STOP SPIDER-MAN!
OHHHH...

IT WOULD HAVE KILLED ANY NORMAL HUMAN-- BUT IT MERELY STUNNED HIM!
QUICKLY! PUT HIM INTO THE SPECIMEN CAGE BEFORE HE COMES TO!

THERE! NOTHING THAT LIVES CAN BREAK OUT OF THAT RESISTO-GLASS ENCLOSURE!
NOW, OUR FINAL PROBLEM IS TO FIND A SUITABLE WAY TO DISPOSE OF THE MEDDLER!

HE IS THE ONLY MORTAL ON EARTH WHO EVEN SUSPECTS OUR PRESENCE HERE--THE ONLY ONE WHO KNOWS OUR MASTER PLAN!
THERE IS NO QUESTION ABOUT IT! HE MUST BE DESTROYED! RELEASE THE AIR FROM THE RESISTO-GLASS PRISON!
7

WITHIN MINUTES, SPIDER-MAN WILL NO LONGER BE A MENACE TO US!
I'VE GOT TO MOVE FAST! THAT CONTROL PANEL ALSO OPENS AND SHUTS THIS CRAZY LITTLE MOUSETRAP!

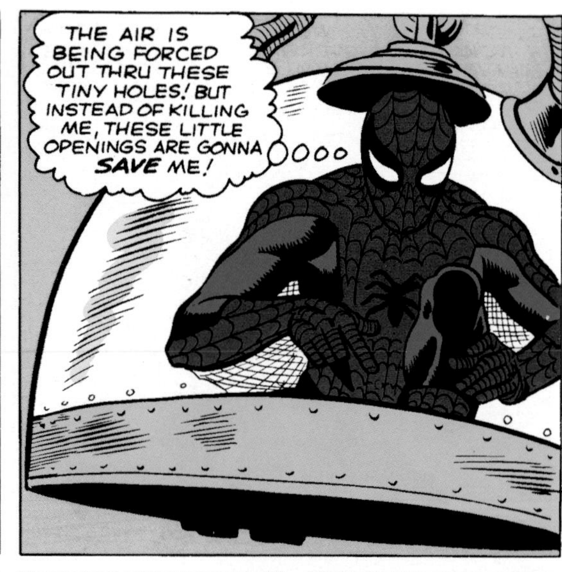
THE AIR IS BEING FORCED OUT THRU THESE TINY HOLES! BUT INSTEAD OF KILLING ME, THESE LITTLE OPENINGS ARE GONNA SAVE ME!

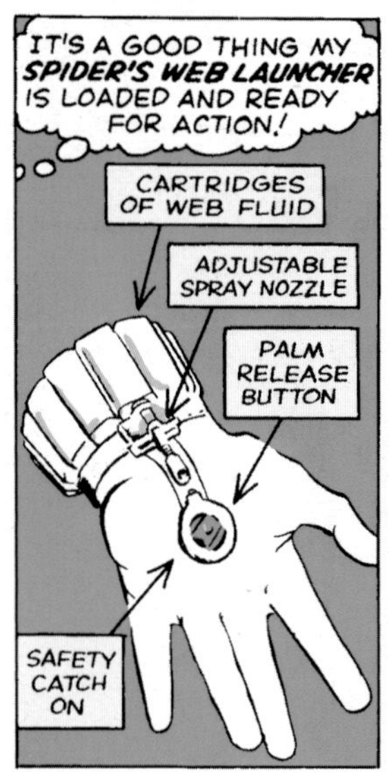
IT'S A GOOD THING MY SPIDER'S WEB LAUNCHER IS LOADED AND READY FOR ACTION!
CARTRIDGES OF WEB FLUID
ADJUSTABLE SPRAY NOZZLE
PALM RELEASE BUTTON
SAFETY CATCH ON

CAN'T AFFORD TO MISS! I'VE GOT TO LINE IT UP PERFECTLY WITH THE HOLE AND THE PROPER CONTROL PANEL BUTTON!

I'VE GOT THE SAFETY CATCH OFF--THE NOZZLE ON TARGET--HAND STEADY--

BULL'S EYE!

IT WORKED! THE CAGE IS OPEN! I'M FREE!
LOOK! IT'S IMPOSSIBLE, BUT--HE'S LOOSE! SPIDER-MAN IS LOOSE!

WHO DO YOU THINK YOU ARE--THE TOWN CRIER??!
YOU FOOL! YOU JARRED MY ARM! I-I'VE DESTROYED OUR CONTROL PANEL!
8

IT WOULD TAKE MONTHS TO REBUILD THAT CONTROL PANEL! WE-- WE HAVEN'T THE TIME!
QUICK! LET US FLEE WHILE WE CAN! SPIDER-MAN IS TOO POWERFUL!
WAIT! DON'T LEAVE ME! DON'T ABANDON ME!

HOLD ON THERE, LAUGHING BOY! YOU'RE NOT GOING ANYWHERE!
THEY WERE JUST DOING THEIR DUTY TO WHATEVER PLANET THEY WERE FROM! BUT YOU, YOU TRAITOR--!

THIS SMOKE! THE BURNING CONTROL PANEL--IT PUT THE WHOLE PLACE ON FIRE! STOP STRUGGLING, TINKERER! I'M TRYING TO SAVE YOU!
NO! LET ME GO! TAKE YOUR HANDS OFF ME! NOBODY TOUCHES THE TINKERER!

CAN'T SEE! THE SMOKE--IT'S BLINDING ME--CHOKING ME-- GOT TO GET AWAY!

JUST IN TIME! COULDN'T HAVE LASTED MUCH LONGER! BUT THE BUILDING IS A TOTAL WRECK! IT'LL BE REDUCED TO ASHES IN MINUTES!
I HEAR SIRENS! FIRE ENGINES! SOMEONE MUST HAVE TURNED IN AN ALARM! I'VE GOT TO DISAPPEAR!

LOOK! IT'S SPIDER-MAN!
MAYBE HE STARTED THE FIRE! BUT-- WHY??
9

MEANWHILE, A STRANGE SPACECRAFT BEGINS TO STREAK AWAY FROM EARTH...
SAFE AT LAST! PRESS THE BUTTON WHICH WILL DESTROY ALL OUR SPY DEVICES BY REMOTE CONTROL!
IT IS DONE! WE CAN NEVER AGAIN RETURN TO EARTH--THEY WILL BE ON GUARD FROM THIS DAY ON!

AND, BACK AT THE LABORATORY OF DOCTOR COBBWELL...
I'VE RE-EXAMINED THE RADIO, AND IT'S PERFECTLY NORMAL NOW! NO DEVICES--NO IMPULSES--NOTHING!
HERE COMES DR. COBBWELL! HE LOOKS EXCITED!
MY BOY, I JUST SAW THE MOST STARTLING SIGHT!

AS I WAS RETURNING FROM THE LECTURE IN MY CAR, I GLANCED SKYWARD--AND I COULD HAVE SWORN I SAW A SPACE SHIP OF SOME SORT, FADING INTO THE ATMOSPHERE!
REALLY? WHAT DID IT LOOK LIKE, SIR?

WELL, IT WAS SORT OF--OHHH, WHAT AM I SAYING?? I MUST HAVE IMAGINED IT! NOBODY WOULD BELIEVE ME, ANYWAY! I HAVE NO PROOF! PEOPLE WILL THINK I'M A TYPICAL ABSENT-MINDED PROFESSOR! FORGET IT, PETER! LET'S GET BACK TO WORK!
SURE, DOC!

AND YET, I WAS SO SURE...
I KNOW HOW THE DOC FEELS! IF NOT FOR THIS MASK I YANKED OFF THE TINKERER AT THE LAST MINUTE, I MIGHT NOT BELIEVE IT MYSELF! BUT I'D BETTER NEVER MENTION THIS TO ANYONE! IT WOULD BE TOO HARD TO EXPLAIN HOW PETER PARKER KNOWS SO MUCH ABOUT THE SPIDER-MAN'S ADVENTURES!
10

the BEGINNING... OF MORE AND GREATER SPIDER-MAN ADVENTURES, STARTING NEXT ISSUE!

APPROVED BY THE COMICS CODE AUTHORITY
the AMAZING SPIDER-MAN
IND.
3
JULY
MARVEL COMICS GROUP 12¢
AMERICA'S MOST EXCITING SUPER-HERO CAPTURED BY THE WORLD'S MOST DREADED SUPER-VILLAIN!
YOU ARE HELPLESS, SPIDER-MAN! I WARNED YOU THAT THE POWER OF DOCTOR OCTOPUS IS FAR GREATER THAN YOURS!
-DITKO-
CAN ANYTHING THAT LIVES, DEFEAT THE MIGHTY DOCTOR OCTOPUS??
A BOOK-LENGTH SUPER-THRILLER!
SPIDER-MAN FACES HIS MOST POWERFUL FOE:
"DR. OCTOPUS!"

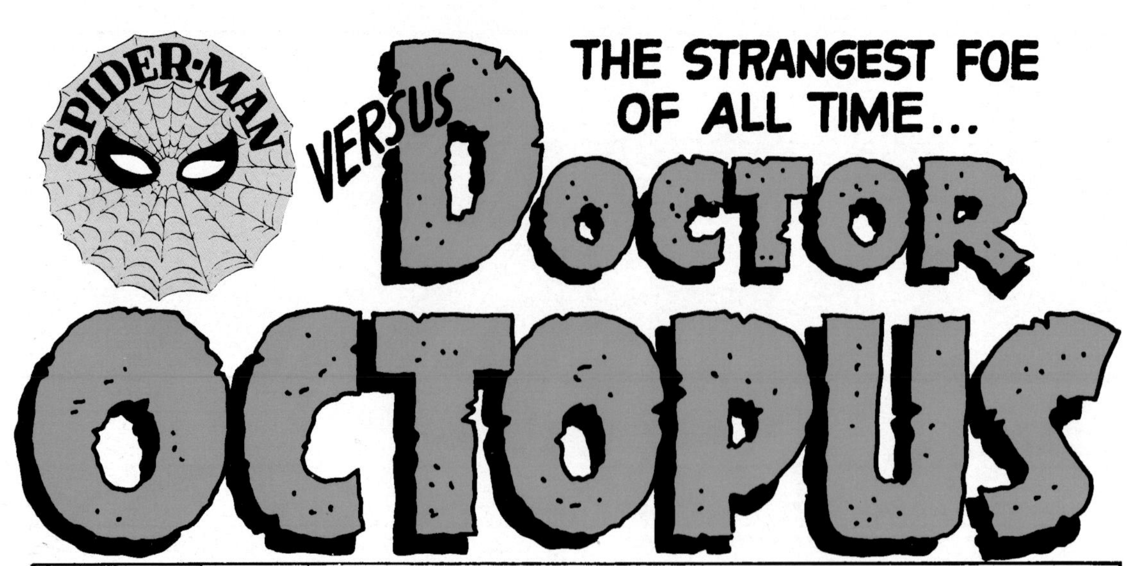
SPIDER-MAN
VERSUS
THE STRANGEST FOE OF ALL TIME...
DOCTOR OCTOPUS

DOCTOR OCTOPUS THE ONLY ENEMY EVER TO DEFEAT SPIDER-MAN!
IN THIS EPIC TALE... SEE THE HUMAN TORCH!
FANTASY! THRILLS!
STORY BY: STAN LEE
ART BY: STEVE DITKO
LETTERER: JOHN DUFFY
AND NOW BEGIN!
X-219
1

A STORY HAS TO START SOMEWHERE, SO LET'S BEGIN WITH A LONELY WAREHOUSE, IN THE DEAD OF NIGHT, WHERE WE FIND A ROBBERY TAKING PLACE...
HOLD IT, YOU GUYS! I THINK I HEARD SOMETHIN'!
RELAX, CHARLIE! IT WAS PROBABLY JUST A MOUSE!

SUDDENLY, THE MOST AWESOME IMAGE IN CRIME-FIGHTING APPEARS ON THE WALL DIRECTLY ABOVE THE STARTLED THIEVES...
MOUSE? YOU'VE NEVER SEEN A MOUSE LIKE THIS BEFORE!
LOOK!! IT--IT'S--

DON'T BE SHY, FELLA! YOU CAN SAY MY NAME! IT'S SPIDER-MAN!
GET 'IM! THERE ARE THREE OF US! HE CAN'T TAKE US ALL!

UGH!
BROTHER, YOU'RE LIVING IN A FOOL'S PARADISE!
OOF!
OW!

MINUTES LATER...
SOME BIG CRIMINAL MASTER-MIND YOU ARE!
AW, SHADDUP! WHOEVER EXPECTED SPIDER-MAN TO BUTT IN!
LOOK, JOE! SPIDER-MAN'S BEEN HERE! AND HOW!

AND, NOT FAR AWAY...
IT'S ALMOST TOO EASY! I'VE RUN OUT OF ENEMIES WHO CAN GIVE ME ANY REAL OPPOSITION! I'M TOO POWERFUL FOR ANY FOE! I ALMOST WISH FOR AN OPPONENT WHO'D GIVE ME A RUN FOR MY MONEY!

AND LITTLE DOES SPIDER-MAN SUSPECT THAT HIS FRIVOLOUS WISH IS ABOUT TO COME TRUE! FOR, AT THAT MOMENT, ON THE OUTSKIRTS OF TOWN...
HERE COMES DOCTOR OCTOPUS!
DOCTOR OCTOPUS? WHY DO THEY CALL HIM THAT?
WATCH! YOU'LL SEE IN A MINUTE!
US
ATOMIC RESEARCH CENTER

SEE? IT'S THAT ESPECIALLY-DESIGNED CONTRAPTION HE WEARS, WHICH ENABLES HIM TO PERFORM HIS EXPERIMENTS BEHIND THE LEAD WALLS WHICH SHIELD HIM FROM RADIATION!!

HE CREATED THAT GET-UP HIMSELF, AND HE'S THE ONLY SCIENTIST PERMITTED TO WEAR IT!
HE'S THE MOST BRILLIANT ATOMIC-RESEARCHER IN OUR COUNTRY TODAY!

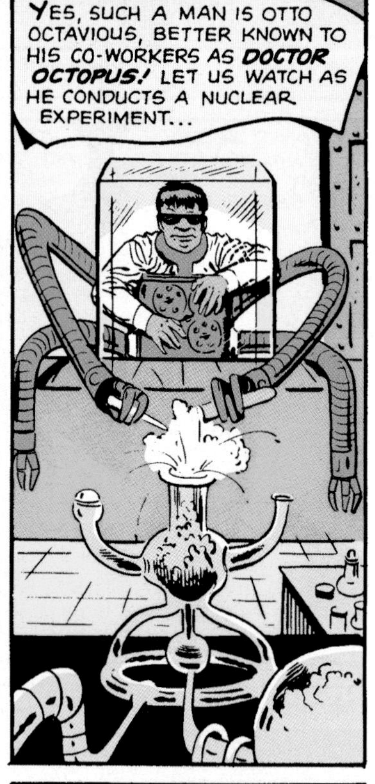
YES, SUCH A MAN IS OTTO OCTAVIOUS, BETTER KNOWN TO HIS CO-WORKERS AS DOCTOR OCTOPUS! LET US WATCH AS HE CONDUCTS A NUCLEAR EXPERIMENT...

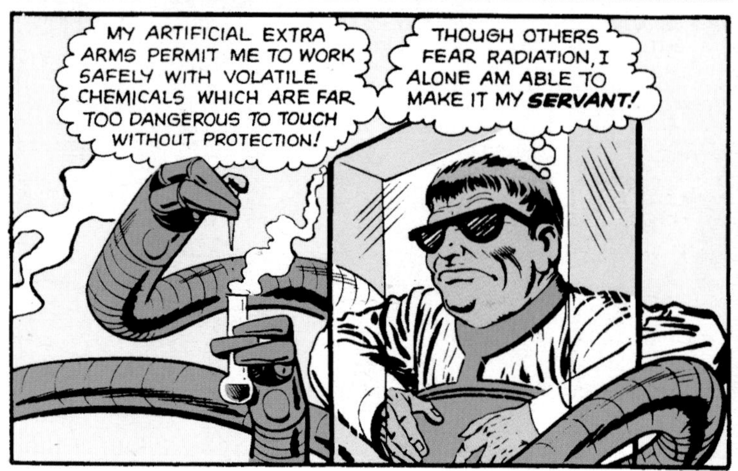
MY ARTIFICIAL EXTRA ARMS PERMIT ME TO WORK SAFELY WITH VOLATILE CHEMICALS WHICH ARE FAR TOO DANGEROUS TO TOUCH WITHOUT PROTECTION!
THOUGH OTHERS FEAR RADIATION, I ALONE AM ABLE TO MAKE IT MY SERVANT!

BUT NOTHING IS EVER PERFECT, NOT EVEN THE PROJECTS OF DOCTOR OCTOPUS! AND, AS THE UNSUSPECTING ATOMIC GENIUS CONDUCTS HIS EXPERIMENT...
LOOK! THE RADIATION-METER HAS GONE WHACKY! SOMETHING IS WRONG! THERE'S GONNA BE A BLOW UP!
SOUND THE ALARM!
3

BUT THE WARNING, ALAS, IS GIVEN TOO LATE! AND BEFORE THE ALARM CAN BE SOUNDED...

THEN, AFTER THE FLAMES AND SMOKE HAVE PARTIALLY CLEARED...
DOCTOR OCTOPUS IS STILL BREATHING! I HOPE WE'VE REACHED HIM IN TIME!
EVEN THOUGH HE'S ALIVE, HE'S ABSORBED A GREAT DEAL OF RADIATION--- POOR GUY!

IN THE HOURS THAT FOLLOW, AFTER EXHAUSTIVE TESTS...
THE X-RAYS SHOW AN UNCERTAIN AMOUNT OF BRAIN DAMAGE! I'M AFRAID HIS MIND HAS BEEN PERMANENTLY DAMAGED!
WE CAN'T REMOVE THOSE ARTIFICIAL ARMS OF HIS YET! THE RADIATION HAS CAUSED THEM TO ADHERE TO HIS BODY IN SOME STRANGE WAY!

FINALLY, DAYS LATER, THE INJURED SCIENTIST RECOVERS CONSCIOUSNESS...
WHAT AM I DOING HERE? LET ME UP! I MUST RETURN TO MY WORK!
NO! YOU'VE BEEN VERY ILL! YOU MUST STAY IN BED! YOU NEED THE REST!

BUT THE BRAIN OF DR. OCTOPUS--THE BRAIN WHICH HAS BEEN DAMAGED BY RADIATION--REACTS IN A BITTER WAY...
THEY'RE JEALOUS OF ME! THEY WANT TO KEEP ME FROM MY WORK! BUT I'LL SHOW THEM! I'M STRONGER THAN ANY OF THEM!

THE WINDOW IS BARRED! THEY'RE TRYING TO MAKE A PRISONER OF ME! THE FOOLS! NO ONE CAN HOLD DOCTOR OCTOPUS AGAINST HIS WILL! NO ONE!
4

THEN SUDDENLY, AT JUST A SUGGESTION OF A THOUGHT BY DR. OCTOPUS, HIS ARTIFICIAL ARMS MOVE AS THOUGH THEY HAVE A WILL OF THEIR OWN...
I'VE GOT TO BREAK THOSE BARS!

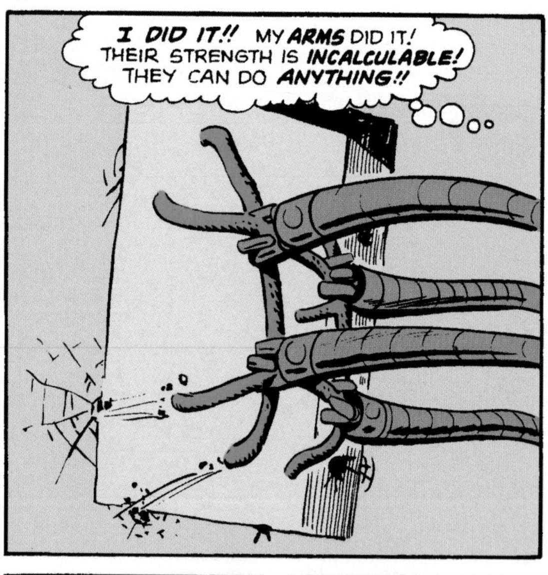
I DID IT!! MY ARMS DID IT! THEIR STRENGTH IS INCALCULABLE! THEY CAN DO ANYTHING!!

SOMEHOW, MY MECHANICAL ARMS HAVE ALMOST BECOME A PART OF ME! THEY OBEY MY EVERY COMMAND! WITH SUCH POWER AND MY BRILLIANT MIND, I'M THE SUPREME HUMAN BEING ON EARTH!

MINUTES LATER...
YOU WANTED TO SEE ME, DR. OCTOPUS?
YES! COME IN! SHUT THE DOOR BEHIND YOU!

WHAT IS IT? YOU-- OH, NO! NO!
HA-HA! YOU DON'T BELIEVE WHAT YOU SEE? BUT IT'S TRUE! I'M ALL-POWERFUL! FROM NOW ON, I GIVE THE COMMANDS HERE!

MEANWHILE, AT THE OFFICE OF J. JONAH JAMESON, PUBLISHER OF THE DAILY BUGLE...
I WANT PICTURES OF THE INJURED SCIENTIST, DR. OCTOPUS, BUT NO ONE IS ALLOWED TO ENTER THE BLISS PRIVATE HOSPITAL ANY MORE!
I NEVER HEARD OF ANY HOSPITAL KEEPING PEOPLE OUT! DON'T WORRY, J.J.! I'LL GET THOSE PIX FOR YOU!

MY BEST MEN HAVE TRIED AND FAILED! BUT SO FAR, YOU'VE SUCCEEDED IN EVERY ASSIGNMENT! I CAN'T IMAGINE HOW A TEEN-AGER LIKE YOU DOES IT!
OUR AGREEMENT, J.J., IS THAT YOU'RE NEVER TO ASK ME HOW I DO IT!

JUST HAVE A CHECK READY FOR ME WHEN I BRING BACK THE PIX OF DR. OCTOPUS!
HE DOESN'T SUSPECT PETER PARKER, THE TEEN-AGER HE ASSIGNED TO THE JOB, IS GONNA HAVE SPIDER-MAN DO IT!
5

AND SO...
HERE'S THE PLACE! STRANGE THAT IT'S LOCKED AND NOBODY IS ADMITTED! WHAT KIND OF A HOSPITAL IS IT, ANYWAY?

WELL, THERE'S ONLY ONE WAY TO FIND OUT-- AND SPIDER-MAN'S JUST THE CAT TO DO IT!

THESE SUCTION FINGERS OF MINE WILL GET ME UP THE WALL IN NO TIME! BOY, IT'S GREAT BEING SPIDER-MAN! I CAN DO ALMOST ANYTHING!

THE ONLY PROBLEM IS--MY JOBS ARE TOO EASY! I'D WELCOME A LITTLE COMPETITION ONCE IN A WHILE!

AND, AS HE STEADILY CLIMBS UP THE SHEER OUTER WALL, LITTLE DOES SPIDER-MAN DREAM THAT HE IS SOON TO GET FAR MORE "COMPETITION" THAN HE EVER BARGAINED FOR!

SECONDS LATER...
ALMOST THERE!

HOLY MACKERAL! WHAT'S THAT?
SILENCE! NOBODY IS TO SPEAK WHEN DR. OCTOPUS SPEAKS!
6

PEERING UNSEEN THROUGH THE LARGE PICTURE-WINDOW, SPIDER-MAN WITNESSES A STRANGE, UNEXPECTED SIGHT...
YOU CAN'T KEEP ALL OF US PRISONERS FOREVER, DOCTOR OCTOPUS! WE'VE DONE WHAT YOU ASKED-- GOTTEN YOU ALL THE EQUIPMENT YOU WANTED! WHEN WILL YOU LET US GO?
NOT UNTIL I'M READY! WITH MY POWERS, NO ONE CAN RESIST ME! YOU'LL REMAIN TO SERVE ME UNTIL I NO LONGER NEED YOU-- AND NOT BEFORE!
WELL, WELL! SO THE GOOD DOC HAS FLIPPED HIS LID, EH? WELL, THIS IS JUST WHAT I'VE BEEN HOPIN' FOR-- A LITTLE ACTION!

BUT THIS IS MAD! YOU HAVE NO RIGHT--
RIGHT?! YOU DARE SPEAK TO ME OF RIGHT?

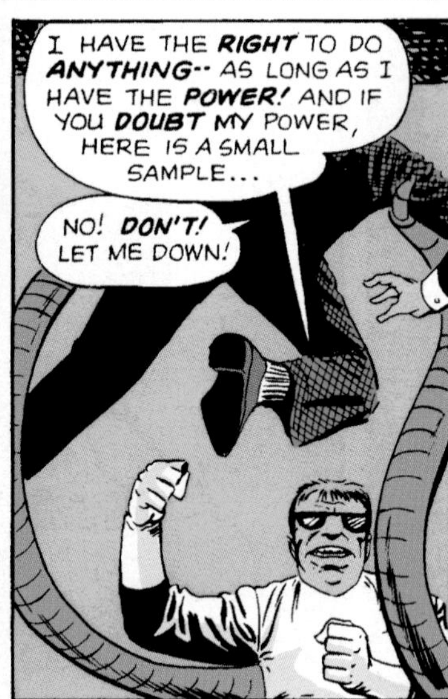
I HAVE THE RIGHT TO DO ANYTHING-- AS LONG AS I HAVE THE POWER! AND IF YOU DOUBT MY POWER, HERE IS A SMALL SAMPLE...
NO! DON'T! LET ME DOWN!

LOOKS LIKE IT'S TIME FOR SPIDER-MAN TO JOIN THE PARTY BEFORE HE REALLY HURTS THAT FELLA!

HOLD IT, DOC! HOW ABOUT PICKIN' ON SOMEONE WHO CAN FIGHT YOU BACK?
SPIDER-MAN!

WELL, I SURE AIN'T ALBERT SCHWEITZER!
YOU DARE SPEAK FLIPPANTLY TO ME! YOU FOOL! WHEN I'M FINISHED WITH YOU, YOU'LL SING A DIFFERENT TUNE!

YOU DON'T THINK THOSE DUMB-LOOKING FLAPPERS OF YOURS CAN MOVE FAST ENOUGH TO CATCH SPIDER-MAN DO YOU?

HEY!! WHA--?
SURPRISED? DOCTOR OCTOPUS IS FAR MORE POWERFUL THAN YOU DREAMED! FAR MORE POWERFUL THAN EVEN YOU!

DON'T LET THAT ONE LUCKY PUNCH GO TO YOUR HEAD, PAL! I'VE A FEW MORE SURPRISES!
AH! MOST INGENIOUS OF YOU! YOUR SPIDER'S WEB!!

BUT, AS YOU CAN SEE, HOLDING ONLY TWO OF MY ARMS ISN'T ENOUGH! I STILL HAVE MORE!
NO TIME TO SHOOT MY WEB AGAIN! HE'S FASTER THAN I EXPECTED!

BUT I CAN STILL GRAB HIS OTHER ARMS!
OOF! IT TAKES ALL MY STRENGTH! HE--HE ALSO HAS SUPER-HUMAN STRENGTH!

MY WEB! HE SNAPPED IT! NOBODY HAS EVER DONE THAT BEFORE!
AND NOW, SUPER-MAN, I GROW BORED WITH THIS GAME! MY TIME IS TOO VALUABLE!
8

NOW, WATCH ME TRAP A SPIDER IN A WEB OF MY OWN-- A WEB MADE OF MY NEW-FOUND ARMS! YOUR STRENGTH IS MERELY THAT OF A SPIDER, BUT MINE IS THE ENERGY OF AN ATOM, BORN OF A NUCLEAR ACCIDENT!
I'M HELPLESS! CAN'T FIGHT ALL THOSE ARMS AT ONCE! DON'T KNOW WHAT TO DO NEXT! HE'S JUST TOYING WITH ME!

YOU DARED TO MOCK ME BEFORE! WHY AREN'T YOU MOCKING ME NOW? WHERE ARE YOUR BRAVE WORDS AND TAUNTS NOW, SPIDER-MAN?

OR DO YOU REALIZE YOU'VE FINALLY MET YOUR MASTER? AND NOW, YOU CAN LEAVE THE WAY YOU ENTERED! YOU'RE NO THREAT TO ME!

WEAK, GROGGY, JUST BARELY CONSCIOUS, SPIDER-MAN HAS HIS FALL BROKEN BY A TREE, AS HE FINALLY SLUMPS TO THE GROUND... IN DEFEAT!
9

HE BEAT ME! I--I NEVER HAD A CHANCE!
I DIDN'T EVEN GIVE HIM A GOOD FIGHT! HE COULD'VE FINISHED ME OFF ANY TIME HE WANTED TO!

WHAT DO I DO NOW? I'VE NEVER BEEN BEATEN BEFORE! BUT THIS TIME, MY SPIDER POWERS WERE NOT ENOUGH! IS THIS THE END OF SPIDER-MAN?

NOT LONG AFTERWARDS, AT THE HOSPITAL...
EVEN THOUGH I DEFEATED SPIDER-MAN, MY PRISONERS ESCAPED DURING THE FIGHT! I MUST LEAVE, BEFORE THE POLICE ARRIVE!

WITH MY ARMS, I CAN GO ANYWHERE... DO ANYTHING! FENCES CAN'T STOP ME! NO ONE CAN CATCH ME!
ATO
RES
CEN

NOW THAT I HAVE REACHED MY OBJECTIVE, ANY UNLOCKED WINDOW WILL FURNISH AN ENTRANCE FOR ME!

THE SECURITY POLICE AREN'T APT TO NOTICE AN EXTRA PIPE OR TWO UP ON THE CEILING! ONCE HE'S GONE, I CAN ACT FREELY!
10

THIS IS WHAT I'M AFTER! THE BRAIN CENTER OF THE ENTIRE ATOMIC LAB! ONCE I TAKE IT OVER, THE GREATEST SOURCE OF ATOMIC POWER IN THE NATION WILL BE MINE!

IT'S AN EASY MATTER FOR DOCTOR OCTOPUS TO UNLOCK A DOOR!

OUT! ALL OF YOU!... I'M TAKING OVER NOW!
D-DID YOU SEE THAT? IT WAS DOCTOR OCTOPUS!
BUT WHAT'S HE UP TO?

NOTHING CAN STOP ME NOW! BETWEEN MY OWN SUPER-STRENGTH AND THE ATOMIC POWER WHICH IS MINE TO COMMAND HERE, I'M THE STRONGEST MAN ALIVE!!
BUT FIRST, I'LL GIVE THE WORLD A DEMONSTRATION OF MY STRENGTH! I'LL DESTROY PART OF THIS PLANT AND REBUILD IT TO SUIT MYSELF!

AND SO...
SOMETHING'S HAPPENED TO THE LEAD SHIELDING! IT'S BEEN LOWERED! THE RADIATION IS STARTING TO ESCAPE!

LOOK! THE GIANT MACHINES ARE RUNNING OUT OF CONTROL -- AS THOUGH SOME MADMAN IS GUIDING THEM!

THERE'S TOO MUCH PRESSURE IN THE MAIN VALVES! THE PIPES ARE OVERHEATING...EXPLODING! IT ISN'T SAFE TO STAY HERE!
11

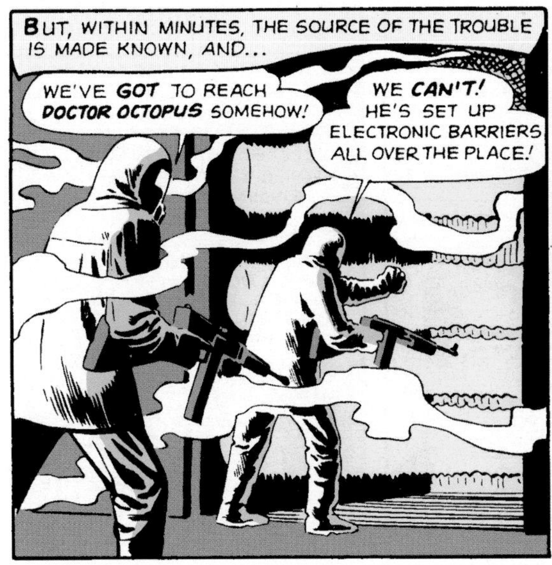
BUT, WITHIN MINUTES, THE SOURCE OF THE TROUBLE IS MADE KNOWN, AND...
WE'VE GOT TO REACH DOCTOR OCTOPUS SOMEHOW!
WE CAN'T! HE'S SET UP ELECTRONIC BARRIERS ALL OVER THE PLACE!

AND, BEFORE LONG, THE ENTIRE PLANT IS EVACUATED, EXCEPT FOR...
THEY REALIZE I CANNOT BE STOPPED AND HAVE GIVEN UP TRYING! I'VE WON!! THE PLANT IS MINE! I AM NOW IN COMPLETE CONTROL!

THE FOREMOST BRAINS OF THE NATION'S ARMED FORCES AND SECURITY AGENCIES CONFER FEVERISHLY, BUT TO NO AVAIL...
WE'VE NEVER BEEN UP AGAINST ANYTHING LIKE THIS BEFORE! A BRILLIANT SCIENTIST, WITH SUPER-HUMAN POWERS, ON A MAD RAMPAGE!
IF WE CAN'T STOP HIM, THEN WE MUST SEE THAT INNOCENT PEOPLE ARE NOT INJURED!

AND SO, THE ORDER GOES OUT--NO ONE IS ALLOWED IN OR OUT OF THE ATOMIC PLANT...
CAN'T FIGURE OUT WHY THEY POST SENTRIES HERE! IF DR. OCTOPUS TRIES TO GET OUT, HOW CAN WE STOP HIM?

MEANWHILE, WHAT OF TEEN-AGE PETER PARKER, ALIAS SPIDER-MAN?
POOR PETER'S BEEN MOPING IN HIS ROOM FOR HOURS! I WISH HE'D TELL ME WHAT'S WRONG?
I'M A FAILURE! SPIDER-MAN IS A JOKE... A NOTHING! THERE'S THE PHONE!
BR-I-I-NG!

MR. JAMESON? NO, I WON'T BE ABLE TO GET THE PICTURES OF DOCTOR OCTOPUS! NO, I PROBABLY WON'T BE ABLE TO GET ANY MORE! SORRY-- YEAH... GOOD BYE!

PETER, DEAR, WHAT'S WRONG? I CAN'T BEAR TO SEE YOU SO UNHAPPY! IS THERE ANYTHING I CAN DO TO HELP?
NO, AUNT MAY... IT'S... IT'S MY OWN PERSONAL PROB-LEM! I'LL GET OVER IT! GOT TO LEAVE NOW-- TIME FOR SCHOOL!
12

HELLO, PETEY!... SAY, WHAT'S WITH HIM? HE DIDN'T **ANSWER!**
AND THERE'S NO ONE I CAN TALK TO... NO ONE WHO'D UNDERSTAND!
HIM? HE'S DOWN IN THE DUMPS! LOOKS LIKE HE LOST HIS FAVORITE TEST TUBE!

PETE, DID YOU HEAR THE BIG NEWS? THE GOVERNOR'S ASKED THE **FANTASTIC FOUR** TO TRY TO CAPTURE DOCTOR OCTOPUS!
THEY'RE BUSY WITH ANOTHER CASE, BUT THEY SENT THE **HUMAN TORCH** TO SEE WHAT HE CAN DO! HE'S SPEAKING TO OUR ASSEMBLY TODAY!
BIG DEAL!

LATER, AT THE SCHOOL ASSEMBLY...
I WAS ASKED HERE TO TACKLE DOCTOR OCTOPUS! BUT I'VE USED MY FLAME SO MUCH RECENTLY, I HAVE TO WAIT A FEW DAYS TO LET IT GET STRONG AGAIN! WHILE I'M WAITING, YOUR PRINCIPAL ASKED ME TO ADDRESS YOU...
IF ONLY I HAD **HIS** POWER... **HIS** CONFIDENCE!... BUT THAT'S EASY WHEN YOU'VE NEVER BEEN BEATEN!

NOW FOR A LITTLE DEMONSTRATION! I CAN'T APPLY MY TOTAL FLAME, BUT HERE ARE SOME FIERY FIGURES FOR YOU!
THIS IS WHAT USUALLY HAPPENS WHEN THE **THING** HELPS ME WITH MY HOMEWORK! I GET RESULTS LIKE **THIS!**
2
2
3

THEN, AFTER A FEW MORE COLORFUL DEMONSTRATIONS...
NOW, FOR A PARTING THOUGHT! STICK TO YOUR SCHOOL WORK AND DO YOUR BEST IN YOUR STUDIES! DON'T BE DISCOURAGED IF IT SOMETIMES SEEMS TOUGH! THE IMPORTANT THING IS NEVER GIVE UP! REMEMBER THAT--**NEVER GIVE UP!**

ABILITY ALONE ISN'T ENOUGH! IT'S **ONE** LESSON I'VE LEARNED FROM MY PARTNERSHIP WITH THE **FANTASTIC FOUR!**
IT'S ALMOST AS THOUGH HE'S TALKING TO **ME!**

EVEN THE **FANTASTIC FOUR** HAVE HAD DEFEATS--BUT WE ALWAYS COME BACK! OUR MOTTO IS NEVER SAY DIE!
HE'S **RIGHT!** BY GOLLY, HE'S **RIGHT!**

LATER, AT THE CONCLUSION OF **THE TORCH'S** LECTURE...
I WANT TO THANK YOU FOR THAT SPEECH! I--I'LL NEVER **FORGET** WHAT YOU SAID TODAY! IT MEANT A **LOT** TO ME!
HUH? OH, SURE--SURE! GLAD YOU ENJOYED IT, FELLA!
13

LIKE A MAN POSSESSED, PETER PARKER RACES HOME TO THE PRIVACY OF HIS ROOM, AND...
I GUESS IF THE FANTASTIC FOUR COULD BE DEFEATED, AND THEN GO BACK FOR MORE, SPIDER-MAN CAN, TOO!

OKAY, DOCTOR OCTOPUS, THIS IS IT!! NOW THAT I KNOW HOW STRONG YOU ARE, YOU WON'T HAVE THE ADVANTAGE OF SUPRISE ON YOUR SIDE AGAIN!

THIS IS ONE EASY WAY TO GET PAST THOSE SENTRIES BELOW!

HEY! DID YOU JUST SEE SOME-ONE FLYING ABOVE US?
SOMEONE FLYING ABOVE US? ARE YOU SOME KINDA NUT OR SOMETHIN'?!

SO FAR, SO GOOD! I LANDED SAFELY ON THE ROOF WITHOUT BEING STOPPED!

NOW, TO GET AS CLOSE AS I CAN TO DOCTOR OCTOPUS BEFORE HE DIS-COVERS ME!

BUT THE STRANGE SCIENTIST HAS EYES EVERYWHERE, AND...
IT'S SPIDER-MAN AGAIN! WELL, THIS TIME HE WON'T BE SO LUCKY! THIS TIME I'LL FINISH HIM FOR GOOD!
14

FROM NOW ON, I ALLOW NO ONE TO INTERFERE WITH MY PLANS! I WILL PERMIT NO ONE TO DEFY ME!

AND, AT THAT MOMENT...
MY SPIDER SENSES WARN ME OF DANGER BEHIND ME!

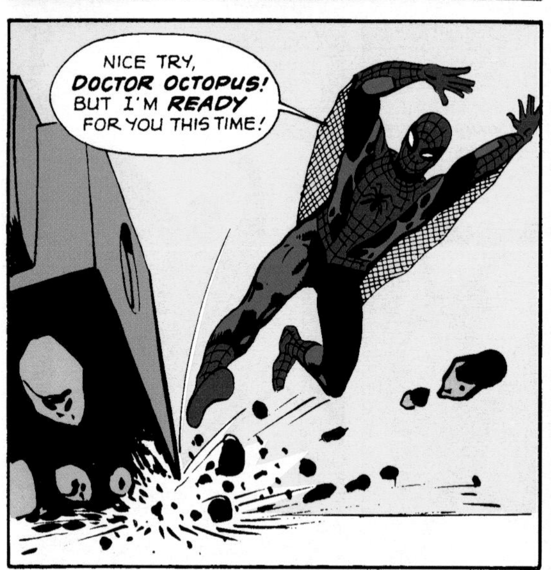
NICE TRY, DOCTOR OCTOPUS! BUT I'M READY FOR YOU THIS TIME!

WITH MY SPIDER SENSES FULLY ALERT, AND MY SPIDER MUSCLES IN TOP CONDITION, HE CAN'T POSSIBLY HURL THOSE ELECTRONIC BOLTS FAST ENOUGH TO HURT ME!

HE KNOWS MY EVERY MOVE! HE MUST BE WATCHING ME ON SOME SORT OF TV HOOK-UP! WELL, I'LL JUST GO SOMEWHERE OUT OF RANGE...AS ONLY I CAN!

HE'S FOUND A WAY TO EVADE MY ELECTRONIC SCANNERS! HMM... HE'S CLEVERER THAN I THOUGHT!

BUT I'LL DEFEAT HIM WITH MY ALL-POWERFUL **ARMS**, AS I DID BEFORE! HE WON'T ELUDE ME **NOW!**

AH, **THERE'S** WHAT I'M LOOKING FOR--THE **CHEM** LAB!
CHEMICAL LABORATORY

I'VE GOT TO MOVE **FAST!** IT WON'T BE LONG BEFORE HE **FINDS** ME!

THERE!! IT'S DONE!

AND NOW THIS WIRING'LL SUIT MY PURPOSE JUST FINE!

MUSTN'T MAKE A MISTAKE! **DOCTOR OCTOPUS** WON'T GIVE ME A SECOND CHANCE IF ANYTHING GOES WRONG!
16

I STILL CAN'T BE SURE THIS WILL WORK, BUT I'VE **GOT** TO TRY IT!

NOW TO FIND **DOCTOR OCTOPUS!**

ONCE AGAIN, AT THE LAST SPLIT-SECOND, **SPIDER-MAN'S** SPIDER INSTINCT SAVES HIM FROM SUDDEN DEFEAT...
HAH! I'VE **GOT** YOU, **SPIDER-MAN!** WHA--?
OH, **NO,** YOU DON'T!

MOVING WITH EVERY OUNCE OF SPEED HE POSSESSES, **SPIDER-MAN** MANAGES TO LOOP ONE OF HIS HASTILY CONSTRUCTED DEVICES AROUND TWO OF **DOCTOR OCTOPUS'** ARMS BEFORE ANOTHER ARM, STRIKING OUT, FORCES HIM TO DROP THE SECOND DEVICE...
OHH!

BUT **SPIDER-MAN** HAS SUPER-HUMAN STRENGTH, EVEN AS **DOCTOR OCTOPUS,** AND HE RECOVERS FROM THE BLOW IN SECONDS, IN TIME TO DIVE OUT OF HARM'S WAY...
NOW TO GET OUT OF REACH AND WATCH WHAT HAPPENS!
YOU **HOPE** TO DEFEAT ME WITH A FOOLISH THING LIKE **THIS?** YOU MUST BE **MAD!**

OH, I SEE! IT'S A CHEMICAL WHICH FUSES MY METAL ARMS TOGETHER! HMM... CLEVER!
BUT I CAN TAKE CARE OF THAT EASILY-- **AFTER** I DISPOSE OF **YOU** FOR GOOD!
17

SLOWLY, INEXORABLY, DR. OCTOPUS FORCES SPIDER-MAN BACK AGAINST THE WALL, BLOCKING HIS WEB WITH HIS SWIFTLY-MOVING ARMS...
HA-HA! EVEN YOUR FAST-SHOOTING WEB ISN'T QUICK ENOUGH FOR ME!

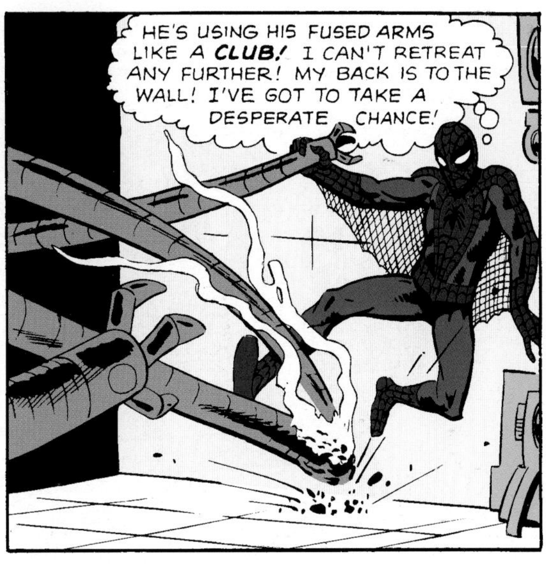
HE'S USING HIS FUSED ARMS LIKE A CLUB! I CAN'T RETREAT ANY FURTHER! MY BACK IS TO THE WALL! I'VE GOT TO TAKE A DESPERATE CHANCE!

MOVING LIKE A PERSON POSSESSED, SPIDER-MAN WHIPS HIS LEGS AROUND ONE OF DOCTOR OCTOPUS' TENTACLE ARMS, WHILE HE SEIZES THE OTHER FREE ARM WITH BOTH OF HIS POWERFUL HANDS...
GOT YOU!
BUT NOT FOR LONG!

THEN, BEFORE DOCTOR OCTOPUS CAN MAKE ANOTHER MOVE, SPIDER-MAN SHOOTS HIS AMAZING WEB DIRECTLY AT THE STARTLED SCIENTIST'S FACE...
I SHOULD HAVE REALIZED SOONER, OCTOPUS, THE BEST DEFENSE IS A SMASHING OFFENSE!

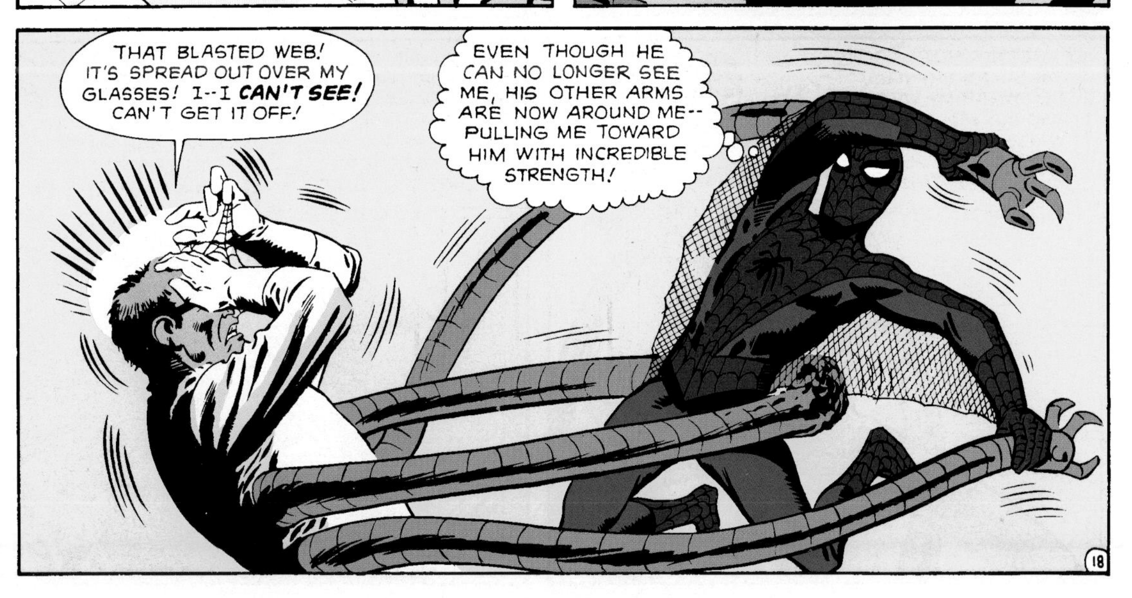
THAT BLASTED WEB! IT'S SPREAD OUT OVER MY GLASSES! I--I CAN'T SEE! CAN'T GET IT OFF!
EVEN THOUGH HE CAN NO LONGER SEE ME, HIS OTHER ARMS ARE NOW AROUND ME-- PULLING ME TOWARD HIM WITH INCREDIBLE STRENGTH!
18

AH... **THERE!!** I GOT THEM OFF!
I'VE GOT HIS TWO FREE ARMS APART! BUT I DARE NOT LET **GO** OF THEM!

GIVE UP, FOOL! SOONER OR LATER YOU'LL **HAVE** TO LET GO, AND THEN I'LL **HAVE** YOU!
I'VE GOT **ONE** CHANCE... BUT I'VE GOT TO TIME IT TO THE SPLIT-SECOND OR I'M **FINISHED!**

SUDDENLY, **SPIDER-MAN** LETS GO OF **DOCTOR OCTOPUS'** ARMS AND, AT THE SAME INSTANT, LASHES OUT WITH A SMASHING RIGHT!
NOW!

I **DID** IT! I KNOCKED HIM OUT!
I HAD TO LET HIM GO, AND THEN STRIKE FASTER THAN HE COULD MOVE!
STRANGE THAT AN OLD-FASHIONED PUNCH TO THE JAW DEFEATED THE MOST DANGEROUS VILLAIN I'VE EVER FACED!

BETTER NOT TAKE ANY CHANCES! I'LL WRAP MY WEBBING AROUND HIM MANY TIMES WHILE HE'S OUT! HE'LL **NEVER** BE ABLE TO SNAP **THIS!**

LATER, AT THE SENTRY POST OUTSIDE THE ATOMIC PLANT...
CAPTAIN! WE'VE BEEN HEARING NOISES INSIDE THERE! LIKE A **FIGHT!**
SOMEONE MUST HAVE SNEAKED PAST US AND-- **LOOK!** OVER THERE!
19

IT'S THE SIGN OF SPIDER-MAN!
THERE HE IS! HE'S WAVING TO US TO COME ON!

CAREFUL, PAL! NO TELLING WHAT'S GOIN' ON!
YOU'RE TELLIN' ME! I'M GONNA SHOOT FIRST AND ASK QUESTIONS LATER!

LOOK! IT'S DOCTOR OCTOPUS! HE'S ALL TIED UP AND HELPLESS!
DON'T JUST STAND THERE! GET ME OUT OF THIS!

THE AUTHORITIES WILL BE ABLE TO HANDLE DOCTOR OCTOPUS NOW!
BUT I STILL HAVE ONE MORE THING TO TAKE CARE OF-- AS SPIDER-MAN!

MINUTES LATER, THE DRAMATICALLY COSTUMED SUPER-HERO CLIMBS THE SHEER WALL OF A NEARBY HOTEL...
HE'S SOMEWHERE IN THIS HOTEL! I'LL FIND HIM EASILY!

MY SPIDER SENSE TELLS ME THAT HIS ROOM IS JUST AHEAD!
20

AND INSIDE THE ROOM IN QUESTION...
GOOD NEWS, TORCH! YOUR TEMPERATURE IS DOWN AND YOUR VIRUS IS GONE! BY NOW, YOUR FLAME SHOULD BE WORKING AT FULL STRENGTH!
GREAT, DOC! I WANNA SHOW MY PARTNERS IN THE FANTASTIC FOUR THAT I CAN TACKLE DR. OCTOPUS ALONE!

FLAME ON!
AND NOW FOR--
RELAX, TORCH! DR. OCTOPUS HAS BEEN CAPTURED ALREADY!

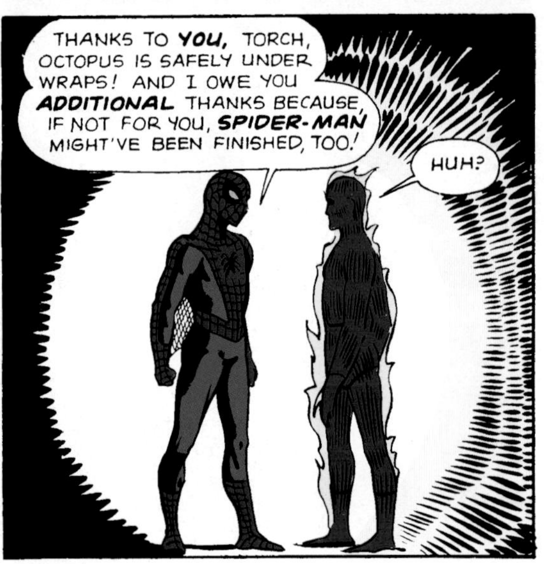
THANKS TO YOU, TORCH, OCTOPUS IS SAFELY UNDER WRAPS! AND I OWE YOU ADDITIONAL THANKS BECAUSE, IF NOT FOR YOU, SPIDER-MAN MIGHT'VE BEEN FINISHED, TOO!
HUH?

SO LONG, TORCH! SEE YA AROUND, PAL!
FLAMIN' FIREBALLS! I DON'T GET IT! WHAT DID I DO??

THE NEXT DAY, THE HUMAN TORCH GIVES A PULSE-POUNDING DEMONSTRATION OF HIS FULL POWERS BEFORE RETURNING TO HIS HEADQUARTERS...
WISH SPIDER-MAN WAS STILL AROUND TO JOIN ME IN THIS SHOW! BUT I DON'T KNOW WHERE HE CUT OUT TO!
NOW THERE'S MY IDEA OF A HERO! THE HUMAN TORCH-- AND A GUY LIKE SPIDER-MAN, TOO! WHY DON'TCHA WATCH AND SEE WHAT A REAL MAN IS LIKE, BOOKWORM?
SOMEDAY I'LL TELL YOU WHY, LOUD MOUTH! AND I'M SURE GONNA ENJOY IT! YES SIR, IT'S GONNA BE A REAL PLEASURE!
AND, FOR THE FIRST TIME, A CASE ENDS WITHOUT PETER PARKER DELIVERING ANY PHOTOS TO MR. JAMESON! BUT, RIGHT NOW, PETER COULDN'T CARE LESS!
The END

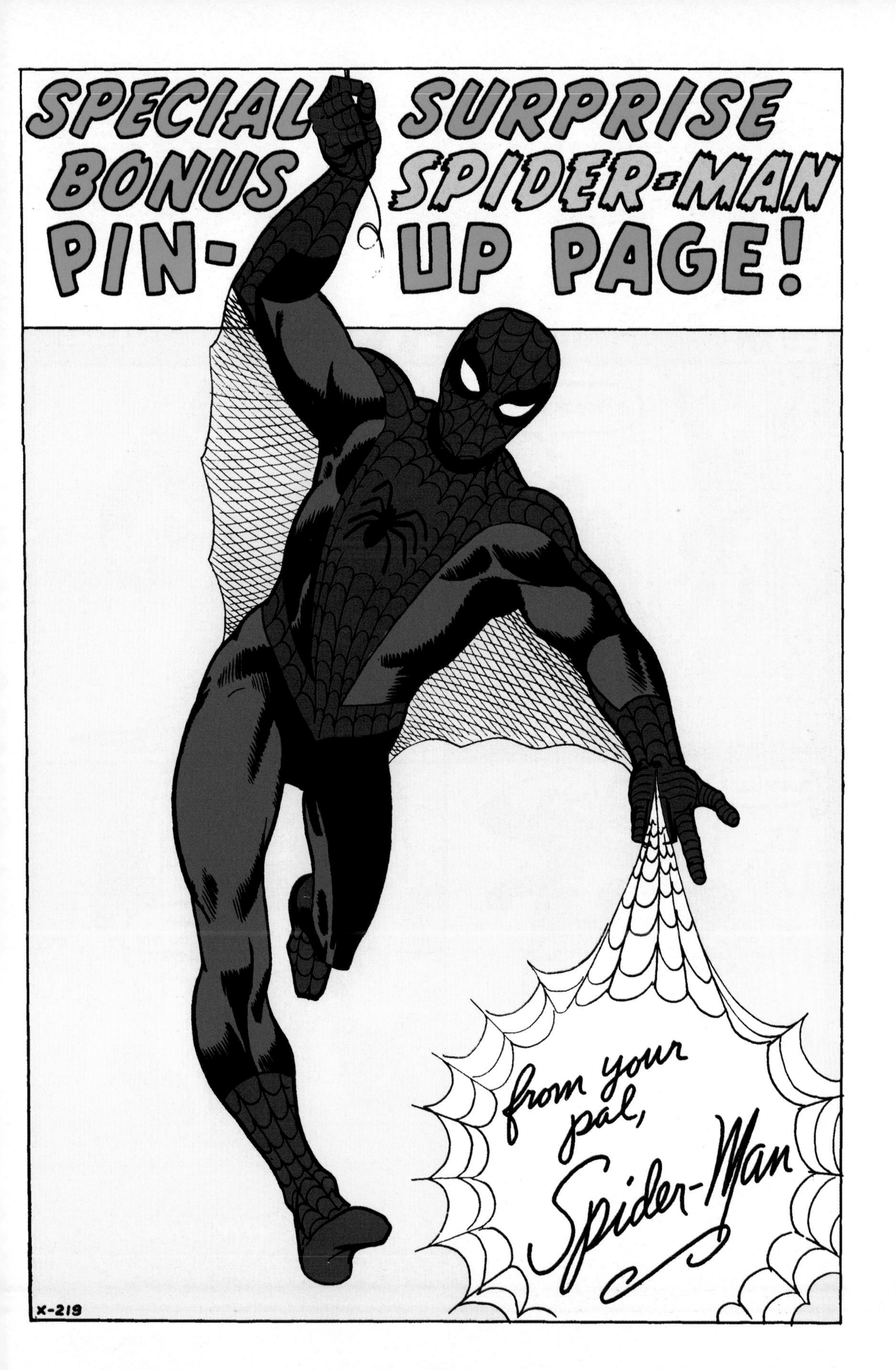
SPECIAL SURPRISE BONUS SPIDER-MAN PIN-UP PAGE!
from your pal, Spider-Man
X-219

the AMAZING SPIDER-MAN

APPROVED BY THE COMICS CODE AUTHORITY

MARVEL COMICS GROUP 12¢

4 SEPT.

HOW CAN SPIDER-MAN DEFEAT A FOE WHO CANNOT BE INJURED?? DON'T DARE MISS.....

"NOTHING CAN STOP... THE SANDMAN!"

SPIDER-MAN

"NOTHING CAN STOP... THE SANDMAN!"

IN THE SPACE OF ONLY THE FIRST THREE ISSUES, YOU READERS HAVE MADE ***SPIDER-MAN*** ONE OF THE GREATEST, MOST PHENOMENAL SUCCESSES IN THE HISTORY OF SUPER CHARACTERS! AND NOW, WITH THIS RECORD-BREAKING FOURTH ISSUE, ***SPIDER-MAN*** SOARS TO STILL GREATER HEIGHTS AS HE BATTLES THE MOST FANTASTIC FOE OF ALL! SO, SETTLE BACK FOR THE THRILL OF YOUR LIFE--THE FATEFUL MOMENT WHEN ***SPIDER-MAN*** MEETS--THE ***SANDMAN!***

by Stan Lee + STEVE DITKO

X-362

1.

KNOW WHAT NEW YORK'S BIGGEST TOURIST ATTRACTION IS? GRANT'S TOMB? EMPIRE STATE BUILDING? NOPE! IT'S A COLORFUL CRIME-FIGHTER NAMED SPIDER-MAN!
LOOKS LIKE OL' J. JONAH IS STILL GUNNIN' FOR ME IN HIS PAPER! SOME GUYS JUST NEVER GIVE UP!
"The SPIDER-MAN MENACE!"
A NEW SERIES BY
J. JONAH JAMESON
STARTING TODAY IN THE DAILY BUGLE

WELL! WELL! IF I EVER SAW THREE PUNKS CASIN' A JEWELRY STORE, I SEE IT NOW!

I WAS RIGHT! NO SOONER DOES THE PROPRIETOR LOCK UP FOR THE NIGHT AND HEAD FOR HOME, THEN THEY START SNEAKIN' UP TO THE PLACE!

HEY! WHAT'S GOIN' ON??
WHO'S THE WISE GUY?
IT FEELS LIKE A PIECE OF WEB DROPPED DOWN ON US! BUT... WHO...?

WELL, IT'S NOT DR. KILDARE!
SPIDER-MAN! WE'RE SUNK!
SHUDDUP, STUPID! I'LL HANDLE THIS!

IF YOU'RE THINKIN' OF PUTTIN' UP A FIGHT, BROTHER, LET ME WARN YOU...
A FIGHT? THE ONLY FIGHT I'LL PUT UP IS IN COURT! I'M SUIN' YOU FOR ASSAULT AND BATTERY, AND I GOT WITNESSES TO PROVE IT!
YEAH, THAT'S RIGHT!

THERE'S NO LAW AGAINST THREE HONEST CITIZENS WALK-IN' IN THE STREET AT NIGHT! THEN YOU COME SWOOPIN' DOWN ON US, SCARIN' US OUTTA OUR WITS! YOU'RE A MENACE... JUST LIKE J. JONAH JAMESON SAYS!
HE'S RIGHT! I WAS A FOOL! I SHOULD HAVE WAITED TILL THEY BROKE INTO THE STORE! NOW I'VE NO EVIDENCE!

DON'T YOU FEEL LIKE A JERK, PARADIN' AROUND IN PUBLIC IN THAT GET-UP??
A FINE WAY TO TALK TO A SUPER HERO! BUT WHAT CAN I DO ABOUT IT?
HEY, LET'S SWEAR OUT A WARRANT AGAINST SPIDER-MAN! I'LL CALL A COP! HELP, POLICE!

THIS IS BATTY! THEM CALLING FOR HELP AGAINST ME!
POLICE!!
BOY, YOU NEVER CAN GET A COP WHEN YOU WANT ONE!
WE'LL HELP YA! HEY, POLICE!
I SEE ONE COMIN' NOW!
2

AWRIGHT, WHAT'S GOIN' ON HERE?
IT'S SPIDER-MAN! HE ATTACKED US FOR NO GOOD REASON!
HE'LL FIND MY WEB ON THE GROUND... AND IT'S THEIR THREE STORIES AGAINST MY ONE!

EVEN A SUPER HERO KNOWS WHEN IT'S TIME TO CUT OUT!
HEY! COME BACK HERE, YOU! I'VE GOTTA FILL OUT A REPORT! I NEED YOUR NAME, ADDRESS... WAIT A MINUTE!

THIS'LL TEACH ME NOT TO GO CHARGING INTO THINGS UNTIL I KNOW WHAT THE SCORE IS!
WELL, IT COULD BE WORSE! AT LEAST I DID STOP 'EM FROM ROBBING THAT STORE!
GET 'IM DOWN FROM THERE! SHOOT THE BUM!

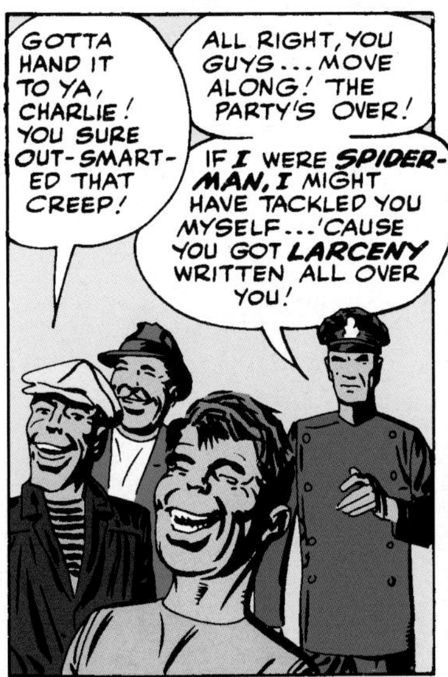
GOTTA HAND IT TO YA, CHARLIE! YOU SURE OUT-SMARTED THAT CREEP!
ALL RIGHT, YOU GUYS... MOVE ALONG! THE PARTY'S OVER!
IF I WERE SPIDER-MAN, I MIGHT HAVE TACKLED YOU MYSELF... 'CAUSE YOU GOT LARCENY WRITTEN ALL OVER YOU!

MEANWHILE, UP ABOVE...
IT'S ALL HIS FAULT! ON ACCOUNT OF JAMESON STIRRING EVERYONE UP AGAINST ME, EVEN CHEAP CROOKS NOW THINK THEY DON'T HAVE TO FEAR ME ANYMORE!

WELL, IT'S TIME I PAID J. JONAH A LITTLE VISIT... AS SPIDER-MAN!
DAILY BUG

HECK! IT'S EMPTY! HE'S NOT IN!
BUT I'LL JUST LEAVE A LITTLE SOUVENIR FOR HIM... TO PROVE I WAS HERE!

MINUTES LATER...
WELL, THAT'S THAT! NOW I'LL... HEY! POLICE CARS BELOW! SOME-THING MUST BE UP! I'D BETTER HANG AROUND!

THAT FELLA CLIMBING FRANTICALLY TO THE ROOF MUST BE THE ONE THEY'RE LOOKING FOR! IT'LL BE DUCK SOUP FOR ME TO GET 'IM!
3.

FIRST, I'LL SHINE MY SPIDER-MAN BEACON IN FRONT OF HIM, TO LET 'IM KNOW WHAT HE'S UP AGAINST!

AND THEN, I'LL JUST... HOLY HANNAH! WHO ARE YOU?!!
I DIDN'T EXPECT A WELCOMING COMMITTEE, BUT, SINCE YOU ASKED...

I CALL MYSELF...THE SANDMAN! NOW, THEN, ANY OTHER DUMB QUESTIONS?
THE SANDMAN! I HEARD OF YOU... BUT I THOUGHT THE REPORTS WERE JUST A GAG!

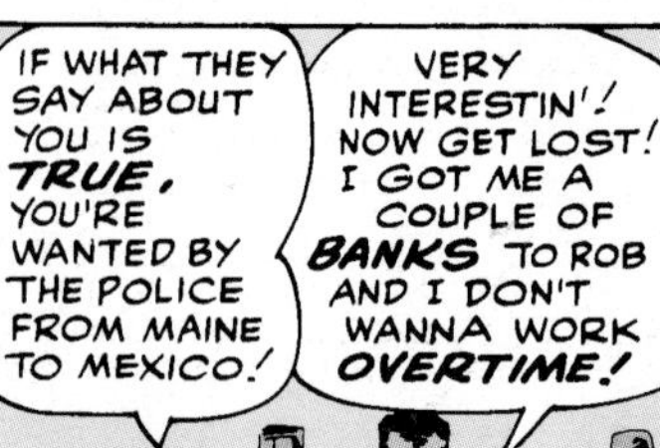
IF WHAT THEY SAY ABOUT YOU IS TRUE, YOU'RE WANTED BY THE POLICE FROM MAINE TO MEXICO!
VERY INTERESTIN'! NOW GET LOST! I GOT ME A COUPLE OF BANKS TO ROB AND I DON'T WANNA WORK OVERTIME!

HOLD IT, GRUESOME! NOBODY GIVES SPIDER-MAN THE BUM'S RUSH!
YOU'RE GONNA GET WORSE THAN THAT IF YOU DON'T LEGGO!

THINK I'M KIDDIN', HUH? OKAY, LET'S SEE YOU HOLD ONTO ME NOW!!
HE..HE'S SLIPPING THROUGH MY FINGERS...JUST LIKE SOFT SAND!

I DON'T KNOW HOW YOU MANAGED TO DO THAT, BUT...
THAT?? THAT'S KID STUFF! YOU AIN'T SEEN NOTHIN' YET!

NOW DO YOU SEE WHY THEY CALL ME SAND-MAN?
IT'S UNBELIEV-ABLE! YOUR BODY ISN'T FLESH AND BLOOD...MY FIST GOES RIGHT THROUGH YOU... WITHOUT HURTING YOU!

BUT I CAN HURT YOU, PAL! ALL I DO IS HARDEN ANY PART OF ME THAT I WANT TO...LIKE THIS!
UGH! YOUR JAW IS LIKE IRON!
4

AND HOW'S THIS?? NO HANDS!!
HE CAN CHANGE HIS BODY AS EASILY AS MISTER FANTASTIC... ONLY SANDMAN ISN'T ON OUR SIDE!
OOOF!
*MR. FANTASTIC: FAMOUS LEADER OF THE FABULOUS FANTASTIC FOUR!

DON'T GO 'WAY, CHUM! THE PARTY'S ONLY STARTIN'!
HE'S JUST TOYING WITH ME! I'VE GOT TO USE MY WEB ON HIM!

But THEN...
OH, NO!! I TORE MY FACE MASK!
CAN'T LET ANYONE SEE ME LIKE THIS! IT'LL BE THE END OF MY SECRET IDENTITY!

EVEN IF I COULD, I DON'T DARE TO CAPTURE HIM NOW!
ONCE MY SECRET IS OUT, J. JONAH JAMESON WILL NEVER STOP HOUNDING ME!
AND AUNT MAY... IF I'M DRIVEN FROM TOWN, WHAT WILL HAPPEN TO HER?
SO YOU GOT ME? SO WHAT? SOON AS THE POLICE GRAB ME, I'LL LET 'EM ALL KNOW WHO YOU REALLY ARE!
TO THINK THAT A PUBLIC MENACE LIVED RIGHT IN OUR MIDST, HIDING BENEATH A MASK OF RESPECT-ABILITY! HE MUST BE EXPELLED FROM SCHOOL... DRIVEN FROM TOWN!!
LOCK HIM UP FOR LIFE! I DON'T WANT DE-CENT TEENAGERS TO ASSOCIATE WITH HIM!
HE'S JUST AN OVER-GROWN DELINQUENT!
DON'T WORRY ABOUT ME, PETER DARLING! I'M JUST AN OLD LADY... IT'S YOU WHO MATTER!
FOR SALE SHOE LACES 10¢

COME BACK HERE, YA BLAMED COWARD! THE AMAZING SPIDER-MAN! BAH!
I'VE GOT TO GET AWAY! CAN'T TAKE A CHANCE ON HIM RECOG-NIZING ME! THE RISKS ARE TOO GREAT!

HE'S GONE! NOW I'LL JUST GET BACK TO BUSINESS!

IT'S EASY FOR A GUY TO JUMP OFF THE ROOF OF A BUILDING ... IF HE CAN TURN INTO SMALL, WEIGHT-LESS SAND PARTICLES!

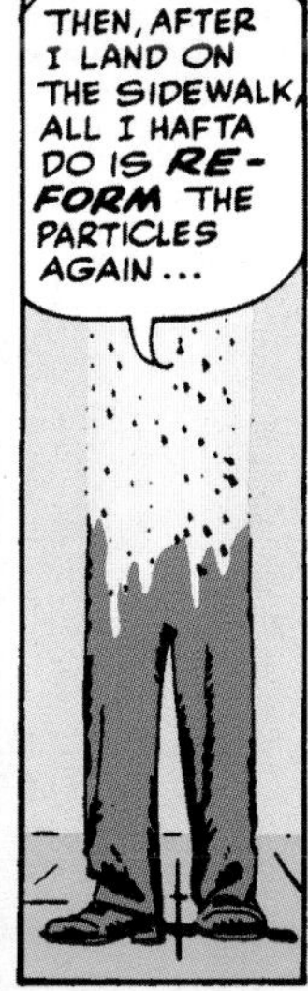
THEN, AFTER I LAND ON THE SIDEWALK, ALL I HAFTA DO IS RE-FORM THE PARTICLES AGAIN...

AND NOW FOR THAT DATE WITH A BANK!!
5

REACHING THE BANK, SANDMAN REFORMS THE PARTICLES OF HIS INDEX FINGER INTO THE SHAPE OF A BLANK KEY...
THIS IS EASIER THAN USIN' BURGLAR TOOLS!

INSERTING HIS FINGER INSIDE THE LOCK, THE "KEY" TAKES THE EXACT SHAPE OF THE LOCK ITSELF, ENABLING IT TO MOVE THE TUMBLERS, THUS OPENING THE DOOR!
CLICK!

ONCE INSIDE THE BANK, SANDMAN THEN SLIDES ALONG THE FLOOR, SLITHERING UNDER THE ELECTRIC EYE BARRIER WITHOUT SETTING OFF AN ALARM!

UNTIL...
SO FAR SO GOOD! NOW TO TACKLE THE MAIN VAULT ITSELF!

MEANWHILE, AT THE HOME OF PETER PARKER, HIGH SCHOOL SCIENCE MAJOR... WE FIND PETER, ALIAS SPIDER-MAN, WRESTLING WITH AN UNUSUAL PROBLEM FOR A SUPER-HERO...
IF THIS DOESN'T TAKE THE CAKE!! I CAN'T GO OUT IN PUBLIC AS SPIDER-MAN UNTIL MY MASK IS SEWN UP, AND WHEN IT COMES TO SEWING, I'M ALL THUMBS!
THIS IS RIDICULOUS! I'M NO COTTON-PICKIN' SEAMSTRESS!! BUT I'VE GOT TO DO IT MYSELF!
I CAN'T WALK INTO A TAILOR SHOP AND SAY "SEW UP MY SPIDER-MAN SUIT, PLEASE" WITHOUT MAKING SOMEBODY JUST A LITTLE SUSPICIOUS ABOUT WHO I AM!
OUCH! DARN NEEDLE! WISH I COULD ASK AUNT MAY, WITHOUT AROUSING HER SUSPI--HEY! WHAT'S THIS??
WE BRING YOU A SPECIAL BULLETIN! THE DREADED SANDMAN HAS BEEN REPORTED IN OUR CITY!
NEWS

"FOR THOSE OF YOU WHO ARE UNFAMILIAR WITH SANDMAN'S BACKGROUND, CHANNEL 17 PRESENTS THIS BRIEF SUMMARY: A FEW MONTHS AGO HE WAS AN INMATE AT ISLAND PRISON..."
"KNOWN AS FLINT MARKO, HE WAS THE MOST INCORRIGIBLE PRISONER AT THAT MAXIMUM SECURITY JAIL! THEN, ONE NIGHT, HE ESCAPED THRU AN UNGUARDED DRAINAGE TUNNEL!"
"VOWING NEVER TO BE RECAPTURED ALIVE, HE HEADED THE F.B.I. LIST OF MOST WANTED CRIMINALS AS HE MANAGED TO REMAIN ONE STEP AHEAD OF THE PURSUING LAWMEN!"
"BUT, AS THE POLICE DRAGNET DREW EVER TIGHTER, HE HID IN THE ONE PLACE WHERE NO ONE WOULD IMAGINE A MAN WOULD HIDE--AN ATOMIC DEVICES TESTING CENTER!"
DANGER KEEP OUT!
6

"REALIZING IT WAS THE ONLY PLACE WHERE HE COULD HAVE A MEASURE OF SAFETY, HE REMAINED ON THE LONELY, FORBIDDEN-AREA BEACH, UNTIL THE FATEFUL DAY THAT A NUCLEAR TEST EXPLOSION CAUGHT HIM UNAWARES!

"BY SOME INCREDIBLE ACCIDENT, THE MOLECULES OF HIS BODY MERGED AT THAT RADIO-ACTIVE INSTANT WITH THE MOLECULES OF THE SAND UNDER HIS FEET, AND HIS BODY TOOK ON THE QUALITIES OF THE SAND ITSELF -- BECOMING VIRTUALLY INDESTRUCTIBLE!"

...AND SO, WE URGE EVERY LISTENER TO STAY INDOORS AND--
CLICK!
UH OH! AUNT MAY'S COMING! GOT TO HIDE MY COSTUME-- FAST!

JUST TIME TO THROW MY ROBE ON! HOPE NONE OF IT IS SHOWING!
PETER, DEAR, YOU'VE BEEN STUDYING SO HARD! I BROUGHT YOU SOME COOKIES AND MILK!

WHY ARE YOU CLUTCHING YOUR ROBE SO TIGHTLY? YOU LOOK SO AGITATED! YOU MUST HAVE A FEVER, DEAR!
THAT'S MY BEST EXCUSE!
I-I THINK MAYBE I AM A LITTLE ILL, AUNT MAY!

NOW YOU JUST GET RIGHT INTO BED, PETER! I'LL BRING UP SOME ASPIRINS AND A THERMOMETER FOR YOU!
GOSH, YOU DON'T HAVE TO BOTHER WITH THAT, AUNT MAY! I'M SURE I'LL BE OKAY IN A LITTLE WHILE!

SHE'S GONE! NOW FOR THE NEWS AGAIN...
...POLICE HAVE THROWN A CORDON AROUND THE BANK! SANDMAN IS SAID TO BE STILL INSIDE!

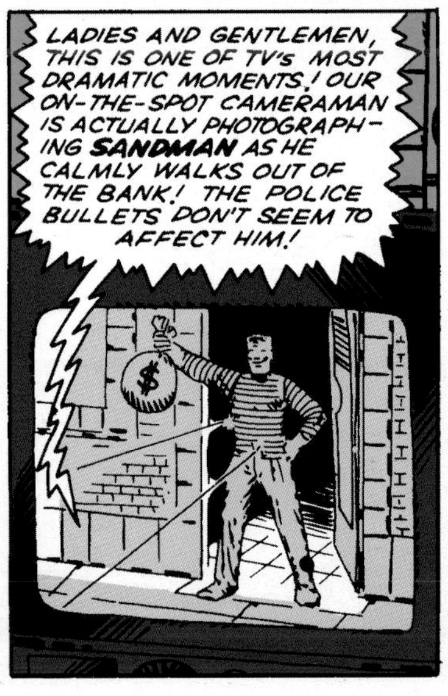
LADIES AND GENTLEMEN, THIS IS ONE OF TV's MOST DRAMATIC MOMENTS! OUR ON-THE-SPOT CAMERAMAN IS ACTUALLY PHOTOGRAPHING SANDMAN AS HE CALMLY WALKS OUT OF THE BANK! THE POLICE BULLETS DON'T SEEM TO AFFECT HIM!
$

MINUTES LATER...
SANDMAN MADE A CLEAN GETAWAY! I'LL BET SPIDER-MAN COULD STOP HIM, IF ONLY I COULD SEW MY MASK AND SLIP AWAY FROM AUNT MAY!
YOU'LL BE JUST FINE AFTER A GOOD NIGHT'S SLEEP, DEAR! YOU'VE JUST BEEN STUDYING TOO HARD!
7

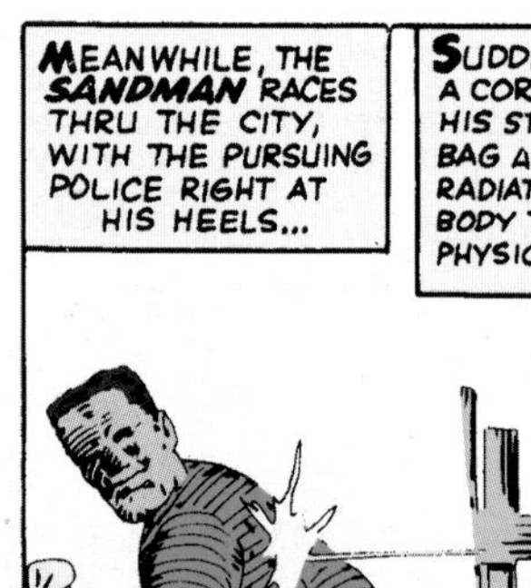
MEANWHILE, THE SANDMAN RACES THRU THE CITY, WITH THE PURSUING POLICE RIGHT AT HIS HEELS...

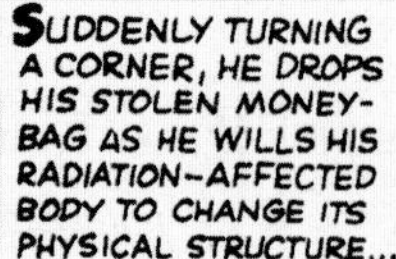
SUDDENLY TURNING A CORNER, HE DROPS HIS STOLEN MONEY-BAG AS HE WILLS HIS RADIATION-AFFECTED BODY TO CHANGE ITS PHYSICAL STRUCTURE...

...AND THE UNSUSPECTING OFFICERS RUN PAST! FOR WHO WOULD THINK TO SUSPECT WHAT LIES BENEATH AN INNOCENT-LOOKING MOUND OF SAND IN A VACANT LOT?!!

THE NEXT MORNING...
...AND, THOUGH SANDMAN HAS MADE GOOD HIS ESCAPE, THE POLICE ARE KEEPING CONSTANT VIGIL...
HMMM, YOU SEEM BETTER THIS MORNING, DEAR, AND YOUR TEMPERATURE IS PERFECTLY NORMAL! I'LL FIX YOU A NICE, WARM BREAKFAST AND YOU CAN GO TO SCHOOL!

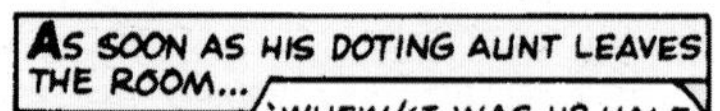
AS SOON AS HIS DOTING AUNT LEAVES THE ROOM...

WHEW! I WAS UP HALF THE NIGHT WORKIN' ON THIS, BUT AT LAST IT'S FINISHED! SO I'LL JUST WEAR MY SPIDER-MAN COSTUME UNDER MY CLOTHES TODAY...

BREAKFAST IS READY, PETER! BE SURE YOU EAT EVERY DROP! I'VE GOT TO LEAVE A LITTLE EARLY TODAY!
THANKS, AUNT MAY! I--EH, I'LL BE A LITTLE LATE COMING HOME TODAY! I'M GOING TO STOP OFF AND SEE MISTER JAMESON ABOUT SOMETHING!

HE'S THAT NICE GENTLEMAN WHO PUBLISHES THE DAILY BUGLE, AND NOW MAGAZINE, ISN'T HE?
JUST BE SURE YOU DON'T EXERT YOURSELF, DEAR! YOU KNOW HOW EASILY YOU CATCH COLD!
AW, AUNT MAY--I WISH YOU WOULDN'T BABY ME SO! I'M PRETTY HUSKY, YOU KNOW!

NOW, NOW, PETER, WE CAN'T BE TOO CAREFUL, CAN WE? HERE, TAKE YOUR UMBRELLA! IT MAY RAIN TODAY!
BOY, IF THE WORLD EVER FOUND OUT THAT SPIDER-MAN HAD TO CARRY AN UMBRELLA AND PROMISE NOT TO EXERT HIMSELF!!!

A FEW MINUTES LATER, AT THE PUBLISHING OFFICE OF J. JONAH JAMESON...
GOOD MORNING, MR. JAMESON!
HRRMPH! BRING ME THE LATEST BULLETINS ABOUT SANDMAN RIGHT AWAY! ALSO, I WANT THE FILE ON SPIDER-MAN!

FIRST SPIDER-MAN PLAGUES THIS CITY, AND NOW SANDMAN!! I WONDER IF THERE COULD BE ANY CONNECTION BETWEEN THE TWO! WHAT A SCOOP IT WOULD BE IF I PROVED THERE IS!
8

SITTING AT HIS DESK CHAIR, JONAH JAMESON ANGRILY FINDS THE LITTLE MEMENTO WHICH **SPIDER-MAN** HAD MISCHIEVOUSLY LEFT THE DAY BEFORE...
WHAT IN THE DAD-BLAMED DING-BUSTED SAM HILL IS ON MY **CHAIR??!!**
I-I HAVEN'T ANY **IDEA,** SIR!

I'M **STUCK** IN THIS BLASTED CHAIR! CAN'T GET OUT!
THERE'S A PIECE OF ADHESIVE **WEBBING** ON THE SEAT!
IT'S THE WORK OF THAT MISERABLE **SPIDER-MAN!** WELL, DON'T JUST STAND THERE **GAWK-ING,** MISS BRANT! GO GET ME ANOTHER PAIR OF **TROUSERS!!**
Y-YES SIR!

OH, THERE'S JJ'S YOUNG PHOTO-GRAPHER, PETER PARKER!
WOULD YOU BRING THESE TROUSERS IN TO MR. JAMESON, PETER? HE'S IN SUCH A BAD MOOD, I HATE TO FACE HIM!
SURE, MISS BRANT!
JJ MUST HAVE FOUND THE LITTLE "**MEMENTO**" I LEFT FOR HIM YESTERDAY! I CLEAN FORGOT ABOUT IT!

OH, IT'S **YOU,** EH? DID YOU BRING ME ANY NEW PICTURES?
NO, MR. JAMESON! I--EH, I'VE BEEN SORT OF BUSY WITH MY STUDIES! BUT HERE'S A PAIR OF **PANTS** FOR YOU!

LISTEN, PARKER, I WANT PICTURES OF **SPIDER-MAN!** YOU'VE MANAGED TO BRING IN GREAT STUFF IN THE PAST, BUT IF YOU CAN'T DELIVER **NOW,** I'LL GET SOMEONE WHO **CAN!** DO YOU **READ** ME?
SAY, WHAT DID YOU COME **UP** HERE FOR, ANYWAY?
I WONDERED IF YOU COULD GIVE ME AN **ADVANCE** ON MY NEXT CHECK?

AN **ADVANCE??!** ARE YOU **KIDDING??** WHAT DO YOU **DO** WITH MONEY, **EAT** IT?? LOOK--THIS IS A **BUSINESS,** NOT A CHARITY! WHEN YOU BRING ME EXCLUSIVE PICTURES, I PAY FOR 'EM... BUT NOT **BEFORE!**

YOU TEEN-AGERS ARE ALL ALIKE --YOU THINK THE WORLD OWES YOU A LIVING! NOW GO OUT AND GET ME SOME SHOTS OF **SPIDER-MAN,** AND DON'T COME BACK TILL YOU **DO!**
I NEEDED THE DOUGH FOR NEW EXPERIMENTS WITH MY WEBBING--BUT I CAN'T TELL **HIM** THAT! OH, WELL, I **TRIED!**

ONCE I GET THOSE PIX OF **SPIDER-MAN,** I'LL RUN THEM NEXT TO SOME PIX OF **SANDMAN,** WITH A CAPTION READING: **ARE THEY THE SAME MAN?** WHAT A FEATURE **THAT** WILL MAKE!
BETTER GET TO SCHOOL BEFORE I MISS THE LAST BELL!

AND SO...
HEY, YOU'RE NOT **SERIOUS** ABOUT HAVING A DATE WITH PUNY PARKER TONIGHT, ARE YOU?
WELL, THE POOR GUY HAS ASKED ME SO **MANY** TIMES, I JUST DIDN'T HAVE THE HEART TO REFUSE HIM AGAIN, FLASH!
I'LL HAVE TO FIND SOME WAY TO PICK UP THE TRAIL OF **SANDMAN** AFTER SCHOOL TONIGHT!
9

HELLO, PETER! WHAT TIME WILL YOU PICK ME UP TONIGHT?
SUFFERIN' CATS! I FORGOT ALL ABOUT MY DATE WITH LIZ TONIGHT! I'LL HAVE TO BREAK IT!
LUCKY FOR YOU, LIZ! NOW YOU CAN GO OUT WITH A REAL MAN-- NAMELY ME!
GOSH, LIZ, I'M SORRY! I CAN'T MAKE IT! SOMETHING KINDA IMPORTANT CAME UP!

GEE, DON'T BE ANGRY, LIZ! YOU SEE--I-I HAVE TO STUDY FOR TOMORROW'S EXAM, AND...
PETER PARKER! YOU'RE THE TOP STUDENT IN THE CLASS! IF YOU CAN'T SPARE ONE EVENING FOR A DATE, THEN I'M SORRY FOR YOU! GOODBYE!
HEY, DIG THE CRAZY UMBRELLA! HOW COME YOU LEFT YOUR GALOSHES HOME, SKINNY??

SOMETIMES I THINK I OUGHTTA HAVE MY HEAD EXAMINED FOR STICKIN' TO THIS SPIDER-MAN BIT! I'M BEGINNIN' TO THINK A SECRET IDENTITY IS FOR THE BIRDS! I WONDER IF MY SPIDER POWER IS AFFECTING MY BRAIN, ALSO! NOTHING I DO SEEMS TO TURN OUT RIGHT!
PARKER! STOP DAY-DREAMING IN CLASS!

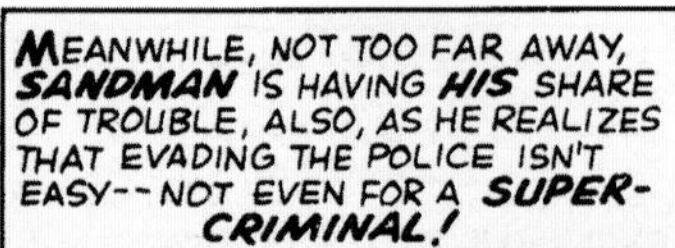
MEANWHILE, NOT TOO FAR AWAY, SANDMAN IS HAVING HIS SHARE OF TROUBLE, ALSO, AS HE REALIZES THAT EVADING THE POLICE ISN'T EASY--NOT EVEN FOR A SUPER-CRIMINAL!

I TURNED MY LEGS INTO SAND JUST IN TIME! THESE BLASTED COPS ARE ALL OVER THE PLACE!

THEY MAY BE HAVIN' A TOUGH JOB HOLDIN' ME, BUT THEY SURE ARE WEARIN' ME DOWN! I'VE GOT TO FIND A PLACE WHERE I CAN HOLE UP AND REST FOR A WHILE!

HMMM, THAT HIGH SCHOOL OVER THERE LOOKS LIKE A GOOD SPOT! NOBODY'D EVER THINK TO LOOK FOR ME IN THERE!

EVERYONE'S IN CLASS, EXCEPT FOR THAT LONE KID! NOW TO FIND AN EMPTY CLASSROOM!
THAT'S WHAT I GET FOR NOT PAYING ATTENTION IN CLASS! I GOT STUCK WITH THE JOB OF CARRYING THESE OLD BOTTLES FROM THE LAB TO THE BOILER ROOM! A REAL GLAMOR BOY, THAT'S ME!

LEAVE 'EM THERE, SONNY! I'LL GET RID OF 'EM AS SOON AS I ADJUST THIS NEW KING-SIZE VACUUM CLEANER!
HE DOESN'T KNOW HOW LUCKY HE IS! NO WORRIES EXCEPT KEEPING THIS SCHOOL CLEAN! NO NUTTY VILLAINS TO CHASE, LIKE I HAVE!

AND, ON THE FLOOR ABOVE...
SOMEONE'S COMIN'! I'D BETTER DUCK INTO THIS ROOM HERE!
10

UH OH! THE BLAMED ROOM IS PACKED!
AND NOW, CLASS, OUR PRINCIPAL WILL SAY A FEW WORDS TO -- WHA--???
IT'S THE SANDMAN!!

LOOK HERE--I'M PRINCIPAL DAVIS! I DEMAND TO KNOW--
QUIET YOU! I'LL DO THE TALKIN'! SO, YOU'RE THE PRINCIPAL, EH? HMMM-- KNOW SOMETHIN'? I NEVER GRADUATED SCHOOL! MEBBE THIS IS MY CHANCE TO GET A DIPLOMA!

I DON'T KNOW WHAT YOU'RE TALKING ABOUT!
WELL, YOU'RE GONNA FIND OUT RIGHT NOW! I FIGURE A GUY LIKE ME DESERVES THE BEST OF EVERYTHING! SO, I WANT YA TO WRITE ME OUT A DIPLOMA--OR ELSE!

NOTHING COULD MAKE ME DO THAT! A DIPLOMA MUST BE EARNED! YOUR THREATS CAN'T MAKE ME VIOLATE MY TRUST, OR MY DUTIES!
SAY! LISTEN TO HIM STAND UP TO THE SANDMAN!
NOW THERE'S A MAN WITH GUTS!

STOP! STAY BACK! THESE STUDENTS ARE IN MY CARE! ALL OF YOU-- RUN! RUN HOME! CALL THE POLICE! I'LL HOLD HIM OFF TILL YOU GET SAFELY OUT!
THAT'S WHAT YOU THINK, MISTER! I'M GONNA TEACH YOU A LITTLE LESSON RIGHT NOW!

BUT, OUTSIDE THE CLASSROOM DOOR, THE RETURNING PETER PARKER HAS OVERHEARD THE COMMOTION, AND, MAKING A RAPID CHANGE, HE SUDDENLY BURSTS INTO THE ROOM LIKE A TORNADO, AS THE AMAZING SPIDER-MAN!!
YOU'VE GOT THAT BACKWARDS, LOUD-MOUTH! YOU'RE THE ONE WHO'S GOT A LOT TO LEARN!
SPIDER-MAN!!
WOW-EEEE! THIS SURE HAS STUDYING CALCULUS BEAT ALL HOLLOW!!
11

GO GET 'IM, SPIDER-MAN!
GIVE 'IM ONE FOR US, PAL!
WONDER IF THEY'D CHEER SO LOUD IF THEY KNEW IT WAS "PUNY" PETER PARKER THEY'RE CHEERING??

THAT WAS A REAL DRAMATIC ENTRANCE, SPIDER-MAN! BUT ENJOY IT WHILE YOU CAN--BECAUSE THIS TIME YOU AINT GETTIN' AWAY FROM ME SO EASY!
I'VE GOT TO GET HIM AWAY FROM HERE! CAN'T TAKE A CHANCE ON ANY OF THESE KIDS GETTING HURT WHILE WE'RE FIGHTING!

BUT MAYBE I CAN QUICKLY FLOOR HIM WITH ONE PUNCH...
UH OH! NOT A CHANCE! MY SPIDER SENSE TELLS ME HE'S MAKING HIS BODY ROCK-HARD AGAIN! I'D JUST BUST MY HAND TRYING!

INSTEAD, I'LL DO THE UN-EXPECTED! I'LL GRAB HIM IN A WRESTLER'S HOLD BEFORE HE CAN CHANGE THE STRUCTURE OF HIS PHYSICAL MAKEUP...

...AND FLIP HIM OVER MY HEAD--LIKE THIS!
HAPPY LANDINGS, BRAGGERT!

PERFECT! I GOT HIM OUT OF THE ROOM! NOW TO FIND A WAY TO HOLD HIM UNTIL THE POLICE CAN GET HERE!

BOY! DID YOU SEE THAT!?!
I WONDER WHERE PETER WENT? HE ISN'T HERE!
WHO, THAT COWARD? HE'S PROBABLY HIDIN' WITH HIS HEAD UNDER A DESK SOMEWHERE!
12

HEY! SANDMAN RECOVERED FASTER THAN I THOUGHT! I'VE GOT TO STAY OUT OF HIS WAY TILL THE SCHOOL CAN BE CLEARED OF THE KIDS!
QUICKLY! EVERYBODY OUT! THIS WAY!

OKAY, SPIDER-MAN! NOW IT'S JUST YOU 'N ME! ONCE I FINISH YOU OFF, NOBODY'LL BE ABLE TO STOP ME!
HE'S PRESSING ME TOO HARD! I NEED MORE ROOM! HE HAS THE ADVANTAGE AT THESE CLOSE QUARTERS! I'LL NEED MY AGILITY TO GET OUT OF RANGE!

AHH, THIS IS MORE LIKE IT! NOW, I'VE GOT TO LURE HIM OUT OF HERE, INTO A BIGGER AREA! I KNOW JUST THE PLACE!

GOOD! HE FOLLOWED ME INTO THE GYM! NOW I'VE REALLY GOT ROOM TO OPERATE!

I'LL COVER HIM WITH MY WEB FROM UP HERE!
TRICKY LITTLE CLOWN, AINTCHA?

BROTHER, YOU DON'T KNOW HOW TRICKY!

WELL, YOU'LL HAVETA BE A LOT TRICKIER THAN THAT TO HOLD ME!
HECK! HE'S POURING RIGHT THRU MY WEB!

ANY OTHER DUMB STUNTS YOU WANNA TRY?
WHY NOT? YOU'RE NOT GOIN' ANYWHERE!
13

I'M TRYING TO SOUND CONFIDENT TO HIM, BUT I'LL BE BLAMED IF I KNOW WHAT TO TRY NEXT!! HE'S SURE NO SITTING DUCK!

GOTTA CATCH MY BREATH FOR A SEC! HE--HE'S GOT ME TRAPPED IN THIS CORNER! CAN'T RUN--AND MY PUNCHES DON'T SEEM TO BE HURTING HIM!
NOW I'VE GOT YOU WHERE I WANT YOU! HOLD STILL, INSECT MAN --THIS WON'T TAKE LONG!

ALL RIGHT, IF YOU WANNA KEEP PUNCHIN' ME, I'LL MAKE IT EASY FOR YA! THERE-- I MADE MYSELF ALL NICE AND SANDY AGAIN! AND NOW--
MY FIST WENT RIGHT THRU HIM! BUT, HE MADE HIS BODY HARD AGAIN! I--I'M STUCK!

I DON'T WANTCHA TO GET BORED, CHUM! SO I'LL HIT YOU A DIFFERENT WAY! EVER GET ANY LOVE TAPS FROM A GUY'S ROCK-HARD HEAD?
UGH! OWW...

IF--IF I DIDN'T HAVE MY SPIDER STRENGTH, I'D BE OUT FOR THE COUNT NOW! CAN'T TAKE MUCH MORE OF THIS! GOTTA DO SOMETHING!!

SUDDENLY, SUMMONING EVERY REMAINING BIT OF STRENGTH IN HIS AMAZINGLY POWERFUL BODY, THE SPIDER-MAN EXERTS ONE LAST MIGHTY EFFORT AND FLIPS SANDMAN OVER HIS HEAD, AGAINST THE IRON STAIRWAY POST!
WHA--??!
14

THE AWESOME CRIMINAL RELEASES HIS HOLD ON SPIDER-MAN AS HE SHATTERS INTO COUNTLESS GRAINS OF SAND...
I'M FREE!

--BUT FOR HOW LONG? HE'S ALREADY REFORMING THE SANDY ELEMENTS OF HIS BODY INTO A SOLID MASS!

NICE TRY, SPIDER-MAN! BUT A FAT LOT OF GOOD IT'LL DO YA!!
BOY! ANYONE WHO WANTED TO TRADE PLACES WITH ME RIGHT NOW WOULDN'T HAVE TO COAX ME VERY HARD!

I'LL JUST LET MY GRAINS OF SAND OOZE OVER THERE TOWARDS YOU... LIKE HAVIN' YOUR LEGS IN QUICKSAND, ISN'T IT?
I'LL BET YOU'D BE GREAT AT A PARTY! YOU'RE JUST A BARREL OF FUN, AREN'T YOU?!!

WELL, THIS LITTLE PARTY'S GONNA END PRETTY SOON! HERE'S WHERE I PUT YOU AWAY FOR KEEPS, YOU COSTUMED PEST!

HE'S TRAPPING ME MORE AND MORE! I CAN'T BREAK LOOSE! WAIT! I'VE GOT AN IDEA!

WHILE HE'S BUSY TRYING TO MAKE ME HELPLESS, I'LL BEND DOWN AND TRY TO MAKE HIM FORM HIMSELF INTO SOME SORT OF A BALL!
I NOTICE YOU'RE NOT GIVIN' OUT WITH ALL THE WISECRACKS NOW, SPIDER-MAN!

IT WORKED! I MANEUVERED HIM NEAR THE BASEMENT STEPS! NOW-- IF I'M LUCKY--
YOU'RE JUST PROLONGIN' THE AGONY, LAMEBRAIN! THIS AIN'T GONNA HELP YA!
15

OOF!
STILL THINK IT WON'T HELP ME??

OKAY, YOU HAD YOUR FUN! NOW I'M THRU FOOLIN' AROUND!
THAT SO? I'M JUST GETTIN' STARTED!

THIS ELECTRIC DRILL WILL BORE THRU ANY-THING! SO YOU'D BETTER KEEP YOUR DISTANCE, SANDMAN!

DON'T YOU EVER LEARN?? ALL I GOTTA DO IS MAKE MY BODY LIKE SAND AGAIN! THAT DUMB THING CAN'T HURT ME!
SO FAR, SO GOOD! HE DOESN'T SUSPECT THAT THAT'S JUST WHAT I WANT HIM TO DO!

STILL NOT CONVINCED, HUH? OKAY, GO AHEAD--WASTE YOUR TIME! HOW'D A NUT LIKE YOU EVER GET TO BE A SUPER-HERO, ANYHOW??
JUST STICK AROUND, BIG MAN! YOU'LL FIND OUT BEFORE YOU KNOW IT!

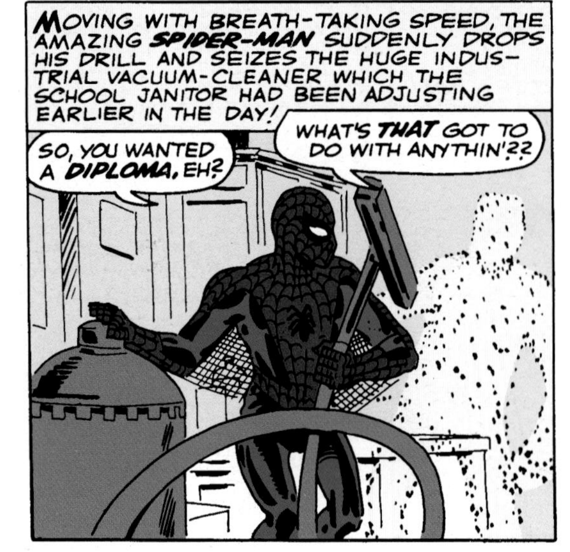
MOVING WITH BREATH-TAKING SPEED, THE AMAZING SPIDER-MAN SUDDENLY DROPS HIS DRILL AND SEIZES THE HUGE INDUS-TRIAL VACUUM-CLEANER WHICH THE SCHOOL JANITOR HAD BEEN ADJUSTING EARLIER IN THE DAY!
SO, YOU WANTED A DIPLOMA, EH?
WHAT'S THAT GOT TO DO WITH ANYTHIN'??

JUST THIS! HERE'S THE FIRST PART OF YOUR EDUCATION--- COURTESY OF YOUR FRIENDLY NEIGHBORHOOD SPIDER-MAN!
OHHHH...
16

WHEW! GOT HIM AT LAST! THAT HEAVY CANVAS BAG WILL HOLD HIM FOR SURE!
TOO BAD! I COULD HAVE GOTTEN SOME PICTURES OF OUR FIGHT! OL' JAMESON WOULD PAY A FORTUNE FOR 'EM! SAY! WHY NOT??

MAYBE WITH A LITTLE INGENUITY I CAN STILL FURNISH THE PIX TO JJ! I'LL JUST TAKE MY CAMERA OUT OF MY BELT...

THERE! I'VE GOT THE TIMER SET TO "AUTOMATIC." NOW, THIS BUCKET OF SAND WILL COME IN REAL HANDY!
FOR FIRE ONLY

I'LL JUST TOSS A MESS OF SAND INTO THE AIR, LIKE THIS!
AND THEN I'LL DIVE THRU IT, AS THOUGH I'M ATTACKING SANDMAN WHILE HE'S IN HIS SAND-GRAIN FORM!
SINCE THIS REALLY HAPPENED A FEW MINUTES AGO, IT CAN'T BE UNETHICAL! IT'S LIKE SHOOTING A RE-TAKE OF A MOVIE! I HOPE THE CAMERA IS FOCUSED JUST RIGHT-- THESE SHOULD BE GOOD SHOTS!

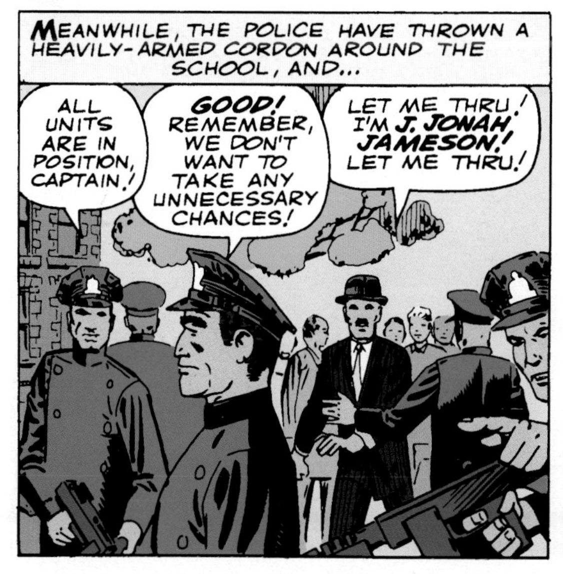
MEANWHILE, THE POLICE HAVE THROWN A HEAVILY-ARMED CORDON AROUND THE SCHOOL, AND...
ALL UNITS ARE IN POSITION, CAPTAIN!
GOOD! REMEMBER, WE DON'T WANT TO TAKE ANY UNNECESSARY CHANCES!
LET ME THRU! I'M J. JONAH JAMESON! LET ME THRU!

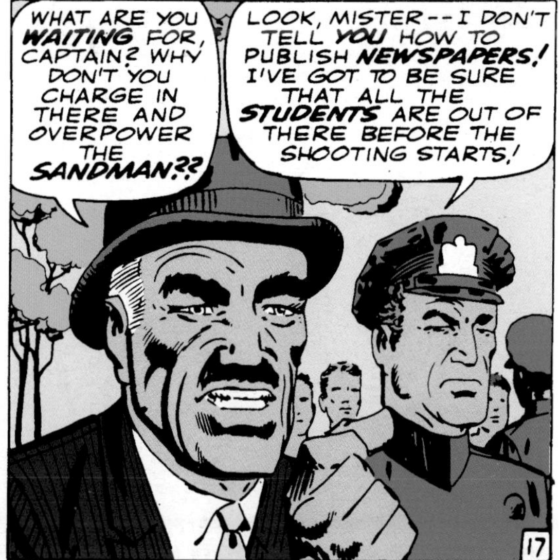
WHAT ARE YOU WAITING FOR, CAPTAIN? WHY DON'T YOU CHARGE IN THERE AND OVERPOWER THE SANDMAN??
LOOK, MISTER-- I DON'T TELL YOU HOW TO PUBLISH NEWSPAPERS! I'VE GOT TO BE SURE THAT ALL THE STUDENTS ARE OUT OF THERE BEFORE THE SHOOTING STARTS!
17

LATER...
ALL RIGHT, THE SCHOOL IS CLEARED OUT, EXCEPT FOR SANDMAN! NOW GET HIM BEFORE HE AND SPIDER-MAN ESCAPE!
YOU'RE OFF BASE THERE, JAMESON! WE'RE NOT AFTER SPIDER-MAN! FAR AS WE KNOW, HE'S HELPING US TO BATTLE SANDMAN!

SO, HE'S GOT YOU FOOLED TOO, HAS HE? I'M CONVINCED THEY'RE IN CAHOOTS! FOR ALL WE KNOW, THEY'RE PLANNING TO LOOT THIS ENTIRE CITY TOGETHER!
JAMESON, WHY DON'T YOU LET ME HANDLE-- WAIT! LOOK!!

YOU CAN BREATHE EASY, CAPTAIN! SANDMAN IS INSIDE, ALL WRAPPED UP FOR YOU!
IT'S SPIDER-MAN!! HE DID IT!
DON'T LET HIM FOOL YOU! IT COULD BE A TRICK! YOU'VE GOT TO CAPTURE SPIDER-MAN! HOLD HIM UNTIL YOU FIND THE SANDMAN!

BETTER COME DOWN FROM THERE, SPIDER-MAN! YOU'LL HAVE TO GIVE US A FULL REPORT!
AND I'VE GOT A FEW QUESTIONS TO ASK HIM, TOO! MY PAPERS WANT TO KNOW MORE ABOUT HIM! WHY IS SPIDER-MAN ALLOWED TO ROAM THE CITY AT WILL--TAKING THE LAW INTO HIS OWN HANDS??

BOY, NOTHING I DO CAN SATISFY JAMESON! I'D BETTER WATCH MY STEP --HE HAS A WAY OF INFLAMING THE CROWD, TURNING EVERYTHING I SAY AND DO AGAINST ME! IF THE POLICE LISTEN TO HIM, I'M LIABLE TO BE LOCKED UP, TOO!
18

HERE--SANDMAN'S INSIDE--BETTER HANDLE WITH CARE!
CAPTAIN, MAKE SPIDER-MAN COME DOWN, TOO! WHY WON'T HE FACE US?? WHAT IS HE TRYING TO HIDE?? AS A TAXPAYER, I DEMAND HE BE APPRE-HENDED!

BUT, INSIDE THE SCHOOL AGAIN, SPIDER-MAN HAS OTHER PLANS...
I'VE GOT TO CHANGE BACK TO PETER PARKER ON THE DOUBLE, BEFORE THEY FIND ME!

A FEW SECONDS LATER...
I SURE HOPE NO ONE TIES MY SUDDEN APPEARANCE IN WITH THE DISAPPEARANCE OF SPIDER-MAN!
HOLD ON THERE, PARKER! I'VE BEEN LOOK-ING FOR YOU!

SO, YOU WERE HIDING IN THE SCHOOL, EH? GOOD BOY! DID YOU GET ANY EXCLUSIVE PICTURES OF THOSE TWO MENACES FOR ME??
YES SIR, I DID! I WAS, EH, KINDA LUCKY THIS TIME!

HERE'S THE FILM, MISTER JAMESON! I DIDN'T HAVE TIME TO HAVE IT DEVELOPED!
THAT'S ALL RIGHT! DON'T WORRY ABOUT IT! I'LL TAKE THE COST OF DE-VELOPING OUT OF YOUR PAY!

NOT A SIGN OF SPIDER-MAN, CHIEF!
WELL, WE'VE NOTHING AGAINST HIM ANYWAY! AND WE DO HAVE SANDMAN UNDER WRAPS!
NOTHING AGAINST SPIDER-MAN??!! WHAT ABOUT THE DAMAGE DONE TO THE INSIDE OF THE SCHOOL?? WAIT TILL MY PAPERS WRITE AN EDITORIAL ABOUT HIM WRECKING PUBLIC PROPERTY!

IF SPIDER-MAN HAD LET THE POLICE HANDLE THIS, SAND-MAN COULD HAVE BEEN STARVED OUT OF THERE AND CAPTURED WITH NO FUSS, NO DAMAGE! BUT ONCE AGAIN SPIDER-MAN TRIED TO STEAL THE GLORY!
MR. JAMESON, THE POLICE APPRECIATE SPIDER-MAN'S HELP! YOU CAN PRINT WHAT YOU WANT TO IN YOUR PAPERS, BUT SOONER OR LATER PEOPLE WILL REALIZE YOU'RE JUST AIRING A PRIVATE GRUDGE OF YOUR OWN!
19

AWW, WHO CARES ABOUT JAMESON!? FOR ONCE, EVERYTHING TURNED OUT OKAY!
I POLISHED OFF SANDMAN, GOT THE MONEY I NEEDED, AND NOW THERE'S NOTHING TO STOP ME FROM DATING LIZ TONIGHT! I'D BETTER GO AND FIND HER!

THERE SHE IS! WAIT UP, LIZ--!
WELL, WELL, LOOK WHO'S HERE! "MR. BOOKWORM OF 1963!"
NOW THAT THE FIGHTING'S OVER, YOU FINALLY CAME OUT OF HIDING, EH?
WHAT IS IT, PETER? I HAPPEN TO BE QUITE BUSY!

GEE, DON'T BE ANGRY, LIZ! I JUST WANTED TO TELL YOU THAT I CAN TAKE YOU OUT TONIGHT, AFTER ALL!
REALLY? PERHAPS WE SHOULD DECLARE THIS A NATIONAL HOLIDAY! SORRY, MR. PARKER, BUT I HAVE MADE OTHER PLANS!
MEANING YOURS TRULY, PUNK! NOW RUN ALONG AND FIND YOUR UMBRELLA!

YOU BRAINLESS LOUDMOUTH! YOU'VE INSULTED ME FOR THE LAST TIME! I'M GONNA WIPE THAT STUPID LEER OFF YOUR FACE RIGHT NOW!
WELL, WELL! SO THE WORM FINALLY TURNED, EH? OKAY, WORM, I'VE BEEN WAITING FOR THIS!

WAIT! WHAT AM I DOING?? I CAN'T AFFORD TO LOSE MY TEMPER LIKE THIS! WITH THE STRENGTH OF SPIDER-MAN, IF I GET INTO A FIGHT WITH A NORMAL GUY, I COULD PULVERIZE HIM!

AWW, FORGET IT! YOU'RE NOT EVEN WORTH THE TROUBLE! I'VE GOT MORE IMPORTANT THINGS TO DO!
SURE, THINGS LIKE CHICKENING OUT OF FIGHTS, AND HIDING WHENEVER THERE'S TROUBLE! THINGS LIKE THAT CAN KEEP A FELLA REAL BUSY, CAN'T THEY, PETEY BOY?
20

WOULD YOU LIKE US TO HELP YOU CROSS THE STREET, SONNY? MEBBE WE COULD--
HEY! WHAT GIVES? YOU OUGHTTA FEEL HIS ARM UNDER THIS JACKET, FLASH! PARKER'S GOT MUSCLES LIKE A WEIGHT LIFTER!
HMMPH! TOO BAD HE DOESN'T HAVE COURAGE TO MATCH!
YOU SAID IT, LIZ! COME ON, CHICK, LET'S GO! THIS COMPANY IS BORIN' ME!

NOW EVEN LIZ THINKS I'M A COWARD! THAT SURE IS PRETTY HARD TO TAKE!
SO LONG, BRAIN WAVE! DON'T LET ANY KINDERGARTEN KIDS RUN AWAY WITH YOUR BOOKS!
THAT'S ENOUGH, FLASH! YOU NEEDN'T BE THAT CRUEL TO PETER!
WOMEN! I THOUGHT YOU WERE MAD AT 'IM!

LATER, WALKING HOME FROM SCHOOL, A THOUGHTFUL PETER PARKER OVERHEARS THE COMMENTS OF HIS NEIGHBORS...
WELL, I SEE THAT SPIDER-MAN CAPTURED THAT AWFUL SANDMAN!
ACCORDING TO THE EDITORIAL, SPIDER-MAN IS JUST AS BAD AS THE OTHER ONE!
JONAH JAMESON WRITES THAT SPIDER-MAN HAS NO BUSINESS TRYING TO CATCH CRIMINALS BY HIMSELF!
IF YOU ASK ME, THAT'S RIGHT! WHO KNOWS WHEN SPIDER-MAN MAY TURN AGAINST SOCIETY?!!
WHAT WOULD MAKE A GUY WEAR A GOOFY COSTUME AND RUN AROUND CHASIN' CROOKS?
I DUNNO! HE MUST BE A NEUROTIC OF SOME SORT! PROBABLY HAS DELUSIONS OF GRANDEUR!
DON'T YOU WISH YOU WERE SPIDER-MAN?
NAH! GIVE ME THE HUMAN TORCH ANY DAY!

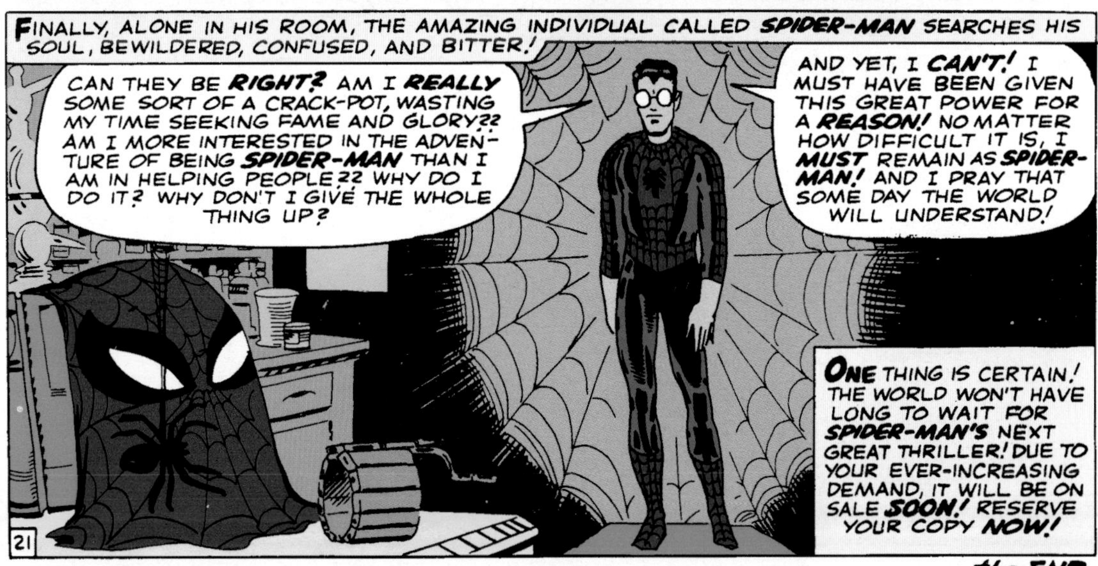
FINALLY, ALONE IN HIS ROOM, THE AMAZING INDIVIDUAL CALLED SPIDER-MAN SEARCHES HIS SOUL, BEWILDERED, CONFUSED, AND BITTER!
CAN THEY BE RIGHT? AM I REALLY SOME SORT OF A CRACK-POT, WASTING MY TIME SEEKING FAME AND GLORY?? AM I MORE INTERESTED IN THE ADVENTURE OF BEING SPIDER-MAN THAN I AM IN HELPING PEOPLE?? WHY DO I DO IT? WHY DON'T I GIVE THE WHOLE THING UP?
AND YET, I CAN'T! I MUST HAVE BEEN GIVEN THIS GREAT POWER FOR A REASON! NO MATTER HOW DIFFICULT IT IS, I MUST REMAIN AS SPIDER-MAN! AND I PRAY THAT SOME DAY THE WORLD WILL UNDERSTAND!
ONE THING IS CERTAIN! THE WORLD WON'T HAVE LONG TO WAIT FOR SPIDER-MAN'S NEXT GREAT THRILLER! DUE TO YOUR EVER-INCREASING DEMAND, IT WILL BE ON SALE SOON! RESERVE YOUR COPY NOW!
21

the END

the AMAZING SPIDER-MAN
APPROVED BY THE COMICS CODE AUTHORITY
IND.
MARVEL COMICS GROUP 12¢
5 OCT.
IT HAD TO HAPPEN! SOONER OR LATER, SPIDER-MAN WAS BOUND TO BATTLE
"DOCTOR DOOM!"
THIS IS YOUR FINISH, SPIDER-MAN! IF THE FANTASTIC FOUR THEMSELVES COULD NOT STOP ME, WHAT CHANCE HAVE YOU?

SPIDER-MAN
"MARKED FOR DESTRUCTION BY DR. DOOM!"
FEATURING
PETER PARKER ALIAS SPIDER-MAN
THE AWESOME DOCTOR DOOM!
J. JONAH JAMESON AND HIS SECRETARY, BETTY BRANT
SPIDER-MAN AND THE ARCH-FOE OF THE FANTASTIC FOUR, FACE-TO-FACE FOR THE FIRST TIME!
FEATURING
FLASH THOMPSON, LIZ ALLAN, AND THEIR ASSORTED CLASSMATES
THE OTHER SPIDER-MAN!
4
AND THE WORLD'S MOST FABULOUS SUPER-TEAM!
WRITTEN BY... Stan Lee
DRAWN BY... S. Ditko
LETTERING... S. Rosen
HAVE YOU EVER NOTICED, WHEN YOU START READING A COMIC MAG, THE OPENING CAPTION TELLS YOU THAT YOU'RE ABOUT TO READ THE MOST EXCITING STORY EVER WRITTEN,..WITH THE MOST DANGEROUS MENACE, AND THE MOST SUSPENSEFUL PLOT?? WELL, WE'RE GOING TO TRY TO BE MORE HONEST! THIS MAY NOT BE THE GREATEST STORY EVER WRITTEN! YOU MAY HAVE READ ABOUT MORE EXCITING VILLAINS! AND YOU MAY HAVE THRILLED TO BETTER PLOTS! BUT, Y'KNOW SOMETHING? WE CAN'T SEE HOW!

YOU ARE LOOKING AT ONE OF THE FEW CANDID ACTION FILMS EVER TAKEN OF SPIDER-MAN BY A NEWSREEL PHOTOGRAPHER!

BY NOW THE WHOLE WORLD KNOWS OF SPIDER-MAN'S EXISTENCE! BUT THE WORLD DOESN'T KNOW HIS TRUE IDENTITY, OR HIS REAL MOTIVES! AND THAT IS WHAT THIS PROGRAM INTENDS TO INVESTIGATE!
SPIDER-MAN... A FORCE FOR GOOD OR EVIL?

MY NAME IS J. JONAH JAMESON, PUBLISHER OF NOW MAGAZINE AND THE DAILY BUGLE! I AM SPONSORING THIS PROGRAM IN THE PUBLIC INTEREST, TO EXPOSE SPIDER-MAN TO THE PUBLIC AS THE MENACE HE IS!

ANY TV SHOW ABOUT THE COLORFUL SPIDER-MAN IS BOUND TO ATTRACT A LARGE AUDIENCE! EVEN TEEN-AGERS IN A LOCAL BOWLING ALLEY INTERRUPT THEIR GAME TO VIEW THE PROGRAM...
BOY, IMAGINE JAMESON SPONSORING HIS OWN PROGRAM, JUST TO ATTACK SPIDER-MAN!
I SAY THAT SPIDER-MAN BELONGS BEHIND BARS!
AW, JAMESON'S NOT SO DUMB! HE'S JUST GETTIN' GOOD PUBLICITY FOR HIS MAG BY MAKING ALL THIS FUSS!
YEAH! PERSONALLY I THINK THAT SPIDER-MAN'S THE COOLEST!

I MUSTN'T SAY ANYTHING TO MAKE THEM SUSPECT ME! I'LL TALK AGAINST SPIDER-MAN!

YOU CAN'T TELL! JAMESON MAY BE RIGHT! NOBODY REALLY KNOWS SPIDER-MAN!

IT'S A CINCH YOU DON'T, PANTY-WAIST! YOU'D PROBABLY FAINT IF YOU EVER CAUGHT SIGHT OF 'IM!

I WOULD, TOO! ...FROM SHEER EXCITEMENT! I'LL BET HE'S REAL HANDSOME UNDER THAT SILLY MASK OF HIS! SIGH!

G'WAN, PARKER, GET LOST! YOU'RE IN THE WRONG PLACE, ANYHOW! THIS IS A BOWLING ALLEY, NOT A KNITTING PARLOR!
THAT'S IT, FLASH! KEEP IT UP! ONE OF THESE DAYS YOU'LL GO TOO FAR, AND YOU'LL NEVER KNOW WHAT HIT YOU! THERE'S EVEN A LIMIT TO SPIDER-MAN'S PATIENCE!

BUT, IN ANOTHER PART OF TOWN, ANOTHER LISTENER HEARS JAMESON'S PROGRAM! A STRANGE AND SINISTER LISTENER!

..MY PAPERS ARE OFFERING A THOUSAND DOLLARS REWARD TO ANYONE WHO CAN DISCLOSE SPIDER-MAN'S TRUE IDENTITY!

SPIDER-MAN?? HMM... HE MAY BE JUST THE ONE I'VE BEEN SEEKING!

2.

EACH TIME I ATTACKED THE FANTASTIC FOUR IN THE PAST, THEY HAVE FOUGHT ME TO A STAND-STILL! ALONE, I DO NOT SEEM ABLE TO DEFEAT THEM!
BUT WITH ONE SUCH AS SPIDER-MAN AT MY SIDE, EVEN THAT ACCURSED QUARTET WOULD NOT BE ABLE TO SAVE THEMSELVES FROM MY WRATH!

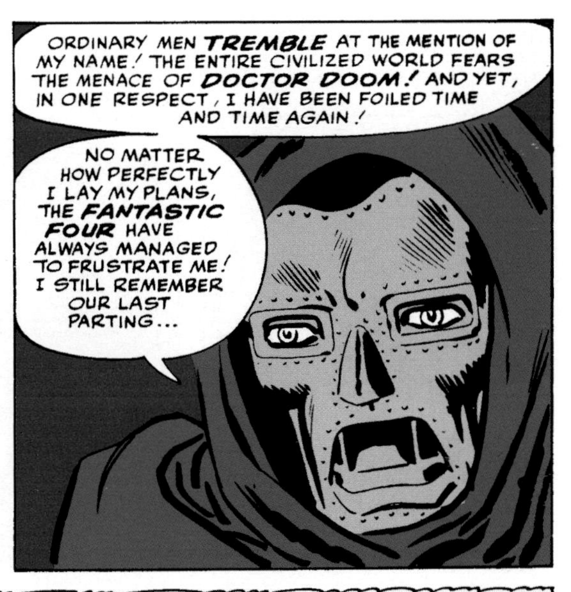
ORDINARY MEN TREMBLE AT THE MENTION OF MY NAME! THE ENTIRE CIVILIZED WORLD FEARS THE MENACE OF DOCTOR DOOM! AND YET, IN ONE RESPECT, I HAVE BEEN FOILED TIME AND TIME AGAIN!
NO MATTER HOW PERFECTLY I LAY MY PLANS, THE FANTASTIC FOUR HAVE ALWAYS MANAGED TO FRUSTRATE ME! I STILL REMEMBER OUR LAST PARTING...

COME BACK! YA CAN'T CHEAT ME OUT OF MY REVENGE THIS WAY!
BEN, GET OUT OF THE WAY! I CAN STILL REACH OUT AND GRAB HIM! BEN... NO! IT'S TOO LATE NOW!

SWIFTLY, SILENTLY, THE AWESOME FORM OF THE GREATEST MENACE OF OUR AGE PLUMMETS EARTHWARD... DOWN... DOWN... DOWN... UNTIL IT IS LOST FROM SIGHT IN THE BILLOWING CLOUDS BELOW...

ONCE UNDER COVER OF THE CLOUDS, THE JET-POWERED FLYING BELT I WORE ENABLED ME TO GLIDE TO SAFETY... TO REPAIR TO A NEW LAIR WHERE I COULD LICK MY WOUNDS LIKE A VANQUISHED BEAST!
BUT NOW, THAT IS ALL BEHIND ME! NOW IT IS TIME TO STRIKE AGAIN! WITH THE AID OF THAT IMPRISONED SPIDER, I WILL TRANSMIT A MESSAGE TO SPIDER-MAN, USING HIS OWN WAVE-LENGTH!

IN SOME STRANGE WAY, HE HAS THE SENSORY POWERS OF A SPIDER... AND SO, IT WAS A SIMPLE MATTER FOR ONE OF MY GENIUS TO CREATE THIS SPIDER-WAVE TRANSMITTER!
CALLING SPIDER-MAN! CALLING SPIDER-MAN! I MUST CONTACT YOU AT ONCE!
3.

MEANWHILE, AT HOME, PETER PARKER PRACTICES HIS AGILITY WITH HIS WEB, IN THE PRIVACY OF HIS ROOM...
IF THE GANG AT THE BOWLING ALLEY COULD SEE ME NOW!

CALLING SPIDER-MAN! CALLING SPIDER-MAN!
I CAN SENSE A MESSAGE! SOMEONE IS TRYING TO REACH ME!

WHO CAN IT BE? HOW COULD ANYONE HAVE FIGURED OUT A WAY TO REACH ME THROUGH MY SPIDER'S SENSE?
WELL, THERE'S ONLY ONE WAY TO FIND OUT!

IT'S A SIMPLE MATTER FOR ME TO FOLLOW THE SENSORY IMPULSES TO THEIR SOURCE! BOY, IT'S GREAT TO BE GETTING BACK INTO ACTION AGAIN!

BUT, PERHAPS SPIDER-MAN WOULD NOT BE QUITE SO ENTHUSIASTIC IF HE KNEW WHO WAS WAITING FOR HIM AT HIS ULTIMATE DESTINATION!
IT SHOULD BE CHILD'S PLAY FOR ME TO PERSUADE SPIDER-MAN TO JOIN ME AGAINST THE FANTASTIC FOUR!

WELL, I GUESS THIS IS THE PLACE! NOW TO... HOLY SMOKE! I'D KNOW THAT GUY ANYWHERE! IT..IT'S DOCTOR DOOM!

SO IT WAS YOU WHO TRIED TO CONTACT ME, DOOM?! IT WOULD HAVE HAD TO BE SOMEONE WITH YOUR TALENT! BUT WHY?
AH, SPIDER-MAN! IS IT NECESSARY FOR YOU TO MAKE YOUR ENTRANCE QUITE SO DRAMATIC, MY IMPETUOUS FRIEND?
4.

MISTER, FROM WHAT I'VE READ ABOUT YOU, YOU HAVEN'T GOT ANY FRIENDS... IMPETUOUS OR OTHERWISE!
FRIENDSHIP IS FOR WEAKLINGS! WHAT I OFFER YOU IS POWER! TOGETHER, WE COULD RULE THE WORLD!

YOU'RE AN OUTCAST, THE SAME AS I! YOU DARE NOT REVEAL YOUR TRUE IDENTITY! AND YET, RIGHT UNDER YOUR NOSE, THE FANTASTIC FOUR BASKS IN THE LIMELIGHT, WHILE YOU ARE SHUNNED AND HUNTED!
I'LL APPEAL TO HIS SENSE OF ENVY... OF PRIDE! THEN, ONCE HE HAS SERVED HIS PURPOSE, I'LL DESTROY HIM WITHOUT A SECOND THOUGHT!

ME TEAM UP WITH YOU, HUH? MAN, WOULDN'T THAT BE A GASSER? JONAH JAMESON WOULD REALLY HAVE SOMETHING TO HOWL ABOUT THEN!
AH, SO YOU WILL DO IT! SPEAK!! GIVE ME YOUR WORD!

NOT SO FAST, TIN-HEAD! SURE, IT'S AN AMUSIN' THOUGHT TO KICK AROUND, BUT JUST BETWEEN US, I NEED YOU LIKE I NEED ANOTHER NOSE! THE ANSWER IS NO, BUSTER!
I WARN YOU... IF YOU ARE NOT WITH ME, THEN WE ARE DEADLY FOES!

DOC, YOU'RE SCARIN' ME PLUMB OUT OF MY WITS! HERE, CHEW ON THIS HUNK OF WEB FOR A WHILE!

THAT'LL KEEP YOU UNDER WRAPS WHILE I FIGURE OUT WHAT TO DO WITH YOU! SAY, HOW COME YOU'RE SO QUIET... SO STILL? CAT GOT YOUR TONGUE?
YOU BRAZEN FOOL! HAVEN'T YOU GUESSED YET?

IT WASN'T YOU AT ALL! JUST A ROBOT... A DUMMY MADE UP TO RESEMBLE THE REAL DOCTOR DOOM!
NATURALLY! YOU ARE NOT FIGHTING ONE OF YOUR USUAL INSIPID ANTAGONISTS NOW, SPIDER-MAN! DOCTOR DOOM CANNOT BE TRAPPED SO EASILY!
5.

BUT SPIDER-MAN CAN! YOU DIDN'T EXPECT A TRAP-DOOR TO OPEN BENEATH YOUR FEET, DID YOU?
SAY, I'LL BET YOU'D BE A WOW AT A CONEY ISLAND FUN HOUSE!

YOU DON'T THINK A FELLER WITH THE REFLEXES OF A SPIDER IS GONNA TUMBLE DOWN A CORNY TRAP-DOOR, DO YOU?
PERHAPS NOT... BUT FOR YOUR SAKE, I HOPE YOU DON'T THINK YOU'VE ESCAPED ME ALREADY!

THE ACCIDENT WHICH YEARS AGO MADE A SHAMBLES OF MY FACE DIDN'T AFFECT MY STRENGTH AT ALL... AS YOU CAN SEE!
OOOF!

AND I AM NOT ENTIRELY WITHOUT LITTLE WEAPONS OF MY OWN.. SUCH AS THIS MOST EFFECTIVE MINIATURE FINGER-GUN!
NICE TRY, RATTLE-TRAP! BUT I SAW THAT COMING SECONDS AGO!

I'LL SAY "SO LONG" FOR NOW, DOC! I DON'T MAKE A HABIT OF BEING A HUMAN TARGET FOR BIG BAD VILLAINS!

IF I TWIST AND TURN JUST THE RIGHT WAY, I'LL MISS THE LEDGE BELOW AND LAND SAFELY IN THE WATER! LOOKS LIKE MY HOURS OF AGILITY PRACTICE ARE REALLY PAYING OFF!

HE ESCAPED ME! WELL, I'LL LET HIM GO FOR NOW! BUT HE SHALL STILL SERVE MY PURPOSE... ONLY, IN A WAY HE CANNOT POSSIBLY SUSPECT!
6.

THE FIRST THING I SHALL DO IS LEARN SPIDER-MAN'S TRUE IDENTITY! THAT WILL MAKE IT EASIER FOR ME TO CAPTURE HIM!
AND THEN, ONCE I HAVE HIM HELPLESS, I'LL USE HIM TO BAIT MY DEADLY TRAP FOR THE FANTASTIC FOUR!

MEANWHILE, HUNDREDS OF FEET BELOW...
I HOPE THAT REFUGEE FROM A NIGHTMARE FACTORY DOESN'T THINK HE'S SEEN THE LAST OF ME!... BECAUSE NOW I'M GONNA TACKLE HIM IN EARNEST!

BUT, BY THE TIME THE COLORFUL CRUSADER REACHES THE ROOF...
HOLY HANNAH! WHAT WAS THAT??
BAROOM!

DOOM WAS ONE STEP AHEAD OF ME! HE BLEW UP THE DESERTED BUILDING BEFORE I COULD GET BACK AT HIM! HE'S PROBABLY MILES AWAY BY NOW, PLANNING HIS NEXT MOVE!

WELL, TIME ENOUGH FOR HIM LATER...
I'LL SNAP A FEW PIX OF THE BURNING BUILDING... OLD SKINFLINT JAMESON MAY BE WILLING TO PAY PETE PARKER FOR THEM, IF THEY'RE EXCLUSIVES!

LOOK! THERE'S SPIDER-MAN!
IT MUST HAVE BEEN HIM WHO BLEW UP THE BUILDING!
JUST MY LUCK! THAT CROWD SEES ME! NOW I'LL PROBABLY BE BLAMED FOR THE FIRE, TOO!

THE NEXT DAY, AT THE OFFICES OF J. JONAH JAMESON..
ALL RIGHT, PARKER, I'LL BUY THOSE PICTURES OF THE FIRE FROM YOU! BUT WHAT I REALLY WANT ARE PIX OF SPIDER-MAN! I'D LOVE TO BE ABLE TO PIN THIS FIRE ON HIM!
HERE'S MY CHANCE TO NEEDLE THE OL' WINDBAG A LITTLE...
I DON'T KNOW, MR. JAMESON! PEOPLE ARE BEGINNING TO SAY YOU ATTACK HIM TOO MUCH! THEY'RE BEGINNING TO WONDER WHAT YOUR REAL MOTIVES ARE!

I THINK PARKER IS RIGHT, SIR! I'VE HEARD SOME OF OUR READERS MENTION THAT THEY THINK YOU'RE JEALOUS OF SPIDER-MAN FOR SOME REASON!
WELL, WELL! I NEVER KNEW I HAD AN ALLY IN J.J.'S SECRETARY! AND I NEVER REALIZED HOW PRETTY BETTY BRANT WAS, EITHER.. TILL NOW!
THAT'S ENOUGH! I'M STILL THE PUBLISHER HERE, AND I'LL DECIDE OUR EDITORIAL POLICY!
7.

I HAVE ONLY ONE REAL MOTIVE...TO MAKE MONEY! THE MORE I ATTACK SPIDER-MAN, THE MORE PEOPLE READ MY PAPERS! IT'S TO OUR ADVANTAGE TO KEEP POUNDING AWAY AT THAT CORNY COSTUMED CLOWN! EVERYBODY IS INTERESTED IN HIM...WHETHER THEY AGREE WITH ME OR NOT DOESN'T MATTER... SPIDER-MAN SELLS PAPERS! UNDERSTAND??
I SURE DO, YOU BIG, BLUSTERING PHONY!

A SHORT TIME LATER, IN ANOTHER PART OF TOWN...
BOY! WHAT A TERRIFIC GAG THIS'LL BE!
POOR PETER! HE'LL NEVER GET OVER IT!
WHERE IS PETER PARKER? I WANT HIM! BRING HIM TO ME!

WELL, HOW DID I LOOK? WILL PUNY PARKER FALL FOR IT?
LIKE A TON OF BRICKS! FLASH, YOU'RE A GENIUS!
THE GALS DID A GREAT JOB ON THE COSTUME! THIS'LL TEACH OUR BOOKWORM BUDDY TO KNOCK SPIDER-MAN!

AND SO, OUR WEB OF FATE DRAWS TIGHTER! NOW, BACK TO THE DEVIOUS DOCTOR DOOM!
THERE! I'VE DEVISED AN INSTRUMENT WHICH WILL REACT TO A SPIDER'S IMPULSES THE WAY A GEIGER COUNTER REACTS TO URANIUM!
ALL I NEED DO IS SCOUR THE CITY UNTIL THE DIAL REGISTERS POSITIVE, AND I WILL HAVE FOUND SPIDER-MAN'S REAL IDENTITY!

WHEN ONE IS A MASTER OF SCIENCE, AS I AM, THERE IS NOTHING WHICH CANNOT BE ACCOMPLISHED! SOONER OR LATER, I SHALL ELIMINATE ALL THOSE WHO DARE OPPOSE ME!

NOT LONG AFTERWARDS...
THERE'S PARKER NOW! WE'VE GOT TO TELL FLASH!
BETCHA HE'LL JUMP CLEAN OUT OF HIS SKIN WHEN HE SEES "SPIDER-MAN"! THIS'LL BE THE GREATEST GAG OF THE CENTURY!
AHHH! MY DEVICE IS BEGINNING TO REGISTER! I'M NEARING MY PREY!
8.

FLASH, HURRY! PARKER'S WALKING BY ALONG FRONT STREET!
OKAY! EVERYTHING'S SET! YOU GUYS HIDE SOMEWHERE AND WATCH THE FREE SHOW!

PARKER'LL BE THE LAUGHING-STOCK OF THE SCHOOL WHEN I'M THROUGH WITH HIM! IF HE'S TOO YELLOW TO FIGHT, THIS IS ONE WAY TO SHOW HIM WHAT WE THINK OF HIM!
ACCORDING TO MY DIAL, THE REAL SPIDER-MAN IS ALMOST DIRECTLY BELOW ME NOW!

THERE HE IS! STRANGE, HE'S WEARING HIS COSTUME IN BROAD DAYLIGHT! WELL, NO MATTER! WITHIN SECONDS, HE'LL BE MY HELPLESS PRISONER!

IT'S TIME TO SHOW MYSELF TO PARKER NOW, AND...
HEY, WHA...? WHAT'S THIS? WHAT'S GOIN' ON??
HE'S SEEN ME! BUT IT'S TOO LATE FOR HIM TO STOP ME! I'VE PLANNED THIS COUP TOO CAREFULLY!

AND AS PETER PARKER, THE REAL SPIDER-MAN, WALKS CALMLY BY, WRAPPED IN HIS OWN DEEP THOUGHTS...
ONE BURST OF THIS FAST-ACTING SLEEPING GAS WILL DO THE TRICK SILENTLY!

AND SO, DOCTOR DOOM MAKES HIS FIRST CARELESS MISTAKE...NOT SUSPECTING THAT HIS GEIGER-LIKE DEVICE HAD REACTED TO PETER PARKER'S PRESENCE, RATHER THAN THE IMITATION SPIDER-MAN'S!
DONE! NOW, ALL THAT REMAINS IS TO CARRY HIM BACK TO THE SHIP! IT WAS EVEN SIMPLER THAN I EXPECTED!
9.

STRANGE THAT HE SHOULD HAVE BEEN SO EASY TO TRAP! PERHAPS SPIDER-MAN POSSESSES LESS SUPER-POWERS THAN PEOPLE THINK!

MEANWHILE...
I DON'T GET IT! WHAT'S FLASH WAITIN' FOR?
PARKER WILL BE GONE IN ANOTHER FEW SECONDS!
MAYBE SOMETHING WENT WRONG! MAYBE FLASH'S COSTUME TORE OR SOMETHING! GEE! WHAT A DIS-APPOINTMENT!

MINUTES LATER, AFTER PETE HAS REACHED HOME...
HI, AUNT MAY! WHAT ARE YOU WATCHING?
THE ED SULLIVAN SHOW, DEAR! I JUST SAW THE CLEVEREST JUGGLING ACT, AND NOW HE'S GOING TO HAVE A CHORUS FROM SOME MIDWESTERN COLLEGE!

SAY! WHAT'S WRONG WITH THE SET?
I DON'T KNOW! OH, DEAR! WE JUST HAD IT FIXED LAST WEEK! I HOPE IT ISN'T THE PICTURE TUBE!

LADIES AND GENTLEMEN, PLEASE STAND BY! THERE IS NOTHING WRONG WITH YOUR SETS' RECEPTION! SOME STRANGE FORCE SEEMS TO BE AFFECTING ALL T.V. TRANSMISSION AT THIS TIME! STAND BY! STAND BY!
BOY, THIS IS A NEW ONE!

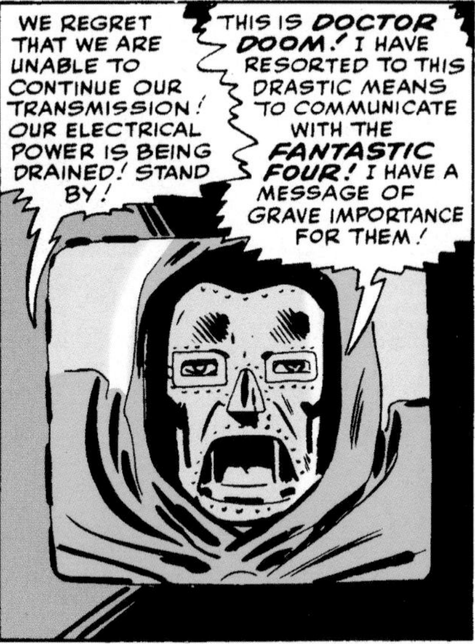
WE REGRET THAT WE ARE UNABLE TO CONTINUE OUR TRANSMISSION! OUR ELECTRICAL POWER IS BEING DRAINED! STAND BY!
THIS IS DOCTOR DOOM! I HAVE RESORTED TO THIS DRASTIC MEANS TO COMMUNICATE WITH THE FANTASTIC FOUR! I HAVE A MESSAGE OF GRAVE IMPORTANCE FOR THEM!

AS YOU CAN SEE, I HOLD SPIDER-MAN A HELPLESS CAPTIVE! UNLESS THE FANTASTIC FOUR PROMISE TO DISBAND AND SURRENDER TO ME, ONE AT A TIME, SPIDER-MAN WILL FORFEIT HIS LIFE! I WILL WAIT EXACTLY ONE HOUR FOR A REPLY!

OH, THAT AWFUL CREATURE! THANK HEAVENS HIS PRISONER IS ONLY SPIDER-MAN WHO IS PROBABLY AS MUCH A MENACE AS DOCTOR DOOM!
I DON'T GET IT! WHO WAS THAT JOKER IN THE SPIDER-MAN COSTUME?? WHAT'S IT ALL ABOUT? IS IT SOME KINDA TRICK?
BRRINNG!
10

I ABSOLUTELY FORBID IT! YOU'RE STILL JUST A BOY! AND, WITH ALL THOSE TERRIBLE PEOPLE ROAMING THE CITY... DOCTOR DOOM, SPIDER-MAN, AND HEAVEN KNOWS WHO ELSE... I WANT YOU HOME WHERE IT'S SAFE!

OKAY, AUNT MAY! YOU KNOW THE DOCTOR SAID YOU MUSTN'T WORRY!

SOME SUPER-HERO I AM! I'VE GOT TO FIND SOME WAY TO GET MY AUNT TO LET ME OUT OF THE HOUSE!

I'LL JUST GO DOWN HERE AND MAKE SURE THE CELLAR WINDOWS ARE LOCKED, AUNT MAY!

HATE TO DO THIS, BUT IT'S THE ONLY WAY! IF I REMOVE THE MASTER FUSE...

OH, PETER, THE LIGHTS WENT OUT! WE MUST HAVE BLOWN A FUSE! AND THERE AREN'T ANY MORE IN THE HOUSE!

I KNOW! NOW I'LL HAVE TO GO OUT TO GET SOME NEW ONES!

BUT PLEASE BE CAREFUL, DEAR... AND HURRY RIGHT BACK!

I'D BETTER GIVE MY EQUIPMENT A FAST SAFETY CHECK! LET'S SEE... PLENTY OF WEB FLUID... SPIDER-MAN LIGHT BEAM OKAY... MASK ON SECURELY...
THAT'S IT! NOW FOR DOCTOR DOOM!

AND AT THAT VERY MOMENT, AT THE FAMOUS SKY-SCRAPER HEADQUARTERS OF THE FANTASTIC FOUR...
WE DON'T HAVE MUCH MORE TIME, REED! WHAT ARE WE GOING TO DO?
WELL, SUE, WE CERTAINLY CAN'T LET ANY HARM COME TO SPIDER-MAN, IF WE CAN HELP IT!
BLASTED AMATEURS! ALWAYS GUMMIN' UP THE WORKS!
SINCE WHEN DID YOU GET A SUPER-HERO UNION CARD, THING, OL' PAL?

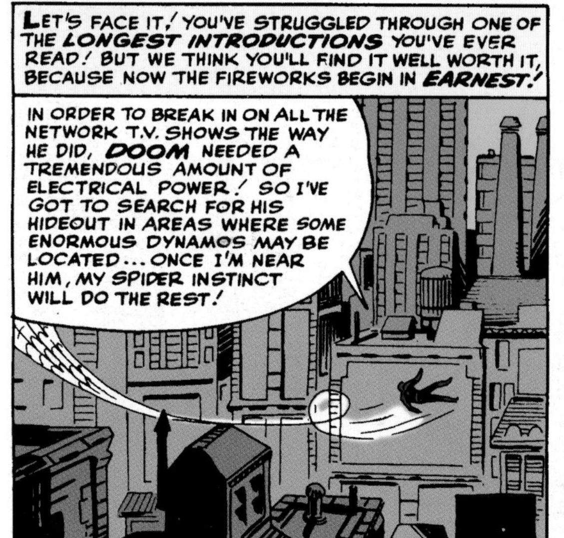
LET'S FACE IT! YOU'VE STRUGGLED THROUGH ONE OF THE LONGEST INTRODUCTIONS YOU'VE EVER READ! BUT WE THINK YOU'LL FIND IT WELL WORTH IT, BECAUSE NOW THE FIREWORKS BEGIN IN EARNEST!
IN ORDER TO BREAK IN ON ALL THE NETWORK T.V. SHOWS THE WAY HE DID, DOOM NEEDED A TREMENDOUS AMOUNT OF ELECTRICAL POWER! SO I'VE GOT TO SEARCH FOR HIS HIDEOUT IN AREAS WHERE SOME ENORMOUS DYNAMOS MAY BE LOCATED... ONCE I'M NEAR HIM, MY SPIDER INSTINCT WILL DO THE REST!

THE TELEPHONE COMPANY INSTALLATION IS BELOW ME, BUT I DON'T SENSE ANY HOSTILE PRESENCE DOWN THERE!

HERE'S THE BROAD-CASTING COMPANY BUILDING... BUT STILL NO TRACE OF LAUGH-ING BOY!

HECK! I'VE COVERED HALF THE CITY BY NOW WITHOUT FINDING HIM! I'VE GOT TO LOCATE DOOM BEFORE THAT HOUR IS UP!

I OUGHTTA HAVE MY HEAD EXAMINED FOR KNOCKIN' MYSELF OUT TO RESCUE A GUY WHO'S MY WORST ENEMY, BUT...
WHOOP! HOLD IT! I'M BEGINNING TO SENSE SOMETHING!
12

GOOD OL' SPIDER SENSE! IT HASN'T FAILED ME YET! I CAN FEEL THE HOSTILE EMANATIONS CLEAR UP HERE FROM THAT ABANDONED FACTORY BELOW!

AND, WITHIN THE SILENT, GLOOMY FACTORY...
LET ME OUT OF HERE! PLEASE! I'M NOT SPIDER-MAN! YOU'RE MAKIN' A BIG MISTAKE! HONEST! YOU'VE GOT TO BELIEVE ME! YOU'VE GOT TO!
SILENCE, YOU CRINGING, SNIVELLING COWARD! THE FAMOUS SPIDER-MAN! BAH! YOU'RE NOTHING BUT A FRIGHTENED WEAKLING!

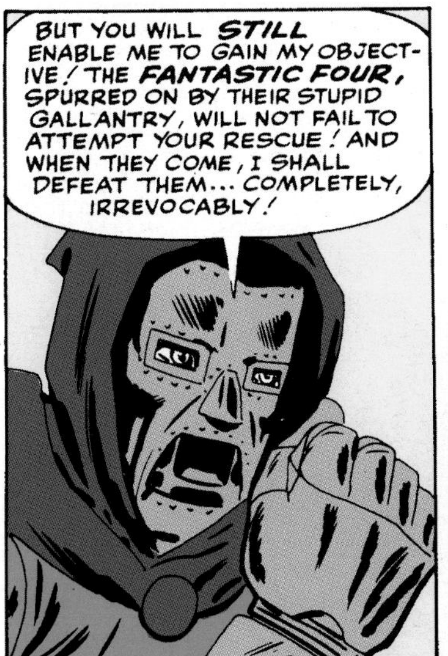
BUT YOU WILL STILL ENABLE ME TO GAIN MY OBJECTIVE! THE FANTASTIC FOUR, SPURRED ON BY THEIR STUPID GALLANTRY, WILL NOT FAIL TO ATTEMPT YOUR RESCUE! AND WHEN THEY COME, I SHALL DEFEAT THEM... COMPLETELY, IRREVOCABLY!

HMM...DOOM PROBABLY EXPECTS THE FF TO TRY TO SAVE HIS PRISONER, SO HE MUST HAVE A ZILLION TRAPS PREPARED! BUT MAYBE I CAN THROW HIM A CURVE BY SLITHERING DOWN THROUGH THIS AIR VENT, AS ONLY SPIDER-MAN CAN DO IT!

IT'S A TIGHT SQUEEZE, BUT I THINK I CAN MAKE IT! WHEW! THIS WOULD BE SOME SPOT FOR A GUY TO GET CLAUSTRO-PHOBIA!

AND NOW, SETTLE BACK AND PREPARE TO WITNESS THE GOL-DANGEST, DING-BUSTEDEST, RIP-SNORTIN'EST SUPER-CHARACTERS FIGHT YOU'VE EVER SEEN!
SPIDER-MAN! BUT... YOU'RE MY PRISONER!... INSIDE! HOW...?
CORRECTION, DOC! I'M THE REAL SPIDER-MAN! YOU JUST CAPTURED YOURSELF A PHONY BRAND-X IN THERE!

IF THAT'S SO, THEN YOU WERE A FOOL TO PLACE YOURSELF IN JEOPARDY AGAIN! THIS TIME I SHALL NOT ALLOW YOU TO ESCAPE!
FUNNY! I WAS THINKIN' THE SAME THING ABOUT YOU!
13

NOTHING LIKE A QUICKLY BUILT WEB COLUMN TO ACT AS A LIFE-SAVING SHIELD!

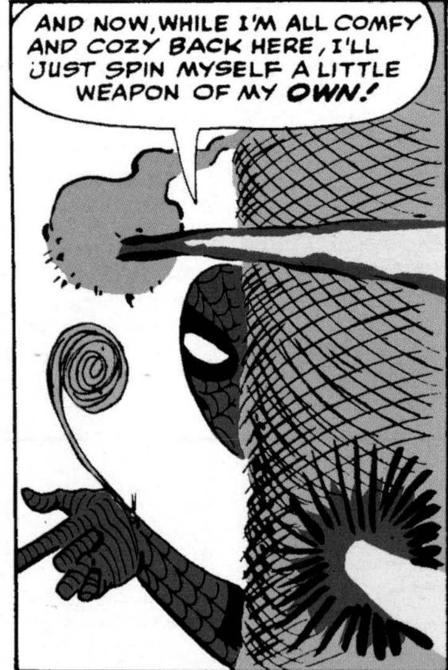
AND NOW, WHILE I'M ALL COMFY AND COZY BACK HERE, I'LL JUST SPIN MYSELF A LITTLE WEAPON OF MY OWN!

HERE WE ARE! HOPE I DIDN'T KEEP YOU WAITING TOO LONG, RUSTPOT! BUT IT TAKES A FEW SECONDS TO MAKE A WEB BALL FILLED WITH WEB FLUID!

YOU'VE GOT TO ADMIT ONE THING, THOUGH... IT'S A GREAT WAY TO TEACH SOMEONE THAT IT ISN'T POLITE TO POINT!
VERY CLEVER, SPIDER-MAN! YOU HAVE TEMPORARILY PUT MY FINGER-BLASTER OUT OF ACTION!

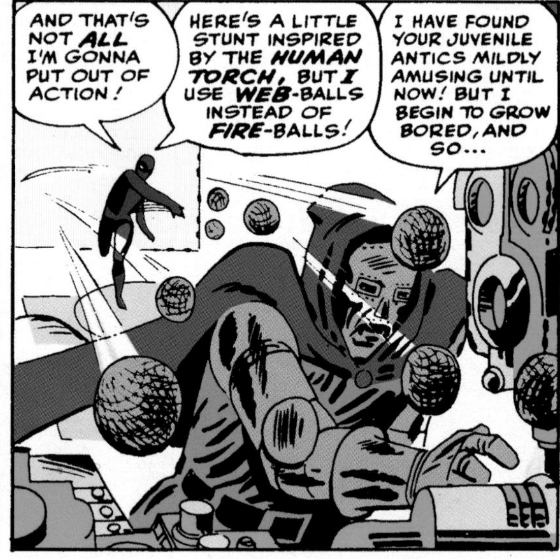
AND THAT'S NOT ALL I'M GONNA PUT OUT OF ACTION!
HERE'S A LITTLE STUNT INSPIRED BY THE HUMAN TORCH, BUT I USE WEB-BALLS INSTEAD OF FIRE-BALLS!
I HAVE FOUND YOUR JUVENILE ANTICS MILDLY AMUSING UNTIL NOW! BUT I BEGIN TO GROW BORED, AND SO...

UH OH! I SENSE DANGER ABOVE ME! HE'S TRYING TO LEAD ME INTO A TRAP! BETTER BUILD ANOTHER SHIELD FOR MYSELF... FAST!

JUST IN TIME! THAT FALLING LIQUID IS TURNING INTO ICE ON CONTACT! IT MIGHT HAVE FROZEN ME SOLID!

WELL, A MISS IS AS GOOD AS A MILE! READY TO TALK TURKEY YET, DOOM??
14.

ON THE CONTRARY, SPIDER-MAN! I WANT TO THANK YOU FOR ACTING AS A GUINEA PIG FOR ME! I'VE BEEN WANTING TO TEST OUT THIS LITTLE DEVICE FOR DAYS NOW!
IRON GLOBES, REVOLVING AT GREAT SPEED AROUND A MAGNETIC CORE!! YOU SURE HAVE SOME INTERESTING HOBBIES DOC!

MORE INTERESTING THAN YOU SUSPECT, BRAGGART! YOU'LL FIND YOUR WEB CANNOT STOP THE IRRESISTIBLE MOTION OF MY LITTLE PLAYTHINGS! THEY ARE FAR TOO POWERFUL!

THEY'RE WHIRLING FASTER AND FASTER! CAN'T DODGE 'EM MUCH LONGER! ONLY ONE CHANCE...

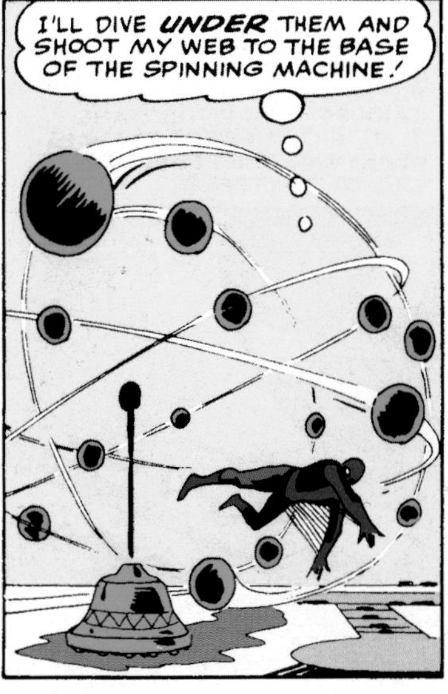
I'LL DIVE UNDER THEM AND SHOOT MY WEB TO THE BASE OF THE SPINNING MACHINE!

IT WORKED! IT JAMMED UP THE MECHANISM! THE BALLS ARE DROPPING-- THEIR POWER SOURCE NO LONGER PROPELLING THEM!

FOR THE LUVVA PETE! DOOM DOESN'T GIVE A GUY A CHANCE TO CATCH HIS BREATH! NOW HE'S GOT LIQUID HEAT SHOOTIN' UP FROM THE FLOORBOARDS!

I'D SURE FEEL SORRY FOR ANYBODY WHO HAD TO FIGHT THAT WALKING RATTLE TRAP...

...IF THEY DIDN'T HAVE THE POWERS OF A SPIDER-MAN!

SO! YOU SWUNG OVER MY HEAT RAYS, OUT OF HARM'S WAY, DID YOU? GOOD! THAT'S JUST WHERE I WANT YOU!
15.

YOU OUTSMARTED YOURSELF THAT TIME! I TRICKED YOU INTO LANDING WHERE YOU DID! AND NOW...
THIS STEEL SECTION OF FLOORING I LANDED ON... YOU'VE GOT IT ELECTRIFIED!

HE'S INCREASING THE CURRENT! CAN'T TAKE MUCH MORE OF IT! IT WOULD HAVE KNOCKED OUT A NORMAL HUMAN BY NOW!

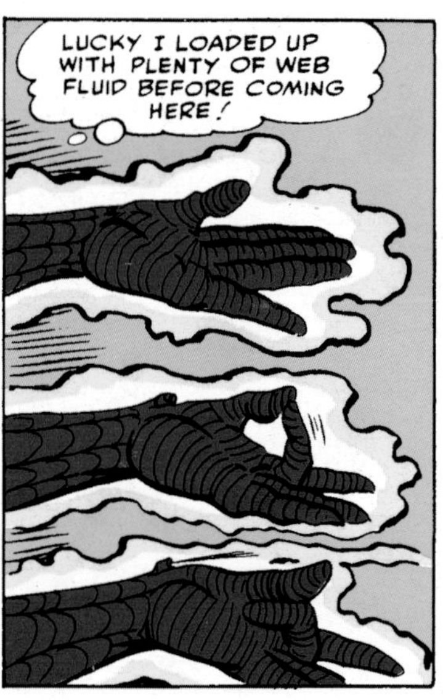
LUCKY I LOADED UP WITH PLENTY OF WEB FLUID BEFORE COMING HERE!

FIGHTING DESPERATELY TO MAINTAIN CONSCIOUSNESS, SPIDER-MAN SHOOTS OUT HIS AWESOME WEB, WHICH CARRIES WITH IT THE SAME ELECTRIC CURRENT WHICH IS WEAKENING THE DESPERATE CRIME-FIGHTER!

AND, AS THE WEB STRIKES THE STARTLED DOCTOR DOOM, THE SAME CHARGE OF ELECTRICITY RUNS THROUGH HIS BODY, MAGNIFIED MANY TIMES BY HIS METAL GARB!
UGH! I'M CAUGHT IN MY OWN TRAP! GOT TO SWITCH CURRENT OFF!

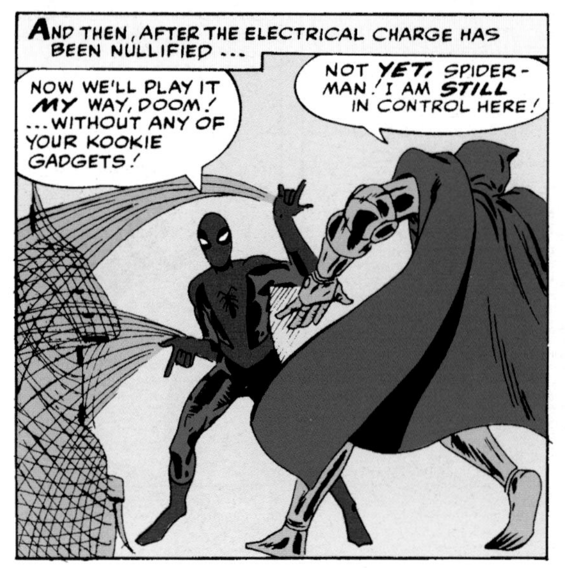
AND THEN, AFTER THE ELECTRICAL CHARGE HAS BEEN NULLIFIED...
NOW WE'LL PLAY IT MY WAY, DOOM! ...WITHOUT ANY OF YOUR KOOKIE GADGETS!
NOT YET, SPIDER-MAN! I AM STILL IN CONTROL HERE!

AH, JUST IN CASE YOU DON'T BELIEVE ME...HERE'S SOMETHING TO CONVINCE YOU!
HUH? BEHIND ME! WHO...? WHAT..?
16

THE ROBOT! WHAT A FOOL I WAS... I FORGOT ABOUT IT!
NATURALLY! NO ONE CAN MATCH THE THINKING ABILITY OF DOCTOR DOOM!

AND NOW, EVEN THOUGH YOU ARE BREAKING FREE, IT IS TOO LATE! EVEN YOU WILL FIND NO DEFENSE AGAINST THIS MACHINE!

BEFORE I WORRY ABOUT ANY NEW MACHINES OF YOURS, HERE'S YOUR PLAYMATE BACK, WITH MY REGARDS!
STILL YOU RELY ON BRUTE STRENGTH, SPIDER-MAN! THAT WILL BE YOUR UNDOING!

WE'LL SEE ABOUT THAT! MY SPIDER'S STRENGTH WILL ENABLE ME TO SMASH YOUR NEW GIZMO BY TOSSING YOUR OWN SATELLITE MACHINE AT IT!
NOT QUITE! NOT IF I CAN FLIP THIS LEVER FIRST!

HOLY SMOKE! HIS MACHINE IS SOME SORT OF DISINTEGRATOR! IT VAPORIZED THE METAL ON THE SPOT! I HAVEN'T A CHANCE AGAINST IT!

WELL, I CAN'T STAND STILL AND LET IT FINISH ME! MAYBE I CAN DIVE PAST THE BOLTS AND REACH THE CONTROL PANEL!
17.

AND THEN, AS THE DEADLY BOLTS FROM THE AWE-SOME MACHINE FLICKER AROUND THEM, THE TWO MIGHTY FOES BATTLE FOR THEIR LIVES!
UGH! HE... HE'S EVEN STRONGER THAN I SUSPECTED!
DIDN'T YOU THINK I EXPECTED YOU TO TRY THAT?

THAT BOLT! IT STRUCK YOU! BUT...
BUT WHAT? DID YOU THINK I'D EXPOSE MYSELF TO MY OWN WEAPON WITHOUT TAKING PRECAUTIONS ??! I'M INSULATED AGAINST THESE BOLTS... THEY CANNOT HARM ME!

BUT YOU, ALAS, ARE NOT SO INSULATED... AS YOU ARE NOW ABOUT TO LEARN!
IT'S UNBELIEVABLE!! HE'S LIKE A HUMAN MACHINE! HE SEEMS TO BE TIRELESS!

ANOTHER INCH AND I'M DONE FOR! SPIDER STRENGTH, IF I EVER NEEDED YOU, I NEED YOU NOW!

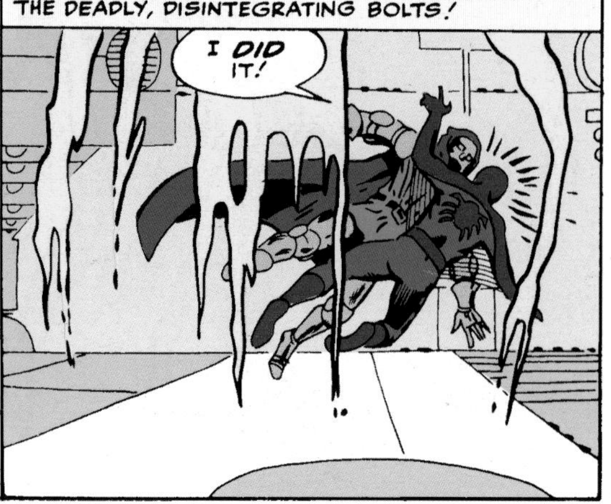
EXERTING EVERY LAST BIT OF POWER CONTAINED IN A SUPER-HUMAN BODY, THE AMAZING SPIDER-MAN, EXECUTING ONE LAST MANEUVER, MANAGES TO TWIST SUDDENLY SO THAT BOTH FIGURES SPRAWL AGAINST THE CONTROL PANEL, HALTING THE DEADLY, DISINTEGRATING BOLTS!
I DID IT!

BUT, ON THE VERGE OF EXHAUSTION DUE TO HIS HERCULEAN EFFORT, SPIDER-MAN CANNOT PREVENT HIS OLDER, MORE EXPERIENCED ADVER-SARY FROM REGAINING HIS BALANCE FIRST AND STRIKING THE INITIAL BLOW!
THIS WILL BE YOUR FINISH, YOU CLUMSY FOOL!
OOOF!
18

IF I HAD A DIME FOR EVERY TIME SOME CORNBALL PREDICTED MY FINISH, I'D... HEY! NOW WHAT??
HAVE PATIENCE! THESE LITTLE FLAKES WILL SOON END THIS BATTLE... FOR GOOD!

HE'S GOT ME ON THE DEFENSIVE AGAIN! SOMETHING IN THOSE GLOWING FLAKES HAS AFFECTED MY EYES! I-I CAN'T SEE! HAVE TO RELY ON MY SPIDER'S SENSE ALONE!

HOW DID HE MANAGE TO DUCK OUT OF THE WAY IN TIME??
OH, I SHOULD HAVE GUESSED! IT'S THAT ACCURSED INHUMAN SPIDER'S SENSE OF HIS!

MY EYES ARE BEGINNING TO CLEAR! IF I CAN JUST KEEP OUT OF RANGE A FEW SECONDS LONGER!
YOU'RE ONLY PROLONGING THE AGONY, SPIDER-MAN! YOU HAVEN'T A CHANCE AGAINST ME!

HEY! WHAT TH...??? IT'S THOSE IRON BALLS FROM THE SATELLITE MACHINE! I DIDN'T NOTICE THEM UNDER-FOOT! CAN'T KEEP MY BALANCE!
AND THUS SHALL I DEFEAT ALL MY MORTAL ENEMIES... INCLUDING THE FANTASTIC FOUR!

BUT, AT THAT FATEFUL SECOND, SOMETHING OUT-SIDE A NEARBY WINDOW CATCHES THE EYE OF DOCTOR DOOM, AND...
IT CAN'T BE! NOT NOW! I..I'M NOT READY FOR THEM YET!
19.

IT'S THE FANTASTI-CAR... WITH THE FANTASTIC FOUR INSIDE! THEY HAVE FOUND ME! I.. I CAN'T FIGHT THEM AND SPIDER-MAN... NOT AT THE SAME TIME!

BLAST THE LUCK! ANOTHER FEW SECONDS AND I'D HAVE FINISHED OFF SPIDER-MAN... FOREVER!!
WELL, AT LEAST I'VE PREPARED A GETAWAY EXIT FOR MYSELF! AS FOR SPIDER-MAN, HE CAN WAIT... THERE'S ALWAYS ANOTHER DAY!
I CAN SEE AGAIN! BUT DOOM IS CUTTING OUT... WHY??

SO THAT'S IT! IT'S THE FF... JUST LIKE THE CAVALRY IN A T.V. WESTERN! WELL, THEIR EYES'LL SURE POP WHEN THEY REALIZE I FOUND DOOM FIRST!

WAIT A MINUTE! I JUST REMEMBERED! AUNT MAY! I LEFT HER ALONE AT HOME! SHE'S PROBABLY BESIDE HER-SELF WITH WORRY ABOUT ME BY NOW!

ACCORDING TO OUR SENSOR-PROBE DIAL, THIS IS THE PLACE!
SKIP THE SCIENTI-FIC DOUBLE-TALK, SKINNY! LET'S GO GET 'IM!
POOR AUNT MAY! CAN'T WASTE A SECOND! GOT TO RUSH BACK HOME!

MEANWHILE, IN DR. DOOM'S NOW-ABANDONED HIDEOUT, FLASH THOMPSON FINDS HIMSELF FREE SINCE THE ELECTRONIC CIRCUITS HAVE BEEN DESTROYED!..
DR. DOOM... HE'S GONE! I DON'T KNOW WHAT HAPPENED, BUT I'M STILL IN ONE PIECE!

WHAT A LUNKHEAD I WAS TO DRESS AS SPIDER-MAN! IF I EVER GET OUT OF HERE ALIVE, I'LL NEVER ASK FOR TROUBLE AGAIN!

LOOK! IT'S SPIDER-MAN!
GRAB HIM!
HUH? W-WAIT! DON'T!
20.

THANKS TO YOUR OVERWHELMING RESPONSE TO PETER PARKER'S OFF-BEAT ADVENTURES, **SPIDER-MAN** IS NOW PUBLISHED **MONTHLY!** DON'T BE A JOHNNY-COME-LATELY! RESERVE YOUR COPY OF THE SENSATIONAL ISSUE #6 AT YOUR NEWSDEALER **NOW!** YOU WON'T WANT TO MISS THE NEW SUPER-VILLAINS, SUPER-ADVENTURES, AND SUPER-SURPRISES IN STORE FOR YOU!

21.

the AMAZING SPIDER-MAN
APPROVED BY THE COMICS CODE AUTHORITY
IND.
MARVEL COMICS GROUP 12¢
6 NOV.
HALF-MAN... HALF-REPTILE...
THE LIZARD
WILL TAKE OVER ALL OF EARTH UNLESS SPIDER-MAN ALONE CAN STOP HIM!
THE MARVEL AGE OF COMICS IS HERE!

SPIDER-MAN
"FACE-TO-FACE WITH... THE LIZARD!"
IT IS COMMON KNOWLEDGE THAT SPIDER-MAN IS THE MOST SUCCESSFUL NEW SUPER-HERO SINCE THE FANTASTIC FOUR!
THIS, THE LATEST, AND POSSIBLY THE GREATEST OF ALL HIS ADVENTURES, WILL SHOW YOU WHY THE MYSTERIOUS MASKED TEEN-AGER HAS BECOME AMERICA'S SUPER SENSATION!
WRITTEN BY: STAN LEE
DRAWN BY: STEVE DITKO
LETTERED BY: ART SIMEK
A 21-PAGE SPIDER-MAN SUPER EPIC!
X-440
1
ANOTHER PROUD PRODUCTION OF THE MIGHTY MARVEL COMICS GROUP!

A SUPER-HERO IS NOTHING WITHOUT A SUPER-VILLAIN! AND, OUR LATEST SUPER-VILLAIN APPEARS, WITHOUT WARNING, IN THE MURKY SWAMPS OF FLORIDA'S EVERGLADES! THIS IS THE FIRST ENCOUNTER BETWEEN MAN-KIND AND--THE LIZARD!
BEGONE!! THIS SWAMP IS MINE!
WHA-WHAT IS IT?
A GIANT LIZARD! BUT--IT TALKS!
IT WALKS LIKE A MAN!

WHATEVER IT IS, IT'S ATTACKING US!! I'LL--LOOK! BULLETS DON'T STOP IT!
YOU DARE DEFY THE LIZARD? YOU'LL PAY FOR THAT FOLLY!

HE SNAPPED THAT HUGE TREE AS IF IT WERE CARDBOARD!
FLEE, PUNY HUMANS! THIS SWAMP IS MINE! HERE THE LIZARD REIGNS SUPREME!
RUN! WE'VE GOT TO GET AWAY FROM HERE!
BOY! HE DOESN'T HAVE TO TELL ME TWICE!

LIKE WILDFIRE, THE REPORTS OF THE HUMAN LIZARD SPREAD THRUOUT THE EVERGLADES... THE STATE... AND THE ENTIRE NATION!
THEY SAY IT WALKS AND TALKS LIKE A MAN!
BULLETS CANNOT HARM IT!! WHAT IS IT? WHO IS IT?
IT HAS THE STRENGTH OF A DOZEN BULL-DOZERS!
NOBODY CAN EVER TRACK IT DOWN... NOBODY WOULD DARE INVADE ITS DARK DOMAIN!

EVEN AS FAR NORTH AS NEW YORK, THE NAME OF THE LIZARD IS ON EVERYONE'S LIPS!
EXTRA! READ ALL ABOUT THE LIZARD! EXTRA! EXTRA!
I'D LIKE A PAPER, TOO! BUT I'LL GET IT MY OWN WAY!

AND SO, QUIETLY--SECRETLY--AMERICA'S MOST MYSTERIOUS SUPER HERO LEARNS ABOUT THE NATION'S NEWEST MENACE FOR THE FIRST TIME!
WHAT KIND OF CORNBALL GAG IS THIS? EVERY PUBLICITY-MAD NUT AND HIS BROTHER TRY TO CHALLENGE ME TO SOME-THING OR OTHER!
EXTRA DAILY BUGLE
THE BUGLE CHALLENGES SPIDER-MAN TO DEFEAT THE LIZARD!
2

WELL, I'LL CHANGE TO PETER PARKER, AND GO SEE MISTER JAMESON! MAYBE HE'LL SEND ME TO FLORIDA TO SNAP SOME PHOTOS OF THAT LIZARD CHARACTER!

A FEW MINUTES LATER, AT THE OFFICE OF THE "DAILY BUGLE"...
YOU'RE OUT OF YOUR MIND, PARKER! I JUST PRINTED THAT "CHALLENGE" HEADLINE TO SELL PAPERS! THE LIZARD IS PROBABLY JUST A PHONY, ANYWAY! I'M NOT PAYING YOU TO WASTE TIME!
BUT IF SPIDER-MAN DOES FIGHT HIM, THINK WHAT A SCOOP WE COULD GET!

DON'T MAKE ME LAUGH! IF THERE REALLY IS A GIANT LIZARD DOWN SOUTH, SPIDER-MAN WILL NEVER TACKLE HIM! HE'D RATHER STAY HERE, FIGHTING TWO-BIT HOODS AND MAKING A REP FOR HIMSELF!
I SHOULD HAVE KNOWN OLD HATCHET-FACE WOULD TURN ME DOWN!

TOO BAD, PETER! I THINK HE SHOULD HAVE SENT YOU TO COVER THE LIZARD STORY! IT MIGHT BE A REAL SCOOP!
THANKS, BETTY! I SURE WISH YOU WERE THE PUBLISHER, INSTEAD OF JUST BEING HIS SECRETARY!

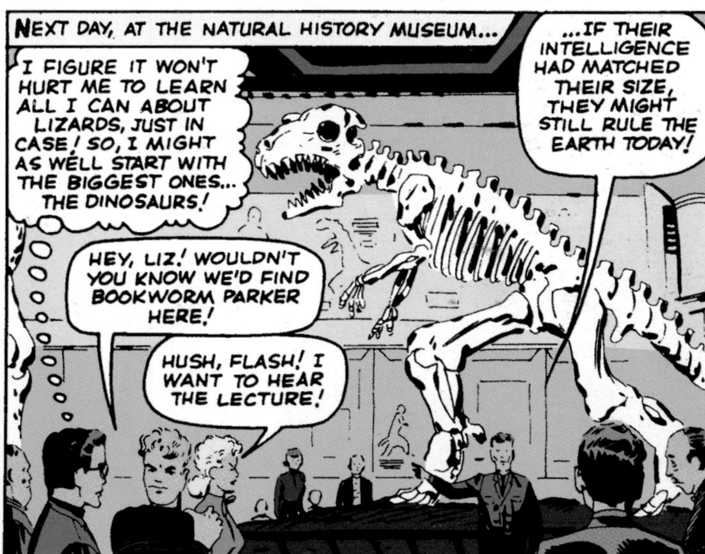
NEXT DAY, AT THE NATURAL HISTORY MUSEUM...
...IF THEIR INTELLIGENCE HAD MATCHED THEIR SIZE, THEY MIGHT STILL RULE THE EARTH TODAY!
I FIGURE IT WON'T HURT ME TO LEARN ALL I CAN ABOUT LIZARDS, JUST IN CASE! SO, I MIGHT AS WELL START WITH THE BIGGEST ONES... THE DINOSAURS!
HEY, LIZ! WOULDN'T YOU KNOW WE'D FIND BOOKWORM PARKER HERE!
HUSH, FLASH! I WANT TO HEAR THE LECTURE!

THEIR HIDES WERE SO THICK THAT IF THEY LIVED TODAY NO GUN SMALLER THAN A CANNON COULD INJURE THEM!
MY SPIDER SENSE IS TINGLING! THOSE TWO MEN COMING IN... IT'S DUE TO THEM!
NO ONE SAW US TAKE THE IDOL'S RUBY! NOW LET'S SCRAM!

THEY LIVED IN OR OUT OF WATER... THEY COULD CRUSH A PRESENT-DAY TANK...
THEY'VE STOLEN SOME-THING! I CAN SENSE IT! HAVE TO FOLLOW THEM!
DON'T LIKE THE WAY THAT KID'S LOOKIN' AT US!
ME, NEITHER! COME ON!
3

AW, HE'S HARMLESS! HE'S GOIN' IN THE OTHER ROOM!
LUCKY FOR HIM! IF HE CAME ANY CLOSER, I'D HAVE LET 'IM HAVE IT!
I'LL DUCK IN HERE AND CHANGE TO SPIDER-MAN!
CLOSED NEW EXHIBIT

THERE'S NOT MUCH MORE I CAN LEARN ABOUT DINOSAURS...
...AND THIS IS A LOT MORE FUN!

UH OH! WHAT'S THE COMMOTION OUT THERE? IT'S THE GUARD! HE'S CHASING THOSE TWO!
HE SAW THEM STEAL SOMETHING! BUT--THEY PULLED A GUN... SEIZED ONE OF THE KIDS... IT'S LIZ!

OKAY, SO YOU SAW US GRAB THAT RUBY! BUT WE'RE GETTIN' OUT OF HERE ANYWAY... AND WE'RE TAKING THIS GAL WITH US--FOR PROTECTION!
PLEASE! LET THEM GO! DON'T TRY TO STOP THEM! THEY--THEY SEEM SO DESPERATE!
YOU TWO WON'T GET AWAY WITH THIS!
I'LL SAY THEY WON'T!

I SEE THAT FLASH THOMPSON, LIZ'S LOUD-MOUTHED DATE, ISN'T DOING HER ANY GOOD!
...BUT "BOOKWORM PARKER" HAS A FEW TRICKS UP HIS LITTLE SLEEVE!

HOLD IT, BOYS! YOU'RE MISSING ONE OF THE MOST INTERESTING EXHIBITS! NAMELY--ME!
IT'S--SPIDER-MAN!
WHAT DO WE DO NOW?

I'LL ANSWER THAT QUESTION! YOU HIT MY EAGER LITTLE FIST WITH YOUR BIG STRONG CHINS... LIKE THIS!
UGH!
OOF!
4

SPIDER-MAN!! YOU SAVED ME FROM THOSE TWO GUNMEN!
THE PLEASURE WAS ALL MINE, BLUE-EYES!

I'M JUST ENOUGH OF A SHOW-OFF TO ENJOY THESE LITTLE INCIDENTS!
...BUT I'D BETTER CUT OUT BEFORE SOMEONE WONDERS WHERE PETER PARKER IS!

MINUTES LATER...
LIZ, COME ON! SNAP OUT OF IT! THIS IS FLASH! DON'T YOU REMEMBER ME?
FLASH? FLASH WHO? ALL I CAN REMEMBER ARE SPIDER-MAN'S STRONG ARMS AROUND ME! -SIGH-
MADE IT! NOBODY EVEN MISSED ME!

HE SAVED ME! HE CALLED ME BLUE EYES! I'LL NEVER FORGET HIM!
NUTS! COMPETITION LIKE YOU I CAN HANDLE, PARKER! BUT WHAT DO I DO ABOUT SPIDER-MAN?
JUST ONE THING, PAL... WORRY!

AT THAT MOMENT, A BOY PASSES BY, LISTENING TO THE NEWS ON HIS TRANSISTOR PORTABLE RADIO...
THE NATION WONDERS WHY SPIDER-MAN HAS AVOIDED GOING AFTER THE LIZARD...
THAT SETTLES IT! I'VE GOT TO FIND A WAY TO GET JAMESON TO SEND ME TO FLORIDA!

AND SO, NOT LONG AFTER...
WH-WHO'S THAT??
WELL, IT'S NOT FATS DOMINO!

UH UH! HANDS OFF YOUR INTERCOM, JONAH, OL' CHUM! LET'S KEEP THIS NICE AND PRIVATE!
A WEB!

GOT TO GET OUT!--GET HELP!
HOLD IT, SMILEY! WHERE'S YOUR HOSPITALITY?
5

JAMESON, YOU'VE BEEN WRITING EDITORIALS AGAINST ME...TALKING ON RADIO AND TV AGAINST ME... AND Y'KNOW SOMETHING? I'M BEGINNING TO THINK YOU DON'T LIKE ME!
L-LET ME DOWN!

WHAT'S THE RUSH? I HAVE A NEWS ITEM FOR YOU! I'M GOING TO ACCEPT THE LIZARD'S CHALLENGE! SO, IF YOU WANT TO SEE WHAT I CAN REALLY DO, YOU'D BETTER SEND A PHOTOGRAPHER TO FLORIDA TO COVER THE STORY!
AS FOR MY WEB, IT'LL LOOSEN IN A MINUTE AND YOU'LL COME DOWN... BOY, WILL YOU COME DOWN!!

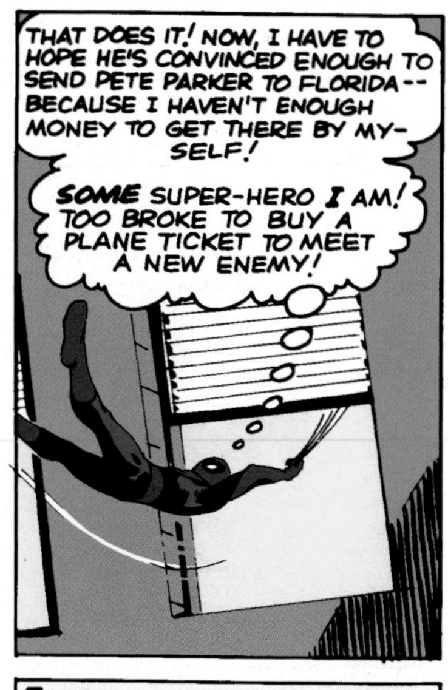
THAT DOES IT! NOW, I HAVE TO HOPE HE'S CONVINCED ENOUGH TO SEND PETE PARKER TO FLORIDA-- BECAUSE I HAVEN'T ENOUGH MONEY TO GET THERE BY MYSELF!
SOME SUPER-HERO I AM! TOO BROKE TO BUY A PLANE TICKET TO MEET A NEW ENEMY!

MISS BRANT, STOP GAPING AND CALL PETER PARKER! I WANT TO SEE HIM HERE AT ONCE! BUT FIRST, PUT SOME SOFT CUSHIONS ON THE FLOOR UNDER ME!
Y-YES, SIR!

WHUMP!
OWW!! NEVER MIND THOSE #!?+! CUSHIONS!
TSK! TSK! POOR GENTLE JONAH!

EXACTLY FIVE MINUTES LATER...
PETER! WHERE HAVE YOU BEEN? MR. JAMESON HAS BEEN LOOKING EVERYWHERE FOR YOU!
NO WONDER HE DIDN'T FIND ME! I HAVEN'T BEEN EVERYWHERE!

YOU KNOW, BETTY... I'VE BEEN WANTING TO ASK YOU SOMETHING...
YES, PETER?
PARKER! GET IN HERE!

I'VE DECIDED TO SEND YOU TO FLORIDA AFTER ALL, TO TRY TO GET SOME PICTURES OF THE LIZARD... AND SPIDER-MAN, IF HE SHOWS UP!
THAT'S GREAT! WHEN DO I START?

START PACKING NOW! WE'RE LEAVING AS SOON AS POSSIBLE!
WE'RE LEAVING--???!
THAT'S RIGHT! IT'S SUCH A BIG STORY THAT I'M GOING WITH YOU!
6

I'M NOT TAKING ANY CHANCES OF A SLIP-UP! BESIDES, I CAN USE A TRIP TO FLORIDA!
OH, BROTHER! IF HE TAGS ALONG, HOW'LL I BE ABLE TO KEEP SWITCHING FROM PETE PARKER TO SPIDER-MAN?
I-I'LL HAVE TO GET PERMISSION FROM MY AUNT MAY!

MINUTES LATER, AT HOME...
YOU WANT TO GO TO FLORIDA?? WITH THAT HORRIBLE LIZARD RUNNING LOOSE DOWN THERE? OH NO, PETER! IT'S OUT OF THE QUESTION!
BUT MISTER JAMESON IS GOING WITH ME!

YOU MEAN J. JONAH JAMESON, THE NICE MAN YOU DO PART-TIME WORK FOR? OH, IN THAT CASE I SUPPOSE IT'S ALL RIGHT! I KNOW THAT HE'LL TAKE GOOD CARE OF YOU!
HE'S LIKE A BIG, FAT GUARDIAN ANGEL, AUNT MAY!

AND SO, THE NEXT DAY...
WHAT ARE YOU LUGGING THERE, PARKER!
A LOT OF CLIPPINGS ABOUT THE LIZARD, AND MAPS OF THE AREA WHERE HE'S BEEN SEEN!

GLAD TO SEE YOU'RE THINKING AHEAD, PARKER! YOU HAVEN'T SOLD ME TOO MANY SENSATIONAL PICTURES LATELY-- YOU BETTER NOT DISAPPOINT ME THIS TIME!
OH, PERISH FORBID!

BUT, UNNOTICED BY JONAH JAMESON, THE SHARP-EYED PETER PARKER SCANS A FEW OTHER ITEMS...
HMM...DR. CONNORS, THE REPTILE EXPERT, LIVES NEAR THE EVERGLADES AREA! HE MIGHT BE OF SOME HELP!
Reptile Expert
DOCTOR CURTIS CONNORS

FINALLY, AT THE AIRPORT IN FLORIDA...
I'LL GO AND GET SOME FRESH FILM AND EQUIPMENT WHILE YOU GET SETTLED IN THE HOTEL!
MAKE IT SNAPPY! WHY DIDN'T YOU BUY THAT JUNK IN NEW YORK INSTEAD OF DOING IT HERE, ON MY TIME?!

AND, ONCE OUT OF SIGHT OF JAMESON AND THE OTHERS...
BECAUSE THEN I WOULDN'T HAVE HAD A CHANCE TO CHANGE TO SPIDER-MAN... THAT'S WHY!
7

HMM... THE LIZARD AREA IS BLOCKED OFF BY ARMED PATROLS!

I WONDER WHAT KIND OF "BLIP" I'D MAKE ON A RADAR SCREEN?

BUT, ALTHOUGH HE IS NOT DETECTED BY RADAR, SPIDER-MAN IS OBSERVED BY SOMETHING FAR MORE DANGEROUS! THE EYES OF... THE LIZARD!
ENEMY COMING...
MUST HIDE! THEN ATTACK!

I DON'T LIKE IT! IT'S TOO QUIET HERE! UNNATURALLY QUIET! IT'S A CREEPY FEELING!

MY SPIDER SENSE IS STARTING TO TINGLE! BUT, I DON'T SEE ANYTHING!

MY FOOT! SOMETHING GRABBED ME FROM BEHIND!
SOMETHING POWERFUL! CAN'T KEEP MY BALANCE...

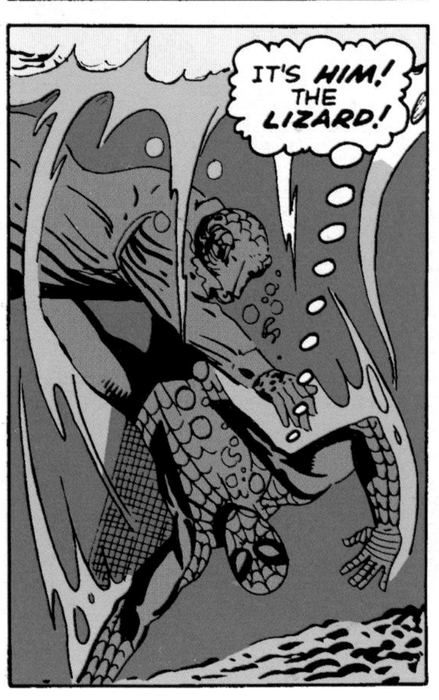
IT'S HIM! THE LIZARD!

LIZARD OR NOT, A GLOB OF MUD PUSHED IN HIS FACE OUGHT TO SLOW HIM DOWN A LITTLE...

WHEW- I'M OUT! COULDN'T HAVE HELD MY BREATH MUCH LONGER!
UH OH! HE'S OUT, TOO!
STILL CAN'T FIGURE OUT WHO, OR WHAT, HE REALLY IS!
8

THE SWAMPLAND IS MINE! I HAVE WARNED THE WORLD! BUT YOU DARED TO INVADE MY DOMAIN! AND SO... YOU ARE DOOMED!
SURE! SURE! EVERY TIME I TURN AROUND I GET "DOOMED" BY SOMEONE ELSE!

HE'S FAST! HIS TAIL ALMOST GOT ME THAT TIME!
STRANGE... HE DOESN'T SEEM TO BE WEARING A DISGUISE... THAT GROTESQUE FORM IS REALLY--HIM!

I'D BETTER KNOCK SOME OF THE FIGHT OUT OF HIM!
IF I CAN JUST HANG ONTO HIS TAIL...

SUFFERIN' SPIDERWEBS!! HE'S A DOZEN TIMES STRONGER THAN I THOUGHT!

BOY, WHEN I MAKE A MISTAKE, IT'S A BEAUT! LOOK OUT BELOW!

-GASP!- HE THREW ME ALMOST HALF A MILE! LUCKY THESE TREES BROKE MY FALL!
SAY... THAT MUST BE DR. CONNORS' HOUSE! HE'S THE REPTILE EXPERT I WANTED TO SEE!

I'D BETTER WARN HIM HOW NEAR THE LIZARD IS!
GOSH! THAT WOMAN IN THERE-- SHE'S CRYING!

DON'T SEE DOCTOR CONNORS AROUND! WELL, I'VE GOT TO SPEAK TO THE WOMAN... WARN HER OF THE LIZARD!
SPIDER-MAN!
DON'T BE AFRAID! I'M HERE TO HELP YOU!

I WANTED TO TALK TO YOUR HUSBAND--ASK HIS ADVICE ABOUT REPTILES--BUT THERE'S NO TIME NOW! YOU'VE GOT TO LEAVE -- THE LIZARD IS NEARBY!
LEAVE? OH, NO-- YOU DON'T UNDERSTAND!
9

MY HUSBAND, DR. CURTIS CONNORS--*IS THE LIZARD!*
WHAT ??!!
To my wife Love, Curtis

"LET ME EXPLAIN... MY HUSBAND WAS A SURGEON--HE LOST HIS RIGHT ARM DURING THE WAR! EVER SINCE THEN, HE HAS STUDIED REPTILE LIFE! HE BECAME ONE OF THE WORLD'S LEADING AUTHORITIES ON REPTILES..."
IF A LOWER ORDER OF LIFE, SUCH AS CERTAIN TYPES OF LIZARDS, LOSE A LEG, OR ANY BASE EXTREMITY, THEY OFTEN SIMPLY GROW A *NEW* ONE!
IF ONLY I COULD LEARN HOW IT IS DONE, AND APPLY THE SECRET TO *HUMANS...* THINK WHAT IT WOULD MEAN!

A MAN MIGHT GROW A NEW PAIR OF LEGS, OR ARMS! PERHAPS EVEN NEW EYES, OR A NEW HEART! I'VE *GOT* TO FIND THE SECRET!
OH, CURTIS... IF ONLY YOU *COULD!*
"CURTIS CONNORS WAS A GOOD HUSBAND, A GOOD FATHER! HIS SON, BILLY, ADORED HIM... AND SO DID I!"
DADDY, WHAT ARE YOU WORKING ON NOW?
SOMETHING TO MAKE YOU *PROUD* OF ME, BILLY! SOMETHING TO HELP ALL MANKIND!
"AFTER MONTHS OF EXPERIMENTATION..."
THE SERUM WHICH I EXTRACTED FROM MY EXPERIMENTAL LIZARDS *WORKED!*
THAT RABBIT GREW A *NEW LEG* WITHIN AN HOUR!

NOW, ALL THAT REMAINS IS FOR ME TO TRY IT ON A *HUMAN!* AND WHAT BETTER SUBJECT CAN THERE BE, THAN--MYSELF!
CURTIS... ARE YOU SURE IT'S SAFE? *CURTIS!!*
"HE DRANK THE BUBBLING SERUM BEFORE I COULD STOP HIM! AND THEN..."
MY RIGHT SHOULDER... SUCH A STRANGE SENSATION!
I-I FEEL *LIFE* RETURNING!

"AND THEN..."
I'VE *DONE* IT! *I'VE GROWN A NEW ARM!*
THIS IS THE GREATEST MEDICAL FEAT OF ALL TIME!
10

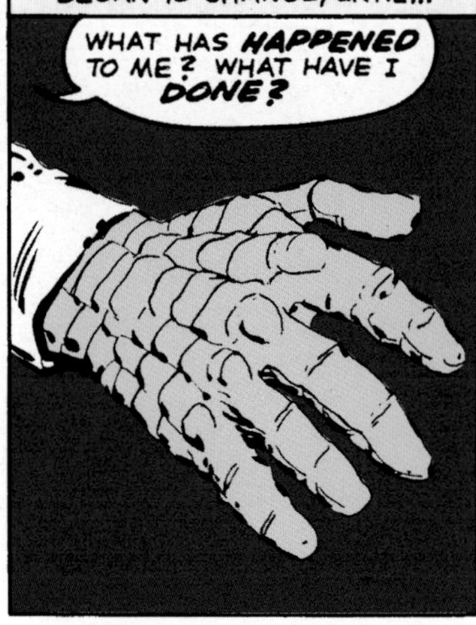
"BUT, THE CHANGE DIDN'T END THERE!! NO-- THE HAND, THE ARM, ALL OF CURTIS CONNORS BEGAN TO CHANGE, UNTIL..."
WHAT HAS HAPPENED TO ME? WHAT HAVE I DONE?

CURTIS!! WHAT IS IT?
NO! NO! STAY AWAY! DON'T LOOK AT ME!! DON'T!

"TREMBLING, SOBBING, LIKE A MAN POSSESSED, THE CREATURE WHO HAD BEEN CURTIS CONNORS RACED OUT INTO THE NIGHT..."
CURTIS!

"HE RETURNED THE NEXT DAY! HE TRIED TO WORK ON A NEW SERUM, ONE WHICH WOULD MAKE HIM HUMAN AGAIN... BUT IT WAS HOPELESS! HIS BRAIN HAD BEEN TOO DULLED-- TOO CHANGED!"
CANNOT DO IT! MUST GIVE UP!

AND THAT WAS THE END! HE LEFT A NOTE... SAYING GOODBYE... HE WAS AFRAID TO REMAIN... AFRAID... BECAUSE OF WHAT HE HAD BECOME!
TAKE BILLY... LEAVE-- NEVER COME BACK--

THEN, AT THAT MOMENT...
MOMMY!!
IT'S BILLY! I THOUGHT HE WAS TAKING HIS NAP!

THE CRY CAME FROM OUTSIDE! PERHAPS MY SPIDER-SENSE WILL LEAD ME TO HIM!

MEANWHILE, NOT FAR AWAY, THE TERRIFIED BOY RACES THRU THE SWAMP... HAVING SEEN A SIGHT WHICH SEEMED TO BE OUT OF A NIGHTMARE!
I-I DID NOT MEAN TO FRIGHTEN YOU!
HELP!

COME BACK!!
THAT SNAKE! I-I CAN'T GET OUT OF ITS WAY IN TIME!
11

SUDDENLY, A COLORFUL, FAST-MOVING FIGURE SWINGS DOWN FROM ABOVE, AND...
GOT YOU!
OH!

NO ONE CAN TAKE HIM FROM ME!
BILLY--STAY UP THERE! DON'T LET GO!!

OWW! HIS SKIN IS HARD AS A DINOSAUR'S ARMOR! I ALMOST BROKE MY HAND... AND HE HARDLY FELT IT!
THUD!

I'LL TRY TO HOLD HIM WITH MY WEB, UNTIL--NO! THAT'S NO GOOD, EITHER! HE SNAPPED IT WITH HIS TAIL AS IF IT WERE MADE OF PAPER!

JUST THEN, A FEMALE VOICE CRIES OUT, AND IT STRIKES A HIDDEN CHORD DEEP WITHIN THE LIZARD'S BREAST! SLOWLY HE TURNS, AND THEN SILENTLY SLITHERS INTO THE MURKY SWAMP...
BILLY! BILLY--WHERE ARE YOU?

MINUTES LATER...
MY HUSBAND! DID YOU SEE HIM? IS HE--?
MOMMY, THAT MAN SAVED ME!
HE'S ALRIGHT... FOR NOW! BUT, HE GETS LESS HUMAN EACH MINUTE!

I KNOW WHO YOU ARE! I SAW PICTURES OF YOU! YOU'RE SPIDER-MAN!
THAT'S RIGHT, BILLY, AND I'M GOING TO TAKE YOU HOME SAFELY NOW!
I WANT TO SEE YOUR HUSBAND'S NOTES, MRS. CONNORS--BEFORE IT'S TOO LATE!

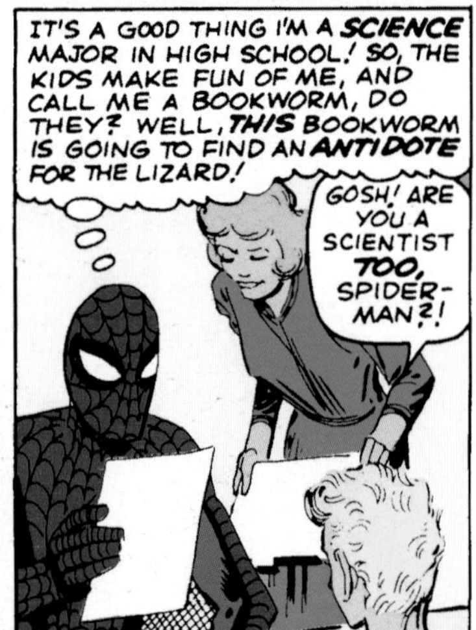
IT'S A GOOD THING I'M A SCIENCE MAJOR IN HIGH SCHOOL! SO, THE KIDS MAKE FUN OF ME, AND CALL ME A BOOKWORM, DO THEY? WELL, THIS BOOKWORM IS GOING TO FIND AN ANTIDOTE FOR THE LIZARD!
GOSH! ARE YOU A SCIENTIST TOO, SPIDER-MAN?!
12

HOURS LATER...
WE'LL SOON FIND OUT IF I'M A SCIENTIST OR NOT! I'LL DROP A PELLET OF THE COMPOUND I CREATED INTO THIS TEST TUBE...
...WHEN IT HITS THE SOLUTION WITHIN, IF IT TURNS GREEN, THEN I'VE SUCCEEDED IN FINDING AN ANTIDOTE!! HERE GOES...

IT CHANGED COLOR! I'VE DONE IT! ONCE THE LIZARD DRINKS THIS FORMULA, HE'LL REVERT TO HIS NORMAL SELF AGAIN!
BUT THERE IS STILL ONE PROBLEM REMAINING...

HOW AM I GOING TO GET HIM TO DRINK IT??
SPIDER-MAN... LOOK!

YOU ARE THE ONLY ONE WHO DOES NOT FEAR ME! ONCE I DESTROY YOU, ALL MANKIND WILL TREMBLE BEFORE THE LIZARD!!

QUICK... TAKE THE TEST TUBE! DON'T LET IT SPILL! I'VE GOT TO REASON WITH HIM!
YOU CAN'T! HE GROWS LESS HUMAN EACH MINUTE! HE--HE DOESN'T EVEN SEEM TO KNOW ME NOW!
AT LAST I SEE FEAR IN YOUR EYES! FOR YOU KNOW I HAVE THE POWER TO RID THE WORLD OF SPIDER-MAN!

MY SKIN IS HARD AS ARMOR, AND MY MUSCLES ARE EQUALLY STRONG! STRONGER BY FAR THAN YOURS!
HE'S RIGHT! HE'S HURLING THAT HUGE OAK DESK AS IF IT'S WEIGHTLESS!

HOW HELPLESS YOU ARE IN THE FACE OF MY BATTERING ATTACK!
DON'T KNOW WHERE TO TURN! HIS ARMS--HIS TAIL--ALL STRIKING AT ONCE--SUCH STRENGTH--IT'S UNBELIEVABLE!
OHH!!

WITHIN A FEW SAVAGE SECONDS, THE UNEQUAL BATTLE IS ENDED...
NOW THERE IS NONE TO STOP ME! NOW I AM SUPREME!
ALL I NEED DO IS FEED MY SERUM TO OTHER LIZARDS, CROCODILES, ALLIGATORS!! I'LL BUILD A MIGHTY LIZARD ARMY!

BUT THE LIZARD HAS MADE HIS FIRST SERIOUS MISTAKE-UNDERESTIMATED THE STRENGTH AND STAMINA OF HIS SUPER-FOE!
SPIDER-MAN! THANK HEAVEN YOU'RE STILL ALIVE!
HE KNOCKED THE WIND OUT OF ME FOR A MINUTE! HE'S STRONGER THAN I HAD GUESSED!
13

IT IS NOT ONLY HIS STRENGTH THAT WAS AFFECTED, BUT HIS BRAIN! HE PLANS TO INJECT HIS SERUM IN GIANT LIZARDS, MAKING THEM LIKE HE IS... CREATING A SAVAGE, SUPER-POWERFUL LIZARD ARMY!
DO YOU REALIZE HOW MANY LIZARDS THERE ARE ON EARTH?? MANKIND WOULDN'T STAND A CHANCE!

HE MUST BE STOPPED, QUICKLY, BEFORE HE CREATES THE FIRST SUPER-LIZARD! OTHERWISE, THEY WILL MULTIPLY TOO FAST TO EVER BE CHECKED!
HERE IS THE ANTIDOTE! BUT HOW WILL YOU GET HIM TO DRINK IT?

I DON'T KNOW YET, BUT THE FIRST THING I MUST DO IS TRACK HIM DOWN NOW! YOU AND YOUR SON REMAIN HERE... I DON'T THINK HE WILL RETURN!
HE IS STRONGER THAN YOU... AND HE HAS BECOME RUTHLESS! PERHAPS YOU SHOULD GET HELP!

THERE ISN'T TIME FOR THAT! WHATEVER MUST BE DONE, MUST BE DONE BY SPIDER-MAN ALONE! I'LL BUILD SOME WEB SWAMP-SHOES FOR MY FEET...
D-DON'T HURT HIM, SPIDER-MAN! HE'S STILL... MY FATHER! -SOB-

THE BOY IS RIGHT! BENEATH THE SAVAGE EXTERIOR OF THE LIZARD, IS A DECENT, TALENTED MAN! BUT HOW CAN I DEFEAT HIM-- AND SAVE MYSELF-- WITHOUT HARMING HIM??

LUCKILY, HIS TRAIL IS STILL RECENT ENOUGH FOR MY SPIDER-SENSE TO TRACK HIM! AND I CAN KEEP THESE SWAMP SNAKES AT BAY AS LONG AS MY WEB FLUID HOLDS OUT!

I SENSE HIM MORE CLEARLY THAN EVER NOW! HE MUST BE INSIDE THAT OLD, ABANDONED SPANISH FORT!

AND NOW... FOR THE SHOWDOWN!

THERE HE IS! BUT... AM I TOO LATE?
14

THE SCENE IS SO AMAZING, SO FRAUGHT WITH DRAMA, THAT SPIDER-MAN TAKES A FEW FAST PICTURES OF IT, AS HE FRANTICALLY TRIES TO PLAN HIS NEXT MOVE!
HE'S SURROUNDED BY HUGE ALLIGATORS! BUT THEY SEEM TO BE OBEDIENT TO HIM!
AND NOW FOR OUR GREAT MOMENT, MY PETS...!

WE SHALL BE THE FIRST! THE FIRST OF EARTH'S NEW RULERS! THE HUMANS WILL HAVE NO PLACE TO RUN...NO PLACE TO HIDE FROM US! FOR THE LIZARDS ARE PART OF THE REPTILE FAMILY, WHICH INCLUDES YOU, THE SNAKES, AND ALL THE CRAWLING HORDES!
THINK OF THE COUNTLESS MILLIONS OF REPTILES IN THESE EVERGLADES ALONE! ONCE I SPILL MY SERUM IN THE MURKY WATERS, NOTHING WILL STOP THE BIRTH OF A NEW RACE OF LIZARD CREATURES!

AND I SHALL BE THE MASTER! MASTER OF AN ENTIRE PLANET! NOW, FOLLOW ME, WHILE I GO TO PREPARE THE SERUM! OUR SUPREME MOMENT IS NEAR AT HAND!
GOOD! THEN I AM STILL IN TIME! HE HASN'T STARTED HIS DEADLY CHAIN REACTION YET!

BUT UNEXPECTEDLY, THE ANCIENT, TIME-WORN MORTER CRUMBLES BENEATH SPIDER-MAN'S WEIGHT, AND...
I'M FALLING!
YOU! YOU STILL LIVE!

WELL, THIS SOLVES MY FIRST PROBLEM... THE PROBLEM OF WHEN TO ATTACK! LOOKS LIKE IT'S NOW OR NEVER!
GET HIM, MY PETS! SPIDER-MAN MUST NEVER LEAVE HERE ALIVE!
15

YOU'VE HAD ALL THE INNINGS SO FAR, FELLA!
NOW IT'S TIME FOR SPIDER-MAN TO SHOW WHAT HE CAN DO!

FIRST, I'LL GET UP TO THE TOP TURRET WHERE THE ALLIGATORS CAN'T REACH ME!
HAH! HE FORGETS THERE ARE THREE THOUSAND DIFFERENT KINDS OF LIZARDS ON EARTH, AND I HAVE THE POWERS OF ALL OF THEM! HAS HE NEVER SEEN A GECKO-LIZARD SLITHER UP A WALL?

HE BEAT ME TO THE TOP!! NOW I'M TRAPPED BETWEEN THE LIZARD AND THE 'GATORS BELOW!

THEY'RE BATTERING THE WALL, TO MAKE IT CRUMBLE!
CAN'T STAY UP HERE MUCH LONGER!

WHEN YOU TALK ABOUT POWERS, PAL, DON'T FORGET THAT SPIDERS HAVE A FEW THEMSELVES! SUCH AS THE POWER OF SWINGING ON THEIR WEBS!
BAH! THAT IS NOTHING!

YOU ARE ONLY POSTPONING THE EVENTUAL OUTCOME! SOONER OR LATER I WILL DESTROY YOU!
I OUGHTTA HAVE A RECORD MADE OF THAT LINE! I HEAR IT ALL THE TIME!
16

DON'T YOU REALIZE YET THAT YOUR WEB ISN'T STRONG ENOUGH TO HOLD ME!?
WELL, YOU CAN'T BLAME A GUY FOR TRYING!
I'VE GOT TO KEEP HIM ON THE MOVE... SO THAT HE FORGETS TO GRAB HIS SERUM AND TOSS IT INTO THE SWAMP! FOR, IF IT SHOULD SPILL INTO THE SWAMP, WE HUMANS WILL NEVER BE ABLE TO STOP THE NEW RACE OF LIZARD CREATURES THAT WILL EMERGE!

YOU MAY BE STRONGER THAN ME, LIZ... BUT I STILL SAY YOU'RE TOO SLOW TO KEEP UP WITH ME!

NOW, ALL I HAVE TO DO IS FLIP BACK AND BOLT THE DOOR BEHIND ME...
THE 'GATORS! HOW DID THEY GET HERE SO FAST??!

GOOD THING THIS DOOR BOLTS FROM BOTH SIDES!
NOW IT'S JUST YOU AND ME, SPIDER-MAN... AND NO WAY FOR YOU TO ESCAPE ME!

WHEREVER YOU GO, I CAN FOLLOW!

CAN'T GO ANY HIGHER! HE'S RIGHT UNDER ME! DON'T DARE LET HIM GRAB ME WITH THOSE POWERFUL ARMS!
NOW--!!

NICE TRY--BUT YOU'VE GOT TO BE FASTER THAN THAT TO SNAG A SPIDER!
THUD!
17

As spider-man plunges toward the floor below, grasping his life-saving strand of web in one hand, he lunges out skillfully, and...
WHA--?
GOT YA!

Then, in mid-air, the amazing costumed crusader summons all his speed, his unerring skill, his lightning-fast reflexes, and whisks a small vial from his belt...
THANKS FOR JOINING ME, LIZARD! IT GETS LONESOME TUMBLING DOWN ALONE!

IF I MISS NOW... THERE MAY BE NO SECOND CHANCE FOR ME!

HOLD IT, LIZ! THIS'LL ONLY TAKE A SECOND!

I DID IT! NOW, IF ONLY... OOOF!!
YOUR TIME HAS RUN OUT, SPIDER-MAN! NOW TO FINISH YOU OFF!!

WHY DOESN'T THE SERUM WORK?? WHAT DID I DO WRONG?? WHAT--?
UGH!! H-HIS TAIL... IT'S LIKE A RUNAWAY SLEDGE-HAMMER!
18

I WARNED YOU THAT YOU WERE NO MATCH FOR ME! AND NOW... WE WILL END THIS... FOREVER!

AS SOON AS I HAVE DISPOSED OF YOU, I WILL SPILL MY SERUM IN THE SWAMP, AND THE WORLD WILL BE MINE!
GOT TO STOP HIM! CAN'T GIVE UP!

BUT, SUDDENLY...
MY HEAD! MY BRAIN! WHAT-- WHAT IS HAPPENING TO ME??

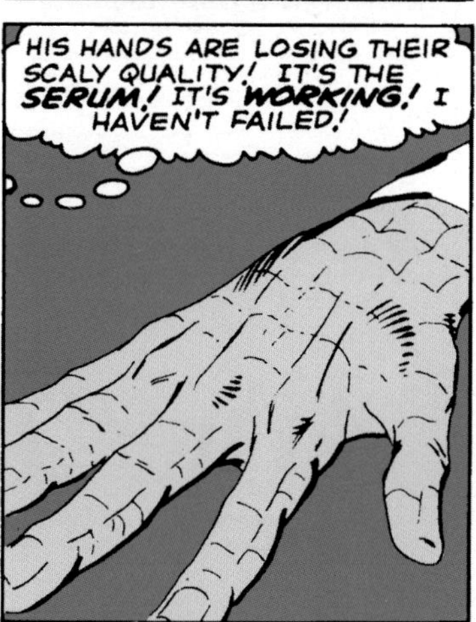
HIS HANDS ARE LOSING THEIR SCALY QUALITY! IT'S THE SERUM! IT'S WORKING! I HAVEN'T FAILED!

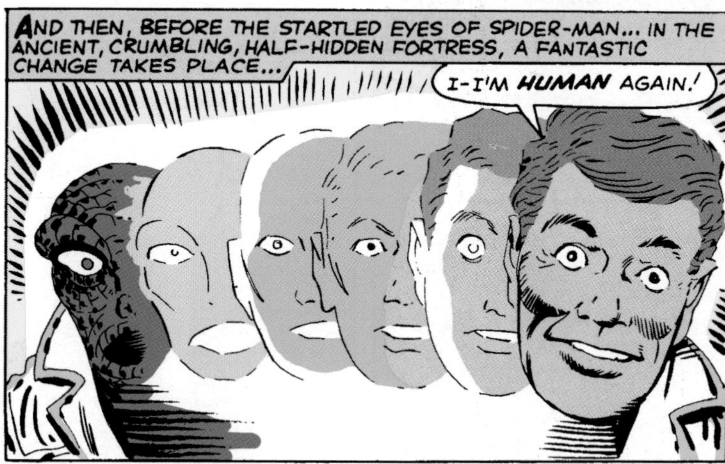
AND THEN, BEFORE THE STARTLED EYES OF SPIDER-MAN... IN THE ANCIENT, CRUMBLING, HALF-HIDDEN FORTRESS, A FANTASTIC CHANGE TAKES PLACE...
I-I'M HUMAN AGAIN!

THE NIGHTMARE HAS ENDED! AT LAST... IT'S OVER!
YOU HAVE ONLY ONE ARM AGAIN! EVERY LAST VESTIGE OF YOUR LIZARD IDENTITY HAS VANISHED!

WITHOUT THE LIZARD CONTROLLING THOSE ALLIGATORS, IT'S A SIMPLE MATTER FOR SPIDER-MAN TO KEEP THEM AT BAY!
AND NOW... I'LL TAKE YOU HOME, DR. CONNORS!

A SHORT TIME LATER...
MY DARLING! IF NOT FOR SPIDER-MAN I MIGHT NEVER HAVE HELD YOU IN MY ARMS AGAIN!
OH, CURTIS... I-I CAN'T BELIEVE YOU'RE REALLY BACK!!
19

I TAMPERED WITH FORCES OF NATURE WHICH MUST NOT BE TAMPERED WITH! WHEN I THINK WHAT MIGHT HAVE HAPPENED...
HUSH, MY DARLING! IT'S ALL OVER NOW! YOU MUST TRY TO FORGET IT!

I'LL BURN MY NOTES! NO ONE ELSE MUST EVER REPEAT MY EXPERIMENTS!
BUT NOW, WHAT PRICE MUST I PAY FOR WHAT I'VE DONE... FOR THE TERRIBLE HAVOK I ALMOST WROUGHT?

YOU'VE BROKEN NO LAW! AND LUCKILY YOU WERE STOPPED BEFORE YOU COULD DO ANY HARM! I SUGGEST WE JUST KEEP THIS WHOLE AFFAIR A SECRET... AMONG THE THREE OF US!
BLESS YOU, SPIDER-MAN!
WE'LL NEVER FORGET YOU!

THE NEXT DAY...
STILL NO SIGN OF YOUR PHOTOGRAPHER, MR JAMESON! WANT US TO SEND OUT AN ALL-STATE ALARM?
ALL I KNOW IS I'M PAYING A FORTUNE IN HOTEL BILLS AND NOT GETTING WHAT I CAME FOR!

SAY, ISN'T THAT PETER PARKER? FITS THE DESCRIPTION YOU GAVE US!
HI, MR. JAMESON! I'VE BEEN LOOKIN' FOR YOU!
YOU'VE BEEN LOOKING FOR ME??! WHY, YOU BRAINLESS, INCOMPETENT...

HOLD IT! DON'T SAY ANYTHING YOU'LL REGRET! JUST LOOK AT THESE PIX OF THE LIZARD! THINK HOW GREAT THEY'D LOOK IN YOUR PAPER!
THE LIZARD!??

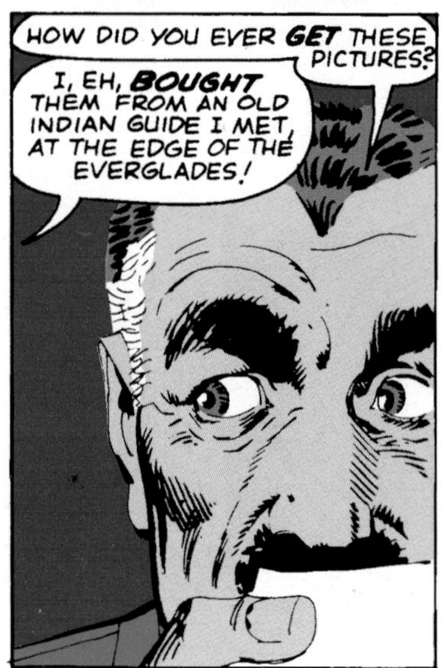
HOW DID YOU EVER GET THESE PICTURES?
I, EH, BOUGHT THEM FROM AN OLD INDIAN GUIDE I MET, AT THE EDGE OF THE EVERGLADES!

WELL, YOU WASTED YOUR MONEY! CAN'T YOU EVEN TELL A FAKE PHOTO WHEN YOU SEE ONE??!
WAIT! STOP! DON'T TEAR THEM!

YOU FOOL! THERE IS NO LIZARD! THE WHOLE THING MUST HAVE BEEN SOME SORT OF PUBLICITY STUNT! BUT WHERE IS SPIDER-MAN?? WHY DIDN'T YOU GET SOME PICTURES OF HIM?!!
20

YOU AND YOUR BIG TALK! YOU PROMISED ME SENSATIONAL PHOTOS... AND ALL YOU BRING ME IS A BATCH OF WORTHLESS FAKES! YOU'VE WASTED ENOUGH OF MY TIME! GET PACKED! WE'RE RETURNING TO NEW YORK!
BUT...
OKAY, I'LL PACK!

WHAT ABOUT THE MONEY YOU PROMISED ME, MR JAMESON?
FOR WHAT??! THE WAY I FIGURE IT, YOU OWE ME FOR YOUR PLANE FARE DOWN HERE AND HALF OF THE HOTEL BILL!

FINALLY, A WEARY PETER PARKER REACHES HIS HOME...
GEE, IT'S GOOD TO BE BACK, AUNT MAY!
NOW DON'T GET TOO COMFORTABLE, PETER! I HAVE A LOT OF CHORES FOR YOU TO DO AFTER YOUR NICE REST IN FLORIDA!

REST?!! BUT...OH, OKAY, AUNT MAY! JUST LET ME CALL BETTY FIRST, AND SEE IF SHE'LL DATE ME TOMORROW! OH... I FORGOT! SHE'S WORKING LATE FOR MR. JAMESON! WELL, THEN I'LL TRY LIZ ALLEN!

HI, LIZ! THIS IS PETER! HOW ABOUT TOMORROW NIGHT?

PETER PARKER! I'LL TELL YOU WHAT I TOLD FLASH THOMPSON! I'LL THANK YOU NOT TO CALL AND TIE UP MY PHONE! I'M WAITING FOR A CALL FROM SPIDER-MAN! AFTER HIM RESCUING ME THE OTHER DAY, AND CALLING ME "BLUE EYES", I'M SURE HE'LL CALL!
AND I DON'T WANT THE LINE TO BE BUSY WHEN MY DREAM MAN PHONES!!

OH NO!! SHE THINKS SPIDER-MAN HAS A CRUSH ON HER! SO SHE WON'T WASTE TIME DATING PLAIN, ORDINARY PETER FROM DULLVILLE!
ONLY A GUY WITH MY NUTTY LUCK COULD END UP BEING HIS OWN COMPETITION!
SLAM!

AND, AT THE OFFICE OF J. JONAH JAMESON, SPIDER-MAN IS ALSO VERY MUCH THE TOPIC OF CONVERSATION...
YOU MEAN HE SENT IT THRU THE MAIL, MISS BRANT?
YES SIR! AFTER ALL, I GUESS SPIDER-MAN CAN MAIL A LETTER LIKE ANYONE ELSE!
21

IT SAYS: "ROSES ARE RED, VIOLETS ARE BLUE... I'M STILL AT LARGE, SO PHOOEY TO YOU!"
WELL, DON'T JUST STAND THERE! TEAR IT UP! BURN IT!
OHH! I'LL GET THAT MASKED MENACE IF IT'S THE LAST THING I DO!

EDITOR'S NOTE: BIG NEWS!! NEXT ISSUE WILL FEATURE THE SENSATIONAL RETURN OF ONE OF THE GREATEST VILLAINS OF ALL... THE ASTOUNDING VULTURE! RESERVE YOUR COPY AT YOUR DEALER'S NOW! SEE YOU SOON...
the END

the AMAZING SPIDER-MAN
IND.
APPROVED BY THE COMICS CODE AUTHORITY
MARVEL COMICS GROUP 12¢
7 DEC.
A MARVEL SUPER-SPECTACULAR: "the VULTURE'S RETURN!"
THE VULTURE LOOKS TOO SURE OF HIMSELF! HE MUST HAVE A FOOL-PROOF PLAN TO DEFEAT ME! BUT--WHAT CAN IT BE?
HERE IS SPIDER-MAN AS YOU LIKE HIM... FIGHTING! JOKING! DARING! CHALLENGING THE MOST DANGEROUS FOE OF ALL, IN THIS-- THE MARVEL AGE OF COMICS!

SPIDER-MAN
THE RETURN OF THE VULTURE
NEVER LET IT BE SAID THAT THE MARVEL COMICS GROUP DOESN'T RESPOND TO THE WISHES OF ITS READERS! EVER SINCE THE FIRST APPEARANCE OF THE VULTURE (IN SPIDER-MAN #2) WE'VE BEEN SWAMPED WITH REQUESTS FOR MORE OF THE SAME! WELL, WE CAN TAKE A HINT! AND SO, WE NOW PRESENT THE VULTURE, AS YOU DEMANDED HIM... IN A BOOK-LENGTH BATTLE WITH THE ONE, THE ONLY, THE AMAZING... SPIDER-MAN!
WRITTEN BY: STAN LEE
ILLUSTRATED BY: STEVE DITKO
LETTERED BY: ART SIMEK
A TALE DESTINED TO RANK AMONG THE VERY GREATEST IN THIS... THE MARVEL AGE OF COMICS!

FOR THOSE OF YOU WHO MISSED SPIDER-MAN#2, IT CONCERNED HIS SPECTACULAR BATTLE WITH ONE OF THE MOST DANGEROUS VILLAINS OF ALL TIME... THE AWESOME FLYING VULTURE! NO MAN KNEW THE SECRET BEHIND THE VULTURE'S ABILITY TO FLY... UNTIL SPIDER-MAN DEDUCED THAT HIS WINGS WERE OPERATED BY A UNIQUE FORM OF MAGNETIC POWER...

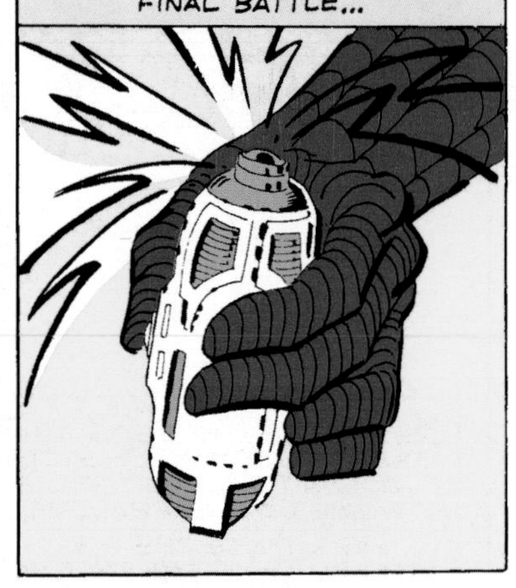
...AND SO, SPIDER-MAN CREATED A POWERFUL ANTI-MAGNETIC INVERTER WHICH HE USED AGAINST THE VULTURE IN THEIR FINAL BATTLE...

WITH HIS MAGNETIC POWER NULLIFIED, DUE TO SPIDER-MAN'S INVERTER, THE VULTURE WAS FORCED TO SPIRAL TO THE GROUND, INTO THE WAITING ARMS OF THE POLICE! AND SO ENDED THAT EPIC BATTLE!
THE VULTURE WILL NEVER THREATEN ANYONE AGAIN!

FOR MONTHS IT SEEMS THAT SPIDER-MAN'S PREDICTION IS CORRECT, AS THE IMPRISONED VULTURE BECOMES A MODEL INMATE OF STATE PRISON...
THE VULTURE IS THE BEST BEHAVED PRISONER IN THE PLACE!
THAT'S WHY THE WARDEN MADE HIM A TRUSTEE AND LETS HIM USE THE MACHINE SHOP!

THE GULLIBLE FOOLS! THEY DON'T SUSPECT THAT I'M PUTTING TOGETHER ANOTHER FLYING DEVICE FOR MYSELF--RIGHT UNDER THEIR NOSES!
I'VE TAKEN ALL THE PARTS I NEED! TONIGHT I'LL MAKE MY FINAL TEST IN MY CELL!
4701

AND, AFTER BED CHECK...
IT WORKS! NOT AS POWERFUL AS MY ORIGINAL FLYING DEVICE...
...BUT GOOD ENOUGH TO GET ME OVER THE WALL--TO FREEDOM!
2

THE NEXT DAY, DURING EXERCISE PERIOD IN THE PRISON COURTYARD...
FAREWELL! IT IS TIME FOR THE VULTURE TO FLY AGAIN!
LOOK! HE MADE HIMSELF A NEW FLYING GIZMO! HE'S GLIDING OVER THE WALL!

HOW EASY IT WAS! BY THE TIME THE GUARDS CAN ORGANIZE A SEARCH PARTY, I'LL BE SAFELY HIDDEN, MILES AWAY!
AND, WHEN NEXT I APPEAR, I'LL HAVE A NEW SET OF WINGS... FAR MORE POWERFUL THAN BEFORE!

MEANWHILE, IN THE SCHOOL YARD AT MIDTOWN HIGH, SOME VOLLEY-BALL PRACTICE IS IN PROGRESS...
HERE, BUTTER-FINGERS! THINK YOU CAN TOSS THAT BIG, BAD, HEAVY BALL ALL THE WAY BACK TO ME?
IF I USED MY SPIDER-MAN STRENGTH, IT WOULD GO CLEAN THROUGH YOU, LOUD-MOUTH!

WE INTERRUPT OUR PROGRAM TO BRING YOU A SPECIAL BULLETIN! THE VULTURE HAS ESCAPED FROM STATE PRISON! ALL CITIZENS ARE URGED TO LOCK THEIR DOORS, AND REPORT ANY SUSPICIOUS...
THE VULTURE-- ESCAPED!!

SPIDER-MAN IS THE ONE BEST SUITED TO CATCH HIM! I'VE GOT TO GET OUT OF HERE--FAST!
I--I DON'T FEEL VERY WELL! I'LL ASK COACH SMITH IF I MAY BE EXCUSED!
WE MIGHT HAVE KNOWN! A FAST GAME OF VOLLEY-BALL IS TOO MUCH FOR POOR PUNY PARKER!

JUST MY CRUMMY LUCK! EVERY TIME I HAVE TO TAKE OFF TO CHANGE TO SPIDER-MAN, EVERY-ONE THINKS I'M CHICKENING OUT BECAUSE OF WEAKNESS!
IT'S NOT TOO MUCH FOR ME, FLASH! I JUST HAVE A--EH, HEADACHE, THAT'S ALL!
STRANGE HOW YOU ALWAYS GET THOSE "HEADACHES" WHENEVER SOMETHING EXCITING IS GOING ON!

LATER, AT HOME...
THIS DOUBLE IDENTITY JAZZ IS FOR THE BIRDS! I CAN'T TAKE MUCH MORE RIBBING AS PETER PARKER! SOONER OR LATER, SOMEONE'S GONNA LOSE A MOUTHFUL OF TEETH!
3

LET'S SEE... I'D BETTER CHECK ALL MY EQUIPMENT! I'VE GOT MY ANTI-MAGNETIC INVERTER WITH ME... AND MY WEB-SHOOTER IS POSITIONED AND READY FOR ACTION...
MY CAMERA IS IN ITS CASE, LOADED WITH FRESH FILM...

...I REFILLED MY WEB-FLUID CAPSULE--AND ALL DEVICES CHECK OUT... A-OKAY!

THIS WEB-SHOOTER IS THE COOLEST THING I EVER DREAMED UP! I CAN DO ALMOST ANYTHING WITH IT! THE VULTURE WON'T HAVE A CHANCE!

I HAD TO WAIT ALMOST TWENTY MINUTES... BUT NOW, ACCORDING TO MY SPIDER-SENSE, THE STREET IS EMPTY!
I CAN'T EVER TAKE THE CHANCE OF SOMEONE SEEING ME LEAVE THE HOUSE IN DAYLIGHT!

A FEW MINUTES LATER...
MOMMY! DADDY! I JUST SAW SPIDER-MAN SWINGING ACROSS THE ROOFTOPS!!
YOU'RE JUST IM-AGINING THINGS, BOBBY!
WHAT WOULD SPIDER-MAN BE DOING HERE, IN A QUIET RESIDENTIAL NEIGHBORHOOD IN FOREST HILLS?

BUT SPIDER-MAN DOESN'T REMAIN IN ANY ONE NEIGHBORHOOD FOR LONG! WITH DAZZLING SPEED, HE HEADS FOR THE HEART OF THE CITY...
THE VULTURE'S A FOOL! I BEAT HIM BEFORE WITH MY ANTI-MAGNETIC INVERTER...
DOESN'T HE REALIZE I CAN DO IT AGAIN?

WHILE HOURS LATER, IN ANOTHER PART OF THE SPRAWLING METROPOLIS...
NOW TO TRY OUT MY NEW MODIFIED WINGS!
AH! I'VE BEEN SIGHTED BY A POLICE HELICOPTER!
WE'RE IN LUCK! THERE'S THE VULTURE!
4

GOOD! THIS WILL GIVE ME A CHANCE TO TEST MY GREATER-THAN-EVER FLYING POWER UNDER ACTUAL COMBAT CONDITIONS!
CALLING HEADQUARTERS! HAVE LOCATED VULTURE!

I CAN MANEUVER PERFECTLY! COMPARED TO MY WINGS, THAT WHIRLEYBIRD IS A SLOW, CUMBERSOME, CLUMSY OLD TUB!
THAT CHARACTER CAN TURN ON A DIME!

NO AIRCRAFT CAN CATCH ME! THERE ISN'T A SHIP BUILT THAT CAN DUPLICATE FEATS LIKE THIS!

HMMM! A JEWELRY SHOWROOM! I MIGHT AS WELL PUT THIS VISIT TO SOME GOOD USE!
THE VULTURE! H-HOW DID YOU GET IN HERE?
THE SAME WAY I SHALL LEAVE... WITH YOUR MOST VALUABLE GEMS! JUST WATCH ME...

HOW EASY THAT WAS! NOTHING CAN STOP A FLYING MAN! I CAN GO ANYWHERE-- DO ANYTHING-- AND ALL OF SPACE IS MY ESCAPE ROUTE!
HELP! I'VE BEEN ROBBED! HELP!

IF I FLY LOW ENOUGH, I CANNOT BE TRACKED BY RADAR! THE POLICE WILL NEVER KNOW WHERE I SHALL STRIKE NEXT!
LOOK! IT'S THE VULTURE!
SOMEBODY DO SOMETHING!
LIKE WHAT?
5

WE CAN'T RISK SHOOTING AT HIM! HE'S CLEVER ENOUGH TO FLY OVER THE CROWD! IF A BULLET SHOULD MISS HIM, IT MIGHT RICHOCHET AND HIT AN INNOCENT BYSTANDER!
THAT'S WHAT HE'S COUNTING ON! HE KNOWS WE WON'T FIRE SO LONG AS HE REMAINS IN THE HEART OF THE CITY!

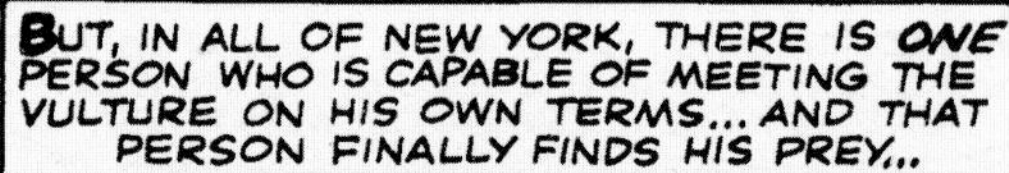
BUT, IN ALL OF NEW YORK, THERE IS ONE PERSON WHO IS CAPABLE OF MEETING THE VULTURE ON HIS OWN TERMS... AND THAT PERSON FINALLY FINDS HIS PREY...

AT LAST! MY SPIDER-SENSE LED ME TO THE VULTURE!

I'VE GOT TO GET CLOSER! MY ANTI-MAGNETIC INVERTER ONLY WORKS AT SHORT RANGE!
SO! WE MEET AGAIN, SPIDER-MAN!

SPIDER-MAN DOESN'T SUSPECT THAT HIS ANTI-MAGNETIC DEVICE, WHICH DEFEATED ME BEFORE, WILL NOT WORK THIS TIME!
THEREFORE, HE WILL ALLOW ME TO GET CLOSE TO HIM... WHICH IS WHAT I WANT TO DO!

HE'S FLYING STRAIGHT TOWARDS ME! PERFECT!
THIS WILL BE OUR FINAL ENCOUNTER, YOU YOUNG FOOL!
I'M GLAD I BROUGHT MY CAMERA, TOO!

WHAT A PICTURE THIS WILL MAKE! JAMESON OUGHT TO PAY ME A FORTUNE!
I'LL SNAP HIM JUST AS MY INVERTER MAKES HIM SPIRAL TO THE GROUND!
NOW!!!
6

IT WORKED! I'M ALMOST DISAPPOINTED! IT WAS TOO EASY!
I'LL PRETEND TO BE FALLING! HE'S SURE TO FOLLOW ME DOWN!

HE'S DESCENDING-- TOTALLY UNPREPARED FOR MY NEXT MOVE! OH, WHAT A BEAUTIFUL REVENGE THIS WILL BE FOR THE VULTURE!

DID I SEE HIM SMILE AS HE STARTED TO FALL?
AW, IT MUST BE MY IMAGINATION!

PERFECT! HE CAN'T TRAVEL AS QUICKLY AS I! HE HAS TO DESCEND LEDGE BY LEDGE! AND NOW, WHILE HE'S ON THAT LEDGE ABOVE, HE CAN'T SEE ME!
HE DOESN'T REALIZE I'M SWOOPING UP TO HIM AGAIN!

MY SPIDER-SENSE IS STARTING TO TINGLE! BUT WHY? THE VULTURE MUST BE A PRISONER ON THE GROUND BY NOW! THERE CAN'T BE ANY DANGER HERE!
IF I TIMED IT RIGHT, HE SHOULD BE JUST REACHING THE EDGE OF THE PARAPET...

OHHH!
SURPRISE, SPIDER-MAN! EVEN YOU CANNOT WARD OFF A DOUBLE UPPER-CUT WHILE YOU'RE COMPLETELY OFF-BALANCE!
7

MOMENTARILY STUNNED BY THE FORCE AND TOTAL UNEXPECTEDNESS OF THE VULTURE'S ATTACK, SPIDER-MAN IS HELPLESS BEFORE HIS POWERFUL FOE'S CONTINUED ONSLAUGHT!
THIS TIME THE VICTORY IS MINE!

LOOK! UP THERE... ABOVE THE ROOFTOPS! IT'S THE VULTURE... BATTLING WITH SPIDER-MAN!
THANK HEAVEN SPIDER-MAN FOUND HIM! HE'S THE ONLY ONE WHO CAN DEFEAT THE VULTURE SINGLE-HANDED!
GUESS AGAIN, LADY! THE VULTURE IS CLOBBERING HIM!

YOU NEVER SUSPECTED I HAD IMPROVED MY WINGS SO THAT THEY COULD CHANGE MAGNETIC POLES INSTANTLY, NULLIFYING YOUR USELESS INVERTER!
SO THAT'S WHY... OOOF!

HAPPY LANDINGS, SPIDER-MAN!
GOT TO SHOOT MY MY WEB--FAST--CATCH ON TO BUILDING--BREAK MY FALL--

MISSED!!

MUST TRY AGAIN! FALLING TOO FAST... TOO FAR...

CAN'T DO IT! IT FELL SHORT! ...NO TIME FOR ANOTHER TRY--!!
8

GOT TO SPIN AROUND IN AIR-- TO SLOW MY RATE OF DESCENT! MUST BREAK FALL! WILL TAKE ALL MY SPIDER STRENGTH! SPIN... KEEP SPINNING--KEEP-- OOOF!!

SPIDER-MAN IS FINISHED! MY REVENGE IS COMPLETE! NOW THE VULTURE IS SUPREME!

LOOK AT THE SHOCKED CROWDS BELOW! THEY SAW WHAT HAPPENED!
NO MAN WILL EVER DARE DEFY ME NOW!

THE VULTURE DEFEATED SPIDER-MAN!
LOOK! HE'S FLYING OFF NOW! LIKE A CONQUERING HERO!
POOR SPIDER-MAN! DESPITE WHAT JAMESON'S EDITORIALS SAID ABOUT HIM, WE COPS ALWAYS FELT HE WAS ON OUR SIDE! HE'LL SURE BE MISSED... WHOEVER HE WAS!

BUT, ALTHOUGH BADLY SHAKEN UP, THE COSTUMED TEEN-AGER IS STILL ALIVE... SAVED BY HIS AMAZING SPIDER STRENGTH!
GOT TO GET UP--CAN'T STAY HERE--CAN'T LET ANYONE DISCOVER ME--
LUCKY TO BE ALIVE! DIDN'T THINK I'D MAKE IT...

OHH! MY ARM! MUST HAVE LANDED ON IT!
FEELS LIKE IT'S BROKEN!

GUESS I CAN'T COMPLAIN! IT PROBABLY SAVED MY LIFE! IF I HADN'T BEEN ABLE TO SPIN AROUND... IF I HAD LANDED ON MY HEAD INSTEAD... ZOWEE!
9

WEARILY, CAUTIOUSLY, SPIDER-MAN REACHES HIS HOME, AND THEN QUIETLY, ENTERS THRU A REAR WINDOW...
DON'T THINK I BROKE ANY BONES...
THE ARM IS PROBABLY JUST SPRAINED!

BUT BOY, DOES IT EVER HURT!! WON'T BE ABLE TO USE IT FOR DAYS! WELL, BETTER CHANGE BACK TO PETER PARKER NOW WHILE I STILL CAN...

BUT, JUST THEN...
PETER, IS THAT YOU? I THOUGHT I HEARD SOMEONE IN THERE!
AUNT MAY! CAN'T LET HER FIND ME HERE LIKE THIS! SHE'S OPENING THE DOOR!!

PETER, DEAR--? OH, FOR GOODNESS SAKES! I MUST HAVE BEEN HEARING THINGS!

ALTHOUGH, IT'S STRANGE THAT HE'S NOT HERE YET! HE KNOWS HOW I WORRY WHEN HE COMES HOME LATE! HE'S SUCH A FRAGILE BOY...NOT A ROUGHNECK LIKE THAT FLASH THOMPSON!

-WHEW- THAT WAS A CLOSE ONE! IF AUNT MAY EVER SUSPECTED THE TRUTH ABOUT FRAGILE ME--WOW!

BOY! IT TOOK ALMOST A HALF HOUR TO CHANGE DUDS! I'M SURE NOT GONNA BREAK ANY SPEED RECORDS WITH THIS ARM OF MINE!

NOW TO SLIP OUT AND COME IN THE FRONT DOOR AS PETER PARKER! HOPE AUNT MAY WON'T MAKE A FEDERAL CASE OUT OF MY SPRAINED ARM!
I'VE GOT TO THINK UP A GOOD EXCUSE FOR IT!
10

THAT NIGHT...
PLEASE STOP WORRYING, MRS. PARKER! I ASSURE YOU IT'S ONLY A SPRAIN--ALTHOUGH IT IS A PAINFUL ONE! YOUR NEPHEW'S ARM WILL BE FINE IN A FEW WEEKS!
A FEW WEEKS! THE VULTURE WON'T WAIT THAT LONG!

OH WELL, I'LL WORRY ABOUT THE VULTURE WHEN THE TIME COMES! RIGHT NOW, MY BIGGEST PROBLEM IS AUNT MAY!
YOU'RE SURE HE SHOULDN'T GO TO THE HOSPITAL, DOCTOR?
POSITIVE, MRS. PARKER!

NOW PROMISE YOU WON'T PLAY THOSE DANGEROUS VOLLEY BALL GAMES IN THE SCHOOL YARD ANY MORE, DEAR!
NOT FOR THE NEXT WEEK, AUNT MAY!

NEXT DAY...
I HATED TO LIE TO AUNT MAY, BUT I COULDN'T VERY WELL SAY I HURT MY ARM WHEN I FELL ON A ROOFTOP FIGHTING THE VULTURE! UH OH! LOOK WHO'S COMING!
WELL, WELL! WHERE'S YOUR PURPLE HEART MEDAL, PETEY BOY?

HOW'D BIG, BRAVE PETER HURT HIS POOR LITTLE ARM? DID YOU TRY TO TURN TOO MANY HEAVY PAGES AT ONE TIME, BOOKWORM? OR DID YOU DROP A NASTY LITTLE TEST-TUBE ON IT IN THE LAB?

LOOK AT PETER BLUSH! OH, FLASH HONEY, YOU'RE A SCREAM!
BLUSH?? THEY DON'T RECOGNIZE I'M LIVID WITH ANGER! IF I EVER LET GO, I'LL SPLATTER THAT CLOWN ALL OVER THE LANDSCAPE!

MEANTIME, THE VULTURE, BASKING IN HIS TRIUMPH, RELAXES AT HIS OLD HIDEOUT, AN INNOCENT-LOOKING ABANDONED FARM SILO ON STATEN ISLAND, NOT FAR FROM THE HEART OF MANHATTAN!
NO ONE WILL EVER THINK TO LOOK FOR ME HERE!

THIS IS THE LIFE! NO MORE SPIDER-MAN TO WORRY ABOUT! NOTHING TO DO BUT PLAN MY NEXT BIG HAUL!
AND I THINK I KNOW WHAT IT'S GOING TO BE!
11

ONE OF THE BIGGEST PAYROLLS IN NEW YORK IS AT THE OFFICE OF **J. JONAH JAMESON!** HE PUBLISHES THE "DAILY BUGLE" AND "NOW" MAGAZINE! HE MUST EMPLOY **HUNDREDS** OF WORKERS!

AND **THAT** MEANS HUNDREDS OF NICE, FAT, JUICY **PAY ENVELOPES,** JUST WAITING FOR THE VULTURE TO FLY IN AND GRAB THEM!
IT'S THE END OF THE WEEK NOW, SO ALL THE DOUGH MUST BE IN THE SAFE, READY FOR PAY DAY! ONLY, IT'S GONNA BE **MY** PAY DAY THIS TIME!

AND, AT THE OFFICES OF THE DAILY BUGLE, WE FIND YOUNG PETER PARKER, TALKING TO J. JONAH JAMESON'S SECRETARY...
OH, PETER, **NOBODY** COULD SPRAIN HIS ARM PLAYING VOLLEY BALL!
WHAT **REALLY** HAPPENED?
OKAY, I'LL TELL YOU THE **TRUTH**...

IT HAPPENED IN THE AIR, WHILE I WAS FIGHTING THE VULTURE FOR DEAR LIFE!
OH, WELL! ASK A SILLY QUESTION!
SO LET'S STICK TO THE VOLLEY BALL STORY! OKAY?
MISS BRANT! SEND PARKER IN NOW!

I'LL **ADMIT** THAT'S A FINE PICTURE OF THE VULTURE, PARKER, BUT I CAN'T PAY MORE THAN TEN DOLLARS FOR IT! AFTER ALL, HE'S BEEN SEEN ALL OVER TOWN! **LOTS** OF PEOPLE HAVE SNAPPED HIM! I WANT SOMETHING **DIFFERENT!**

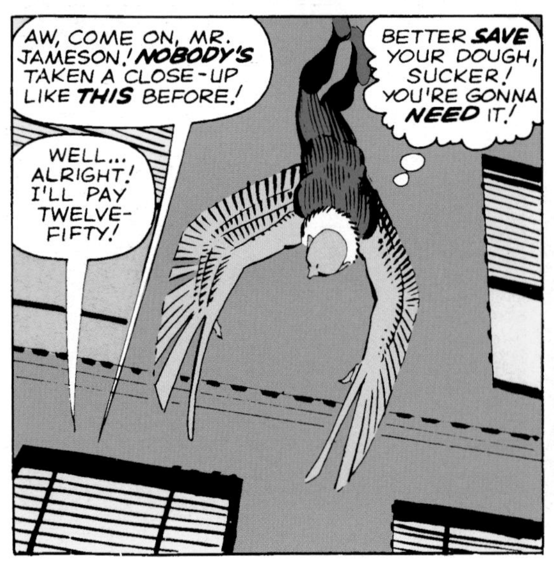
AW, COME ON, MR. JAMESON! **NOBODY'S** TAKEN A CLOSE-UP LIKE **THIS** BEFORE!
BETTER **SAVE** YOUR DOUGH, SUCKER! YOU'RE GONNA **NEED** IT!
WELL... ALRIGHT! I'LL PAY TWELVE-FIFTY!

GREETINGS, JAMESON! IF YOU'LL PAY FOR A MERE **PHOTO** OF ME, WHAT WILL YOU GIVE FOR THE VULTURE IN THE **FLESH??!**
HOLY COW! IT'S **HIM!**
THE **VULTURE!!**
12

I TELL YOU WHAT... I'LL SET THE PRICE MYSELF! SO, OPEN YOUR SAFE AND EMPTY IT OUT FOR ME!
NO! NO! YOU CAN'T ROB MY PAYROLL! YOU MUSTN'T! IT'S ALL I'VE GOT! IT WOULD PUT ME OUT OF BUSINESS!

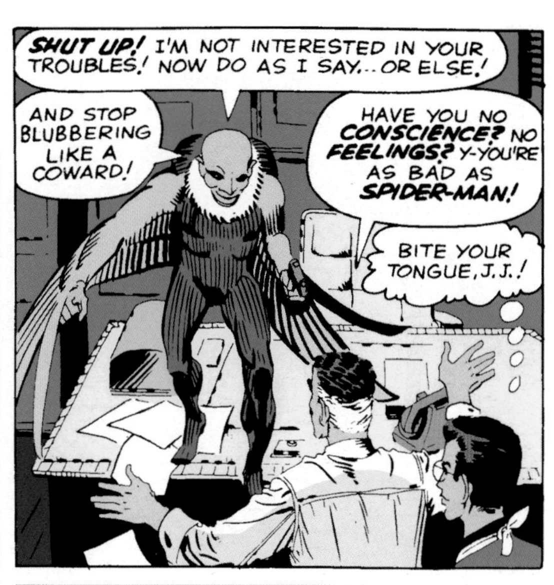
SHUT UP! I'M NOT INTERESTED IN YOUR TROUBLES! NOW DO AS I SAY... OR ELSE!
AND STOP BLUBBERING LIKE A COWARD!
HAVE YOU NO CONSCIENCE? NO FEELINGS? Y-YOU'RE AS BAD AS SPIDER-MAN!
BITE YOUR TONGUE, J.J.!

I'VE SPENT YEARS BUILDING UP THIS BUSINESS... IT MEANS EVERYTHING TO ME! YOU CAN'T...
OH, CAN'T I?? THE VULTURE CAN DO ANYTHING... AS YOU'RE ABOUT TO LEARN!!

JAMESON IS SUCH A SKINFLINT, HE'D PROBABLY RATHER GET SHOT THAN PART WITH HIS DOUGH! I'LL HAVE TO SLIP OUT NOW AND TRY TO SAVE HIM--WHETHER HE LIKES IT OR NOT!
LOOK--MAYBE WE CAN MAKE A DEAL? I CAN GIVE YOU PUBLICITY...
ALL I WANT IS MONEY, MISTER!! YOUR MONEY!

WHERE GREENBACKS ARE CONCERNED, JAMESON CAN OUT-TALK ANYBODY! -OWW- IT'S SOME JOB PUTTING MY COSTUME ON WITH THIS BLAMED ARM OF MINE!

I'LL TRY TO ALTER MY WEBBING SLIGHTLY SO IT'LL ACT LIKE A SLING! WITH LUCK, NO ONE WILL NOTICE!

I OUGHT TO HAVE MY HEAD EXAMINED FOR TACKLING THE VULTURE WITH A BAD ARM... BUT THIS'LL SURE MAKE ME SEEM HEROIC... WHEN THEY WRITE MY OBITUARY!
13

ALL RIGHT, VULTURE--PLAYTIME IS OVER! HERE'S WHERE WE SEPARATE THE MEN FROM THE BOYS!
SPIDER-MAN!!
YOU'RE STILL ALIVE ??!!

WELL, YOU WON'T STAY THAT WAY FOR LONG! EVEN YOU CAN BE STOPPED BY A BULLET!
MAYBE SO! BUT FIRST YOU'VE GOT TO BE ABLE TO FIRE THE BULLET!
THWUP!

BAH! GUNS AREN'T MY STYLE, ANYWAY! WHAT DOES THE MIGHTY VULTURE NEED A WEAPON FOR! I'VE GOT MY WINGS!
YOU'LL HAVE A HARP, TOO, BY THE TIME I GET THROUGH WITH YOU!
OWW!

HE'S USING JAMESON AS A SHIELD! I CAN'T LET GO WITH A GOOD PUNCH!
OOF!!
SPIDER-MAN! LOOK OUT, YOU FOOL! I'LL BE HURT! LET ME GO!

THAT STOPPED HIM LONG ENOUGH FOR ME TO BREAK OUT OF THERE!
I CAN'T FIGHT AS WELL AT CLOSE QUARTERS! I NEED ROOM--SPACE TO USE MY WINGS TO THEIR BEST ADVANTAGE!
WHA-- WHAT'S GOING ON??

YOU STAY HERE, JAMESON! FROM NOW ON, IT'S A PRIVATE BATTLE BETWEEN THE VULTURE AND ME!
NO! NO! YOU TWO WILL WRECK THE PLACE! LET HIM GO! LEAVE HIM TO THE POLICE!
14

THERE ISN'T TIME! IF HE GETS A CHANCE TO FLY OFF, WE MAY NEVER TRAP HIM AGAIN!
OOP! GET TO THE SIDE OF THE ROAD, GAL!
THIS MUST ALL BE A BAD DREAM!

POLICE! SOMEONE CALL THE POLICE! THOSE TWO MANIACS MUST BE STOPPED!
MISS BRANT! WHERE IN BLAZES ARE YOU??!
H-HERE, MISTER JAMESON... WHERE IT'S SAFE!

HE'S TRYING TO FIND A WINDOW HE CAN FLY THROUGH! I'VE GOT TO STOP HIM!
I WARN YOU, SPIDER-MAN! STAY OUT OF MY WAY, WHILE YOU STILL CAN!

MISTER, I THRIVE ON WARNINGS! IN FACT, SOME DAY I'M GOING TO WRITE AN ARTICLE FOR THE READERS' DIGEST TITLED: "THE MOST UNFORGETTABLE WARNING I'VE EVER KNOWN!"
VER-RY FUNNY!!
GET DOWN FROM THERE!
HAH! YOU MISSED BY A MILE!

MY LEDGERS! MY FILES!! LOOK WHAT YOU'RE DOING!
AW, GO SLIDE DOWN A BARBED-WIRE FENCE!

CAN'T MAKE IT TO THE WINDOW UP THERE! I'LL TRY A LOWER FLOOR! SPIDER-MAN CAN NEVER DEFEAT ME!
IF I EVER CATCH THAT MASKED MENACE, I'LL SUE HIM FOR ALL HE'S WORTH! I'LL PUT HIM IN JAIL FOR LIFE! I'LL-- I'LL MAKE HIM PAY FOR THIS!!
15

THIS ISN'T EXACTLY FLYING... BUT IT'LL SERVE MY PURPOSE!
WHO'S CHASING WHO?
THE PLACE IS HAUNTED!

THIS IS MORE LIKE IT! I'M IN THE PRESS ROOM! I'VE ENOUGH FLYING SPACE AGAIN! I'LL DESTROY SPIDER-MAN FOREVER NOW, IF HE'S FOOL ENOUGH TO FOLLOW ME HERE!

I HAD A HUNCH THE VULTURE WOULD LAND DOWN HERE!
THE ODDS ARE ALL IN HIS FAVOR NOW... BUT THAT NEVER STOPPED ME BEFORE!
HE DOESN'T SEE ME YET...SO HERE GOES NOTHING!

HEY!! WHA--??
IT'S YOU AGAIN!!
WELL, IT SURE ISN'T THE LONE RANGER!
DIDN'T EXPECT ME SO SOON, DID YOU?

YOU JUST MADE YOUR LAST FATAL MISTAKE, SPIDER-MAN!!
I'LL SHAKE YOU OFF LIKE A DOG SHAKES A FLEA!
I THINK YOUR MODESTY IS WHAT I LIKE BEST ABOUT YOU!

LET'S SEE IF A WISE-CRACK WILL HELP YOU ONCE YOU'RE FALLING INTO THOSE BIG PRESS ROLLERS!
I'VE GOT TO KEEP RIB-BING HIM! MY ONLY CHANCE IS TO MAKE HIM SO ANGRY THAT HE WON'T NOTICE MY INJURED ARM!
16

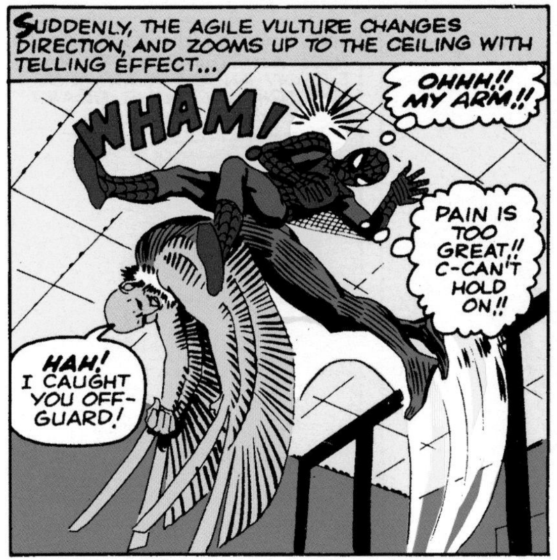
SUDDENLY, THE AGILE VULTURE CHANGES DIRECTION, AND ZOOMS UP TO THE CEILING WITH TELLING EFFECT...
WHAM!
OHHH!! MY ARM!!
PAIN IS TOO GREAT!! C-CAN'T HOLD ON!!
HAH! I CAUGHT YOU OFF-GUARD!

IF I HIT THOSE GIANT ROLLERS, I'M DONE FOR!
MY WEB HAS TO SAVE ME NOW... THIS TIME THERE'LL BE NO SECOND CHANCE!

MADE IT! NOW TO DESCEND SLOWLY, AND... OH NO! THE VULTURE IS CUTTING MY LIFE-SAVING STRAND!!
I HAD A HUNCH YOU'D TRY THAT, SPIDER-MAN!

BUT, WHILE DANGLING ABOVE, THE COLORFUL TEEN-AGER HAS TIME ENOUGH TO ESTIMATE THE DISTANCE... AND, WITH ONE MIGHTY LEAP...
WHEW THAT WAS A CLOSE ONE!

GOT TO REACH THE VULTURE BEFORE HE FLIES OUT OF RANGE!!
BUT HOW ??!

UH OH! MY SPIDER SENSE WARNS ME HE'S WAITING ABOVE! IT'S A TRAP!
BUT I'LL LET HIM SPRING IT!
17

HAH! YOU BLUNDERED RIGHT INTO MY TRAP... AS I KNEW YOU WOULD!
WELL, MERCY ME!

I'LL TAKE YOU UP SO HIGH THAT YOU'LL BE COMPLETELY HELPLESS! EVEN A SPIDER IS POWERLESS IN THE SKY!
ARE YOU SURE YOU WERE NEVER VACCINATED WITH A PHONOGRAPH NEEDLE?

YOUR FLIPPANCY IS WASTED ON ME, SPIDER-MAN! YOU'RE JUST WHISTLING IN THE DARK! I KNOW AN ICY FEAR MUST BE GRIPPING YOUR HEART RIGHT NOW!
WELL, I'LL ADMIT I'VE HAD HAPPIER MOMENTS!

BEFORE I DROP YOU, SPIDER-MAN, I WANT TO SAY I ADMIRE YOUR COURAGE! ANYONE ELSE WOULD BE BEGGING FOR MERCY NOW! I'M ALMOST SORRY TO HAVE TO DO THIS...
YEAH! I CAN SEE THAT YOU'RE ALL BROKEN UP!

WELL, I'M GONNA TELL YOU A SECRET... THIS LITTLE PARTY ISN'T OVER YET! WATCH...!

YOU--YOU PINNED MY WINGS WITH YOUR WEB!! YOU FOOL! IF I CANNOT FLY... WE BOTH WILL PERISH!
WELL, WHO WANTS TO LIVE FOREVER ?!
18

I DON'T WANT TO DIE! SAVE ME! -SOB- DO SOMETHING! PLEASE--PLEASE! SAVE ME!
I CAN'T! I'M TOO BUSY ADMIRING YOUR TIGHT-LIPPED COURAGE!

WELL, ANYTHING TO STOP YOUR MOANING! SUPPOSE I SPIN A LITTLE WEB WHILE WE FALL--?!
AT A TIME LIKE THIS ??!

SURE! IT MIGHT BE FUN! 'SPECIALLY IF I MAKE IT WITH MY NEW SEMI-SOLID FLUID WHICH ENABLES IT TO ACT LIKE A PARACHUTE!

LOOK! IN THE SKY! A GIANT PARACHUTE!
THERE ARE TWO FIGURES DANGLING FROM IT!!
WHO ARE THEY??
CAN'T TELL! TOO HIGH UP! WAIT--THEY'RE GETTING CLOSER! I-I CAN MAKE A OUT A COSTUME--!
IT'S SPIDER-MAN! AND THE VULTURE!
SPIDER-MAN'S BEATEN HIM!
BY SOME MIRACLE, SPIDER-MAN WON!

YOU HAD THIS PLAN IN MIND ALL THE TIME!!
DARN RIGHT I DID, CURLY! I DON'T DEPEND ON MY WINGS TO DO MY THINKING FOR ME, LIKE SOME GUY I COULD MENTION!

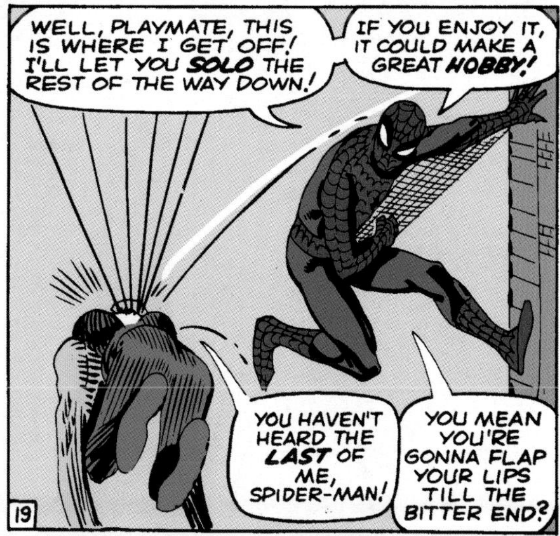
WELL, PLAYMATE, THIS IS WHERE I GET OFF! I'LL LET YOU SOLO THE REST OF THE WAY DOWN!
IF YOU ENJOY IT, IT COULD MAKE A GREAT HOBBY!
YOU HAVEN'T HEARD THE LAST OF ME, SPIDER-MAN!
YOU MEAN YOU'RE GONNA FLAP YOUR LIPS TILL THE BITTER END?
19

SPIDER-MAN! WAIT!!
WELL, IF IT ISN'T LAUGHING-BOY JAMESON! HE PROBABLY WANTS TO APOLOGIZE AND OFFER ME A BIG REWARD!
AND WHO AM I TO REFUSE?
YES, MR. JAMESON?

I WANT YOU TO KNOW THAT I HOLD YOU RESPONSIBLE FOR ALL THE DAMAGE DONE TO MY BUILDING! IT'S ALL YOUR FAULT FOR BUTTING IN!
SAY, WHAT ARE YOU?
A PROFESSIONAL NUT?

I'LL SHOW YOU WHO'S A NUT! SOONER OR LATER I'LL LEARN WHO YOU REALLY ARE! AND WHEN I DO...
YEAH? THEN WHAT?

--I'LL GET WHAT'S COMING TO ME! IN SPADES!
MISTER, I'M ABOUT TO GIVE YOU SOMETHING RIGHT NOW THAT'S BEEN COMING TO YOU FOR MONTHS!

NO! NO! YOU-YOU WOULDN'T DARE!! DON'T--!
WHY NOT? WHAT HAVE I GOT TO LOSE? YOU COULDN'T HATE ME ANY MORE THAN YOU DO NOW!
THWUP!

BUT, ANYHOW, I WON'T HAVE TO LISTEN TO YOU FOR A WHILE! THAT WON'T WEAR OFF FOR AT LEAST AN HOUR!
MMPFF! GLBBFF! PHHMF!

MINUTES LATER, A SILENT FIGURE NOISELESSLY ENTERS THE BUILDING IN HIS OWN INIMITABLE MANNER...
SO FAR, SO GOOD! THE COAST IS CLEAR!

HOPE NOBODY FOUND MY CIVVY CLOTHES--
NOPE! THEY'RE JUST WHERE I HID THEM!
20

AND, WITHIN SECONDS, THE AMAZING SPIDER-MAN VANISHES, TO BE REPLACED BY A SLING-WEARING, INNOCENT-LOOKING PETER PARKER!
THE WORST THING ABOUT BEING SPIDER-MAN IS CHANGING CLOTHES A ZILLION TIMES A DAY!
OH WELL... IT KEEPS ME OUT OF THE POOL ROOM!

HI, BETTY! WHAT ARE YOU DOING BEHIND THAT DESK?
IT'S THE ONLY SAFE PLACE, PETER! THIS OFFICE WAS A MADHOUSE A FEW MINUTES AGO!

MIND IF I JOIN YOU?
BE MY GUEST!

BY THE WAY, WHERE WERE YOU WHILE SPIDER-MAN WAS BATTLING THE VULTURE?
ME? OH... I WAS HIDING IN A CLOSET!

I'M AFRAID I'M JUST NOT THE HEROIC TYPE!
NEITHER AM I! MAYBE THAT'S WHY I LIKE YOU SO MUCH, PETER! AT LEAST, YOU DON'T PRETEND TO BE WHAT YOU'RE NOT!
BOY! IF SHE ONLY KNEW!!

*!!MMPPFF!!!
GRRMMPFF!! *!!*!!?!
LOOK! MISTER JAMESON CAN'T TALK! I WONDER WHAT'S WRONG WITH HIM?
WRONG? IT'S AN IMPROVEMENT!

PETER, SOMETIMES I GET THE FEELING THAT YOU'RE LAUGHING AT A SECRET LITTLE JOKE THAT'S ALL YOUR OWN!
IF YOU KEEP USING THAT COOL PERFUME, BETTY, I MAY BREAK DOWN AND TELL YOU ABOUT IT SOME DAY!
21

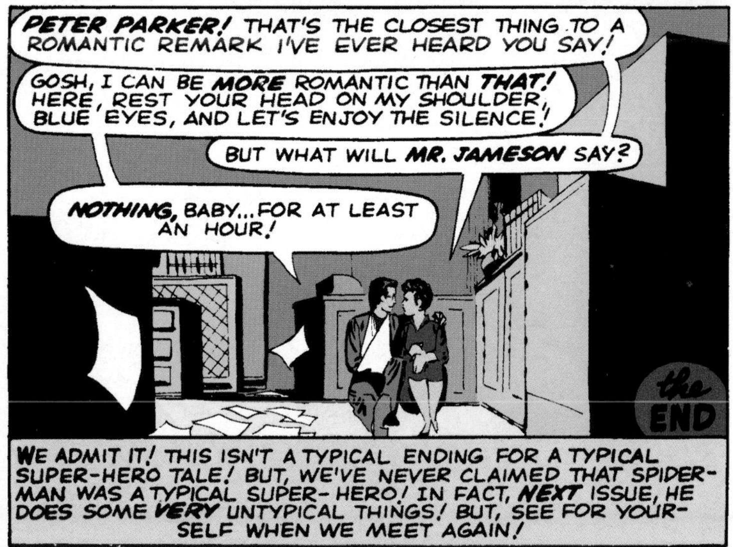
PETER PARKER! THAT'S THE CLOSEST THING TO A ROMANTIC REMARK I'VE EVER HEARD YOU SAY!
GOSH, I CAN BE MORE ROMANTIC THAN THAT! HERE, REST YOUR HEAD ON MY SHOULDER, BLUE EYES, AND LET'S ENJOY THE SILENCE!
BUT WHAT WILL MR. JAMESON SAY?
NOTHING, BABY... FOR AT LEAST AN HOUR!
the END
WE ADMIT IT! THIS ISN'T A TYPICAL ENDING FOR A TYPICAL SUPER-HERO TALE! BUT, WE'VE NEVER CLAIMED THAT SPIDER-MAN WAS A TYPICAL SUPER-HERO! IN FACT, NEXT ISSUE, HE DOES SOME VERY UNTYPICAL THINGS! BUT, SEE FOR YOURSELF WHEN WE MEET AGAIN!

SPECIAL "TRIBUTE-TO-TEEN-AGERS" ISSUE!!

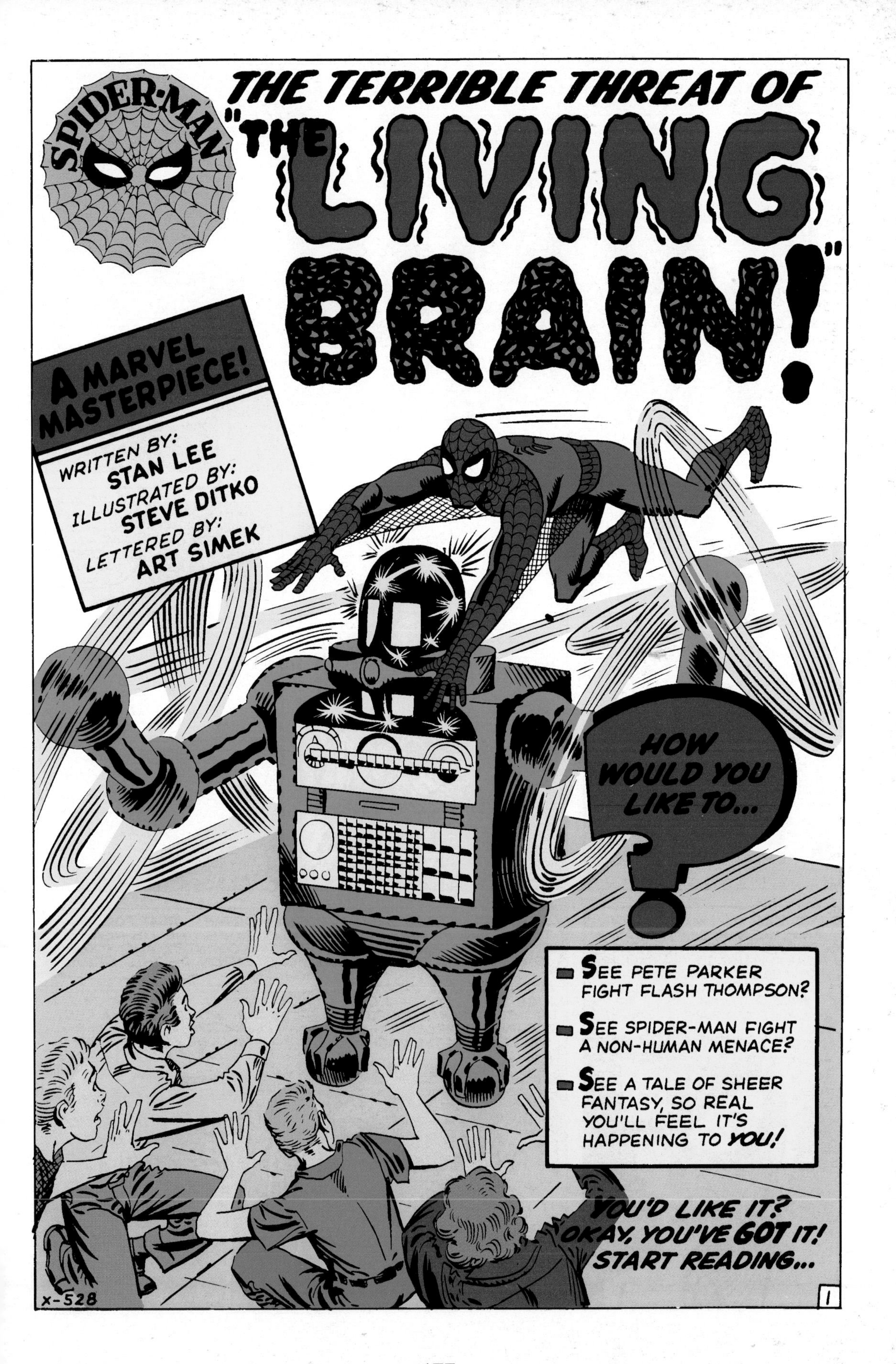
SPIDER-MAN
THE TERRIBLE THREAT OF
"THE LIVING BRAIN!"
A MARVEL MASTERPIECE!
WRITTEN BY: STAN LEE
ILLUSTRATED BY: STEVE DITKO
LETTERED BY: ART SIMEK
HOW WOULD YOU LIKE TO...?
SEE PETE PARKER FIGHT FLASH THOMPSON?
SEE SPIDER-MAN FIGHT A NON-HUMAN MENACE?
SEE A TALE OF SHEER FANTASY, SO REAL YOU'LL FEEL IT'S HAPPENING TO YOU!
YOU'D LIKE IT? OKAY, YOU'VE GOT IT! START READING...
X-528
1

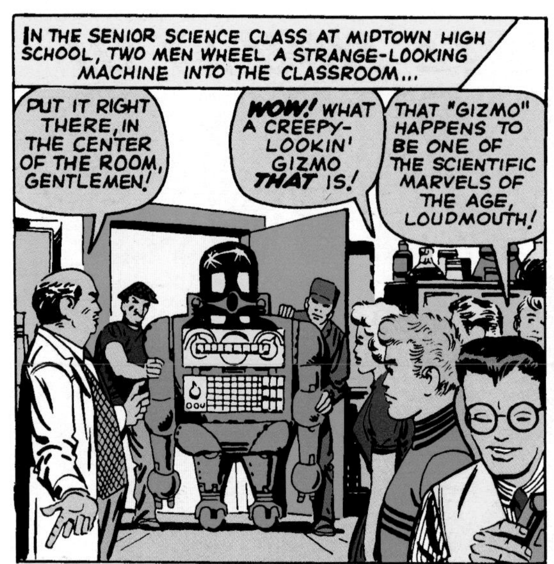

IN THE SENIOR SCIENCE CLASS AT MIDTOWN HIGH SCHOOL, TWO MEN WHEEL A STRANGE-LOOKING MACHINE INTO THE CLASSROOM...
PUT IT RIGHT THERE, IN THE CENTER OF THE ROOM, GENTLEMEN!
WOW! WHAT A CREEPY-LOOKIN' GIZMO THAT IS!
THAT "GIZMO" HAPPENS TO BE ONE OF THE SCIENTIFIC MARVELS OF THE AGE, LOUDMOUTH!

WELL, WELL! LISTEN TO PETER PARKER, THE DEMON SCIENTIST!
YOU SURE TALK BIG AND BRAVE WHEN THE TEACHER'S AROUND, EH, PUNY PARKER?
LOOK OUT, YOU DUMB CLOWN! MY GLASSES--!!

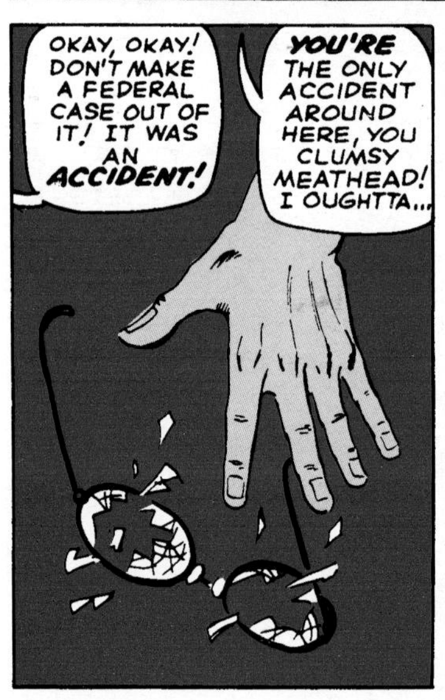

OKAY, OKAY! DON'T MAKE A FEDERAL CASE OUT OF IT! IT WAS AN ACCIDENT!
YOU'RE THE ONLY ACCIDENT AROUND HERE, YOU CLUMSY MEATHEAD! I OUGHTTA...

YOU OUGHTTA WHAT, WEAKLING??
BOYS! KEEP YOUR VOICES DOWN! REMEMBER--YOU'RE STILL IN CLASS!
OKAY, LIZ! BUT FLASH HAS GONE TOO FAR THIS TIME!

LOOK, SCARECROW! WE'LL SEE IF YOU STILL TALK SO BIG AFTER CLASS!
JUST HANG AROUND, UGLY! YOU'VE GOT A LITTLE SURPRISE COMING!

I'VE HAD IT! I'M THROUGH PRETENDING TO BE A PANTYWAIST TO CONCEAL MY REAL IDENTITY! I DON'T NEED THOSE SPECS ANYWAY!
UH OH! MISTER WARREN'S CALLING THE CLASS TO ORDER!

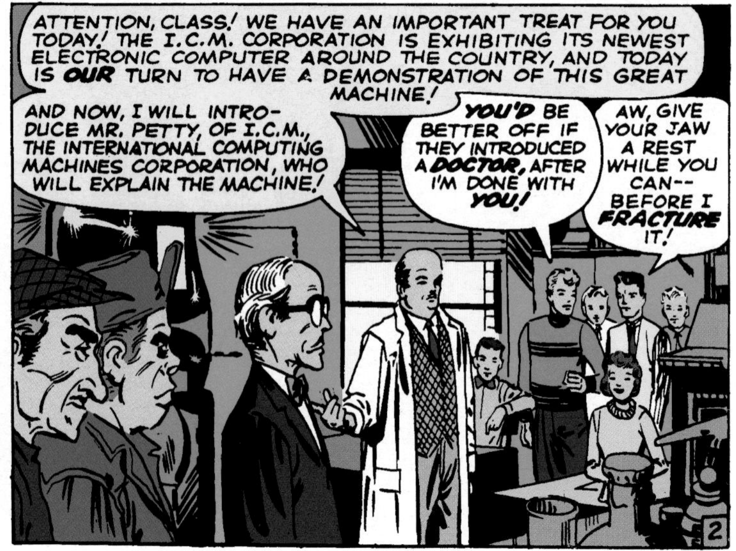

ATTENTION, CLASS! WE HAVE AN IMPORTANT TREAT FOR YOU TODAY! THE I.C.M. CORPORATION IS EXHIBITING ITS NEWEST ELECTRONIC COMPUTER AROUND THE COUNTRY, AND TODAY IS OUR TURN TO HAVE A DEMONSTRATION OF THIS GREAT MACHINE!
AND NOW, I WILL INTRODUCE MR. PETTY, OF I.C.M., THE INTERNATIONAL COMPUTING MACHINES CORPORATION, WHO WILL EXPLAIN THE MACHINE!
YOU'D BE BETTER OFF IF THEY INTRODUCED A DOCTOR, AFTER I'M DONE WITH YOU!
AW, GIVE YOUR JAW A REST WHILE YOU CAN--BEFORE I FRACTURE IT!
2

THANK YOU FOR YOUR INTRODUCTION MR. WARREN! AND NOW, CLASS...
WE BUILT OUR COMPUTER IN THE FORM OF A HUMAN BODY IN ORDER TO DRAMATIZE ITS POWERS! IT IS THE GREATEST MECHANICAL BRAIN EVER BUILT! IN FACT, WE CALL IT THE LIVING BRAIN!

NOTICE HOW ITS LEGS HAVE BALL-BEARING ROLLERS ON THEM, ENABLING THE BRAIN TO MOVE UPON COMMAND!

AND ITS ARMS ARE SO CONSTRUCTED THAT THEY TOO CAN PERFORM SIMPLE MOTIONS...

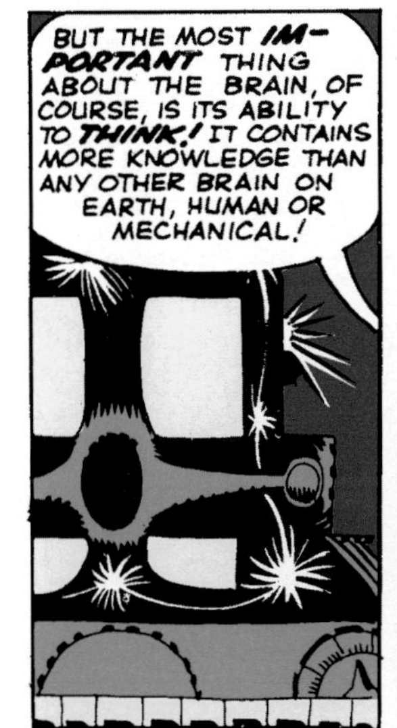
BUT THE MOST IMPORTANT THING ABOUT THE BRAIN, OF COURSE, IS ITS ABILITY TO THINK! IT CONTAINS MORE KNOWLEDGE THAN ANY OTHER BRAIN ON EARTH, HUMAN OR MECHANICAL!

IT WILL ANSWER ANY QUESTION WHICH IS FED TO IT... BASING ITS ANSWER ON THE VAST STOREHOUSE OF INFORMATION WHICH IT POSSESSES! AND, UNLIKE THE HUMAN BRAIN, IT NEVER FORGETS A THING!
NOW, MR. WARREN, WOULD YOU SELECT A STUDENT TO ASSIST ME, PLEASE?

PETER PARKER IS OUR TOP SCIENCE STUDENT! PARKER, WILL YOU STEP UP HERE FOR A MOMENT?
I'LL BE GLAD TO, SIR!
SURE YOU'D BE GLAD TO! HOW DOES IT FEEL TO BE A PROFESSIONAL TEACHER'S PET??
QUIET, FLASH! LET'S SEE WHAT THEY WANT PETE TO DO!

MOMENTS LATER...
NOW THAT I'VE EXPLAINED THE BRAIN'S OPERATION TO YOU, LET'S SEE YOU--
SAY! YOU LEARN PRETTY QUICKLY, SON!
THANKS, MISTER PETTY! ACTUALLY, I'VE READ A LOT ABOUT ELECTRONIC BRAINS! I'VE ALWAYS BEEN REAL INTERESTED IN THEM!
NOW, CLASS, YOU THINK OF A QUESTION FOR THE LIVING BRAIN, AND THEN PARKER WILL FEED IT TO HIM AND SEE IF HE CAN ANSWER IT!

DIDJA HEAR HIM CALL THE BRAIN "HE"--LIKE IT WAS A REAL PERSON??
IT'S SMARTER THAN ANY REAL PERSON! IT CAN FIGURE OUT HORSE RACE WINNERS, ELECTIONS, ANYTHING! WE COULD GET RICH IF WE OWNED IT!
3

WHAT SHOULD WE ASK THE BRAIN??
GOSH, I DON'T KNOW! WHAT DO YOU THINK?
SEARCH ME?? GOT ANY IDEAS, LIZ?
YES! I THOUGHT OF SOMETHING EVERYBODY WOULD LIKE TO KNOW! LET'S SEE HOW SMART THE BRAIN REALLY IS...
WHAT IS SPIDER-MAN'S REAL IDENTITY??
NOW

HEY! THAT'S TERRIFIC!
WHAT A GREAT QUESTION!
THIS IS TERRIBLE! WHAT IF THE BRAIN IS SMART ENOUGH TO ANSWER THAT?? WHAT'LL I DO??
IMPOSSIBLE AS THAT QUESTION SEEMS, IF THE LIVING BRAIN IS FED ENOUGH INFORMATION ABOUT SPIDER-MAN, HE MIGHT BE ABLE TO ANSWER IT!

AND SO, THE CLASS CALLS OUT ALL THE FACTS THEY CAN THINK OF ABOUT THE COSTUMED MYSTERY MAN...
HE'S ABOUT FIVE FEET, TEN INCHES TALL!
WEIGHS ABOUT ONE-HUNDRED SIXTY POUNDS!
HE'S BEEN SIGHTED IN THE FOREST HILLS AREA A LOT!
HE'S THE MOST WONDERFUL, HEROIC, GLAMOROUS MAN IN THE WHOLE WORLD!
IF YOU ASK ME, HE'S A NEUROTIC NUT!

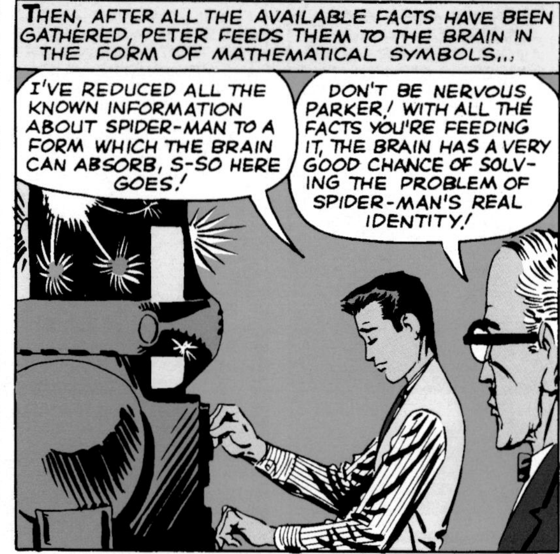
THEN, AFTER ALL THE AVAILABLE FACTS HAVE BEEN GATHERED, PETER FEEDS THEM TO THE BRAIN IN THE FORM OF MATHEMATICAL SYMBOLS...
I'VE REDUCED ALL THE KNOWN INFORMATION ABOUT SPIDER-MAN TO A FORM WHICH THE BRAIN CAN ABSORB, S-SO HERE GOES!
DON'T BE NERVOUS, PARKER! WITH ALL THE FACTS YOU'RE FEEDING IT, THE BRAIN HAS A VERY GOOD CHANCE OF SOLVING THE PROBLEM OF SPIDER-MAN'S REAL IDENTITY!

I KNOW IT! THAT'S WHAT I'M NERVOUS ABOUT!!
PARKER IS SPID

UH OH! THE BRAIN IS SIGNALLING! THE ANSWER IS READY! BOY, IT SURE DIDN'T TAKE LONG!

VERY WELL, PARKER! AS YOU CAN TELL BY THAT WINKING LIGHT, THE ANSWER IS READY FOR YOU! YOU MAY TAKE IT NOW!
YES, SO I SEE! I-I'LL GET IT...
4

AS YOU KNOW, THE ANSWER IS GIVEN IN THE FORM OF MATHEMATICAL CODE SYMBOLS! IT WILL BE UP TO YOU TO TRANSLATE THEM OVERNIGHT, PARKER!
WHEW-- GOOD! AT LEAST THAT'LL GIVE ME TIME TO TRY TO THINK OF SOMETHING!

MEANTIME, THE TWO ATTENDANTS ARE MAKING PLANS OF THEIR OWN...
THEN IT'S A DEAL? FIRST CHANCE WE GET WE STEAL THE BRAIN!
WE'LL MAKE A FORTUNE OUT OF IT AND SKIP TO SOME OTHER COUNTRY!

AND, AT THAT MOMENT...
LET ME HAVE THAT PAPER, PARKER! YOU'RE TOO WEAK TO TAKE CARE OF SOMETHING SO VALUABLE! I'LL DECODE IT!
GET YOUR GRUBBY HANDS OFF THIS, THOMPSON! YOU COULDN'T DECODE YOUR OWN NAME UNLESS SOMEONE SPELLED IT OUT FOR YOU!

YOU HEARD ME, BIRDBRAIN! GIVE ME THAT PAPER!
WELL, WELL! SO THE WORM TURNS, EH? AND IN YOUR CASE, I DO MEAN "WORM"!

ALL RIGHT, YOU TWO! BREAK IT UP-- AND I MEAN RIGHT NOW!
YES SIR!
SORRY, MISTER WARREN!

I'VE HAD MY EYE ON YOU TWO FOR A WHILE NOW! IF YOU BOTH ARE SUCH ENEMIES, I SUGGEST YOU SETTLE YOUR FEUD ONCE AND FOR ALL-- IN THE GYM!
IT'S A DEAL!
SUITS ME JUST FINE!

AND SO, AFTER CLASS...
POOR PARKER! THIS IS ONE TIME YOU COULDN'T GET OUT OF A FIGHT, HUH?
WELL, DON'T WORRY, STRINGBEAN! IT WON'T LAST LONG! YOU'LL NEVER KNOW WHAT HIT YOU!
THE ONLY THING I'M WORRIED ABOUT IS BEING ABLE TO PULL MY PUNCHES ENOUGH SO I DON'T REALLY CLOBBER THAT BAG OF WIND!
ANYWAY, EVERYONE FORGOT ABOUT THE PAPER WITH SPIDER-MAN'S IDENTITY ON IT!

DON'T END IT TOO SOON, FLASH BOY! GIVE US A LITTLE SHOW, HUH?
DON'T WORRY! IT'S TAKEN MONTHS TO GET PARKER TO AGREE TO FIGHT! AFTER WAITING SO LONG, I WANNA REALLY ENJOY THIS!
DON'T BE TOO ROUGH ON HIM, FLASH! HE CAN'T HELP IT IF HE'S NOT THE HE-MAN YOU ARE!
5

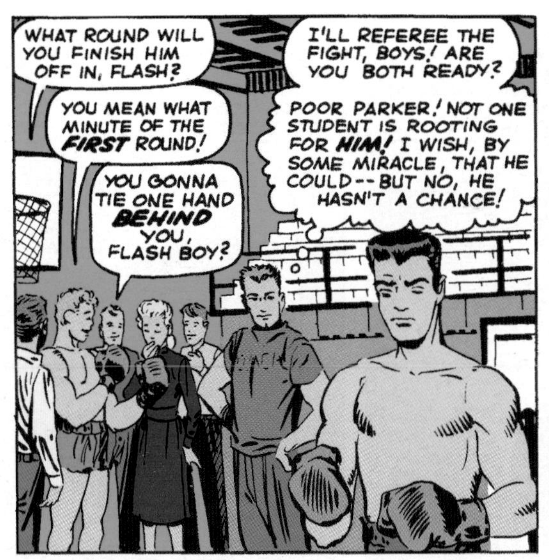
WHAT ROUND WILL YOU FINISH HIM OFF IN, FLASH?
YOU MEAN WHAT MINUTE OF THE FIRST ROUND!
YOU GONNA TIE ONE HAND BEHIND YOU, FLASH BOY?
I'LL REFEREE THE FIGHT, BOYS! ARE YOU BOTH READY?
POOR PARKER! NOT ONE STUDENT IS ROOTING FOR HIM! I WISH, BY SOME MIRACLE, THAT HE COULD-- BUT NO, HE HASN'T A CHANCE!

FINALLY, THE FIGHT BEGINS! PETE'S SPIDER INSTINCT AND LIGHTNING-FAST REFLEXES ENABLE HIM TO MOVE AWAY FROM FLASH'S BLOWS AT THE SPLIT-SECOND THAT FLASH BEGINS TO THROW THEM! BUT, TO THE WATCHING STUDENTS, IT LOOKS AS THOUGH...
PARKER'S A COWARD! LOOK AT HIM STAYING OUT OF FLASH'S REACH!
I AVOID FLASH'S SWINGS SO FAST THAT THE OTHERS THINK I'M JUST STAYING OUT OF RANGE! MY REFLEXES ARE TOO GOOD!

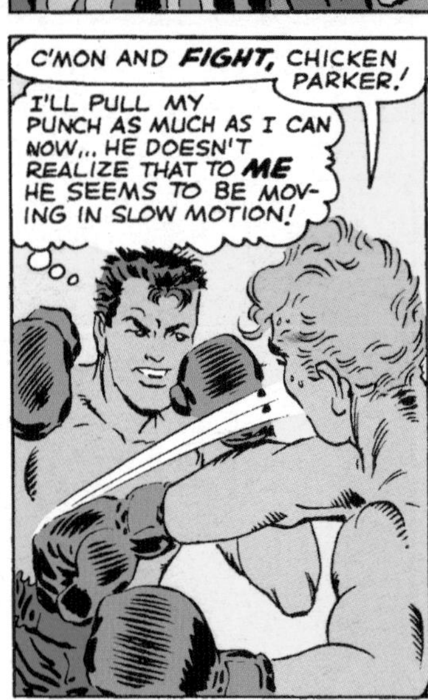
C'MON AND FIGHT, CHICKEN PARKER!
I'LL PULL MY PUNCH AS MUCH AS I CAN NOW... HE DOESN'T REALIZE THAT TO ME HE SEEMS TO BE MOVING IN SLOW MOTION!

THERE! I PUT ONLY THE SMALLEST FRACTION OF MY POWER INTO THAT BLOW!
WHAM!

HOLY COW! DID YOU SEE THAT??!
I'M NOT SURE! IT HAPPENED SO FAST, IT WAS LIKE A BLUR TO ME!

THIS IS WHAT I'VE ALWAYS FEARED! EVEN THOUGH I HIT HIM AS EASY AS I COULD, IT WAS STILL TOO HARD!

PRETTY CLEVER, EH, FLASH? YOU'RE JUST CLOWNIN' AROUND --TRYING TO MAKE PARKER THINK HE'S A POWER-HOUSE BEFORE YOU FINISH HIM OFF, EH?
HUH? OH, YEAH --SURE! THAT'S WHAT I'M DOIN'! JUST TRYING TO HAVE A FEW LAUGHS BEFORE I CLOBBER HIM!

BUT, DESPITE HIS BRAVE WORDS, FLASH THOMPSON APPROACHES HIS FOE WITH FAR MORE CAUTION THAN BEFORE...
IT MUSTA JUST BEEN A LUCKY PUNCH! B-BUT HOW DID HE KNOCK ME CLEAN THROUGH THE ROPES???
IT ALL HAPPENED SO FAST-- I PROBABLY TRIPPED! SURE, THAT MUST BE IT! I JUST TRIPPED OVER THE ROPES!
6

MEANWHILE, ON THE FLOOR ABOVE, WE FIND THE TWO TECHNICIANS ALONE WITH THE GIANT COMPUTING MACHINE...

NOW'S OUR CHANCE TO TAKE THIS MEAL TICKET AND CUT OUT OF HERE!
RIGHT! 'MOST EVERYBODY'S DOWN IN THE GYM, WATCHING THE FIGHT!

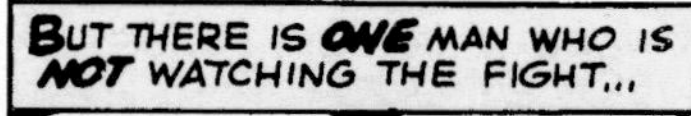
BUT THERE IS ONE MAN WHO IS NOT WATCHING THE FIGHT...

WAIT! WHERE ARE YOU TWO GOING WITH THE BRAIN??!
IT'S PETTY! WE'VE GOT TO SHUT HIM UP, FAST!

THERE! BY THE TIME HE WAKES UP, WE'LL BE GONE!
HEY-- LOOK OUT! YOU MADE ME BUMP INTO THE BRAIN'S CONTROL PANEL!

OH NO! I MUST HAVE SHORT-CIRCUITED IT! LOOK-- IT'S MOVING BY ITSELF! IT--IT NEVER DID THAT BEFORE!
IT'S COMING TOWARDS US --AS THOUGH IT WANTS TO HARM US! H-HOW DO WE STOP IT?

WE CAN'T STOP IT! CAN'T GET NEAR IT WHILE ITS ARMS ARE SWINGIN' THAT WAY!
ANYTHING CAN HAPPEN NOW! LET'S GET OUT OF HERE-- WHILE WE CAN!

IT KEEPS BLOCKING THE EXITS! I'D SWEAR IT DOESN'T WANT US TO LEAVE!
WITH ITS STRENGTH, AND ITS INTELLIGENCE, NOTHING CAN STOP IT IF IT'S ON A RAMPAGE!

BUT SUDDENLY, THE LIVING BRAIN TAKES A RANDOM TURN, AND...
LOOK! IT-IT'S THE GIANT COMPUTING MACHINE!
BUT NOBODY'S CONTROLLING IT!
IT'S RUNNING WILD! STAY CLEAR OF THOSE SWINGING ARMS!

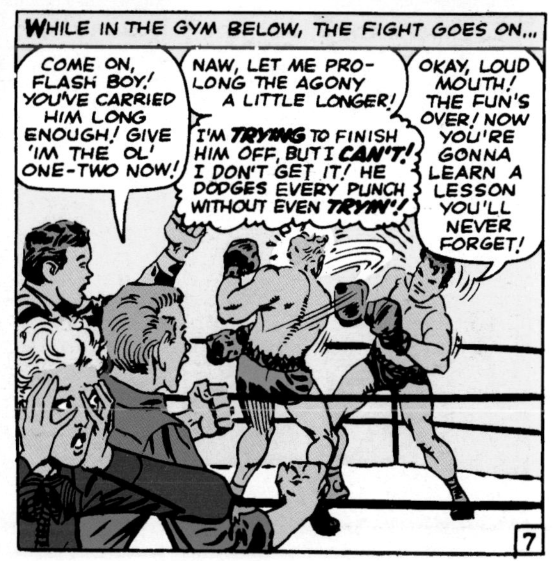
WHILE IN THE GYM BELOW, THE FIGHT GOES ON...
COME ON, FLASH BOY! YOU'VE CARRIED HIM LONG ENOUGH! GIVE 'IM THE OL' ONE-TWO NOW!
NAW, LET ME PROLONG THE AGONY A LITTLE LONGER!
I'M TRYING TO FINISH HIM OFF, BUT I CAN'T! I DON'T GET IT! HE DODGES EVERY PUNCH WITHOUT EVEN TRYIN'!
OKAY, LOUD MOUTH! THE FUN'S OVER! NOW YOU'RE GONNA LEARN A LESSON YOU'LL NEVER FORGET!
7

I'VE FINALLY FIGURED OUT HOW TO HIT HIM WITHOUT SPLATTERING HIM ALL OVER THE GYM! I'LL JUST SWAT HIM BY FLIPPING MY WRIST INSTEAD OF MY WHOLE ARM!!

HERE IT COMES, FLASH! NOW SMILE--I WANT TO REMEMBER YOU AS YOU LOOK RIGHT NOW!

BUT JUST THEN, A FRANTIC CRY RINGS OUT... AND FLASH AUTOMATICALLY TURNS HIS HEAD IN THE DIRECTION OF THE SOUND!
HELP! THE BRAIN IS OUT OF CONTROL! HELP!
CAN'T STOP MY BLOW!

THAT DID IT! B-BUT IF ONLY HE HADN'T TURNED HIS HEAD!
WHOOM!

BOOOO! YOU HIT HIM WHEN HIS HEAD WAS TURNED! IT WAS A FOUL!
THAT WAS A CRUMMY THING TO DO, PARKER! POOR FLASH WASN'T EVEN LOOKING!

AT THAT MOMENT...
MR. PETTY! WHERE'S MR. PETTY?? HE'S THE ONLY ONE WHO CAN DO ANYTHING!
THE LIVING BRAIN IS RUNNING AMOK, AND NO ONE KNOWS HOW TO STOP IT!

I'LL BRING FLASH TO THE LOCKER ROOM! HE'LL BE OKAY--JUST HAD THE WIND KNOCKED OUT OF HIM!
AND THEN, SPIDER-MAN BETTER SEE WHAT'S GOING ON UPSTAIRS!

EXACTLY THIRTY SECONDS LATER...
I DON'T SEE HOW THE BRAIN COULD GO OUT OF CONTROL--UNLESS IT WAS TAMPERED WITH!

ANYWAY, HOW CAN AN ELECTRONIC THINKING MACHINE CAUSE SUCH ALARM?? I'M SURE IT'S JUST--
SIZZLIN' SPIDER-WEBS!! LOOK AT THAT! NO WONDER THEY'RE SCARED!
8

RUN! RUN! THE BRAIN'S GETTING CLOSER!
NOTHING CAN STOP IT! IT'S TRYING TO CATCH US ALL!
LOOK-- THERE'S SPIDER-MAN! MAYBE HE CAN DO SOMETHING!

KEEP RUNNING, ALL OF YOU! I'LL TAKE OVER NOW!
IT'S LIKE A HUGE, INVULNERABLE ENGINE OF DESTRUCTION! PERHAPS I CAN LAND ON TOP OF IT, FROM THE CEILING!

MADE IT!

WHAP!
OWW! I FORGOT --THE MACHINE CAN THINK, IN ITS OWN FASHION! IT SWATTED ME OFF EASY AS PIE!

SOMERSAULTING IN MID-AIR, THE AGILE SPIDER-MAN REGAINS HIS BALANCE AND LANDS LIGHTLY ON HIS FEET AS THE RAMPAGING MACHINE CONTINUES TO RUMBLE DOWN THE HALL!
I'VE GOT TO GET AHEAD OF IT AND WARN THE OTHER KIDS TO RUN TO SAFETY!

CLEAR OUT OF HERE--ALL OF YOU! HURRY!
LOOK! ON THE WALL-- IT'S SPIDER-MAN!
DO AS HE SAYS! RUN FOR THE EXIT! QUICKLY!

AND NOW I CAN CONCENTRATE ON THE BRAIN! I'LL TRY TO SLOW HIM DOWN WITH A QUICK-FORMING WEB!

IT WORKED!! IT'S STOPPING HIM!!
9

HE'S GRASPING THE WEB! I-I COULD SWEAR HE'S TESTING IT... ANALYZING ITS STRENGTH!

I HEAR HIS GEARS MOVING... AS THOUGH HE'S DECIDING HOW MUCH PRESSURE TO APPLY!!
AW, THAT'S IMPOSSIBLE! HE CAN'T BREAK MY WEB!

BUT THE MIGHTY MACHINE PLOWS THROUGH THE DECEPTIVELY STRONG WEBBING AS THOUGH IT DOESN'T EXIST!
WHEW! HE'S STRONGER THAN I THOUGHT! HAVE TO TRY SOME-THING ELSE!

FIRST, I'LL TEST HIS THINKING ABILITY! I'LL LET HIM HEAR ME RUNNING--THEN I'LL SEE WHAT HE DOES!

HE DOES THINK! LIKE A HUMAN! AT THE SOUND OF MY FOOTSTEPS HE TURNED...

HE'S EXTENDING HIS ARMS, STRIKING AT ME... AS A MAN WOULD! AND HE'S FAST! FASTER THAN I WOULD HAVE GUESSED!

HE KNOWS I'M AN ENEMY! HE'S AFTER ME!
I'VE GOT TO STAY OUT OF REACH OF THOSE POWERFUL ARMS!

OH, NO! THE BRAIN FIGURED OUT MY SPEED, AND INCREASED HIS OWN ENOUGH TO OVER-TAKE ME!!

HE OUT-MANEUVERED ME! HE REALLY IS THE FASTEST THINKING MACHINE ON EARTH!! I-I'M TRAPPED!
10

BUT ALTHOUGH HE CAN OUT-THINK A HUMAN, HE CAN'T OUT-GUESS ONE! IF I CAN MAKE AN UNEXPECTED MOVE... LIKE THIS!

BUT HE'LL REMEMBER THAT MANEUVER! I'LL NEVER BE ABLE TO TRICK HIM WITH IT AGAIN!

I'VE GOT TO KEEP LEAPING FROM WALL TO WALL! CHANGE MY MOTION PATTERN ALL THE TIME! IF I REPEAT ANY ACTION, HE'LL REMEMBER IT AND GET ME!

MORE KIDS! I THOUGHT THEY WERE ALL SAFELY OUT!
TURN AROUND-- RUN! THE LIVING BRAIN IS RIGHT BEHIND ME!
B-BUT THE EXIT DOOR IS JAMMED! WE CAN'T OPEN IT!

THERE! NOW SCATTER! HURRY!
WOW! DID YOU SEE THAT??!
HE PULLED THAT LOCK APART LIKE IT WAS PAPER!

THE KIDS ARE ALL SAFE NOW! BUT I'VE GOT TO REMAIN! GOT TO STOP THE LIVING--
SAY! WHERE IS IT? WHERE DID IT GO??

I DON'T LIKE THIS! IT'S TOO CUNNING!
I MUSTN'T FORGET THAT EVEN THOUGH IT'S ONLY A MACHINE, IT THINKS LIKE A MAN! IT'S PLANNING A TRAP FOR ME!

AND, A FEW SECONDS LATER, SPIDER-MAN'S WORDS COME TRUE...
THUD!
OH!

IT WAS HIDING BEHIND THAT DOOR-- WAITING! BUT IT HASN'T YET LEARNED HOW GREAT MY STRENGTH IS-- IT THINKS THIS WILL STOP ME!
11

IT'S GONE! THINKS IT FINISHED ME OFF! BUT I'LL HAVE TO BE MORE CAREFUL NEXT TIME!
THE BRAIN NEVER FORGETS! ONCE IT SEES ME AGAIN, IT'LL REALIZE THE EXTENT OF MY STRENGTH, AND IT WILL FIGHT HARDER THAN EVER!

BUT, SUDDENLY...
NOW'S OUR CHANCE! THE BRAIN IS GONE! LET'S CLEAR OUT OF HERE!
YEAH, BEFORE ANYONE REALIZES WE CAUSED ALL THE TROUBLE BY MESSING UP ITS CONTROLS WHEN WE TRIED TO STEAL IT!
AHHH ...SO THAT'S IT!
I KNEW THE BRAIN COULDN'T HAVE BECOME A MENACE BY ITSELF! BUT MY FIRST JOB IS STILL TO FIND IT, AND RENDER IT HARMLESS!

IF I COULD ONLY FIND A WAY TO REACH ITS CONTROL PANEL! MAYBE I COULD FIGURE OUT...
THAT NOISE DOWN THE HALL! IT MUST BE STRAIGHT AHEAD!

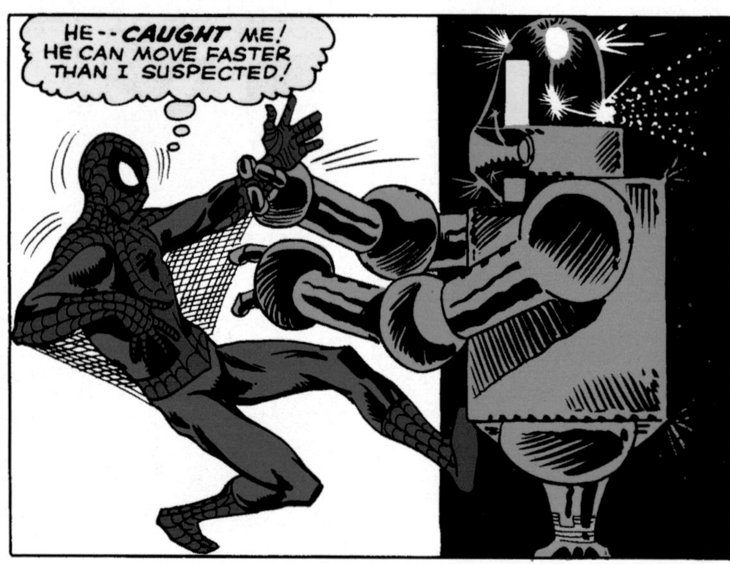
HE--CAUGHT ME! HE CAN MOVE FASTER THAN I SUSPECTED!

HE THINKS SO FAST THAT HE CAN ACTUALLY SECOND-GUESS MY ACTIONS!

AND HIS ELECTRONIC CIRCUITS CAN ADJUST HIS MECHANICAL BODY AS FAST AS HE CAN THINK!
WHEN I EXERT MORE PRESSURE, HE AUTOMATICALLY INCREASES HIS OWN POWER TO NULLIFY MINE!
12

THEN, THE LIVING BRAIN SUDDENLY SPINS SPIDER-MAN AROUND AND RELEASES HIM, IN AN EFFORT TO DASH HIM AGAINST THE WALL!
HE REALIZES MY STRENGTH NOW! HE'S TAKING NO CHANCES WITH ME!

BUT THE MASKED TEEN-AGER SAVES HIMSELF BY A LIGHTNING-FAST MANEUVER...
GOOD THING I LOADED MY VIAL WITH ENOUGH WEB FLUID THIS MORNING!

THWUP!
GOOD OL' TRUSTY WEB! IT HELD! STOPPED ME FROM HITTING THE WALL!

AND NOW, I'M IN MY OWN ELEMENT!

BETTER CLING TO THE CEILING WHILE I PLAN MY NEXT MOVE!

LUCKILY, I'M JUST OUT OF HIS REACH!
BUT I CAN'T STAY UP HERE FOREVER!

SAY, WHAT'S HE TRYING TO DO NOW??

HOLY SMOKE! I'LL SAY HE CAN THINK! HE'S TRYING TO DISLODGE ME BY HITTING THE WALLS!

--AND HE'S USING THAT DOOR LIKE A FLY-SWATTER!
13

HE CAN THINK, BUT HAS NO CONSCIENCE! TO HIM, THERE IS NO RIGHT OR WRONG!

HE DOESN'T EVEN HATE ME! JUST WANTS ME TO STOP BOTHERING HIM!
BUT WHETHER HE MEANS IT OR NOT, IF HE CONNECTS, IT'S GOODBYE SPIDER-MAN!

WHATEVER I'M GOING TO DO, I'D BETTER DO IT FAST!

WELL, HERE GOES NOTHING!
THWAP!

IF I HOLD TIGHT ENOUGH, HE WON'T BE ABLE TO REACH THE WALL TO POUND ANY MORE!
BUT I CAN'T HOLD ON MUCH LONGER --HE'S EXERTING TOO MUCH PULL!

HE'S SPINNING AROUND-- CAUSING ME TO SPIN, ALSO!!
THAT HUNK OF MACHINE CAN ACTUALLY OUT-THINK A HUMAN BRAIN!
HOW'LL I EVER BEAT HIM??

H-HE SHOOK ME LOOSE!
LOOK OUT BELOW!

HE'S LEAVING! HE FEELS THERE'S NOTHING I CAN DO TO STOP HIM! I'M NOT WORTH BOTHERING ABOUT ANY MORE!

OH NO! SOME FOOL KIDS CAME BACK INTO THE SCHOOL TO SEE WHAT'S GOING ON! HE'S HEADING TOWARDS THEM! THEY WON'T HAVE A CHANCE!
14

SEEING THE LIVING BRAIN BEARING DOWN ON THEM, THE STUDENTS TURN AND FLEE... BUT, IN THEIR HASTE, ONE TRIPS, AND...
CHARLIE, GET UP! HURRY! IT'S ALMOST ON TOP OF US!

I'VE GOT TO REACH THE BRAIN BEFORE IT CAN GET TO THOSE KIDS!

OL' SPIDER-STRENGTH, IF I EVER NEEDED YOU, I NEED YOU NOW!

GOT HIM! NOW, IF I CAN JUST REACH THAT CONTROL PANEL...
LOOK! SPIDER-MAN SAVED US!
YEAH! BUT NOW WHO'S GONNA SAVE SPIDER-MAN??

AT LEAST I DIVERTED HIS ATTENTION FROM THOSE KIDS!
BUT HE'S MOVING SO FAST I CAN'T REACH HIS CONTROLS!

THIS IS THE SHOWDOWN! HE WON'T REST NOW UNTIL I'M COMPLETELY DESTROYED! I'VE JUST GOT TO HOPE HE CAN'T THINK OF A WAY TO DO IT BEFORE I CAN DO SOMETHING!

WHAT A PICKLE! IF I FALL OFF, I'M DONE FOR!
AND IF I STAY ON HERE, I'LL SOON BE A SITTING DUCK FOR HIM!

THERE! I FINALLY REACHED HIS CONTROL SWITCHES!
BUT HE'S HEADING FOR THE STAIRS! I'VE GOT SECONDS TO FIGURE THESE THINGS OUT!

I DID IT! I FLIPPED THE MAIN CUT-OFF SWITCH! HE'S INCAPABLE OF FURTHER INDEPENDENT ACTION!
BUT HE CAN'T STOP HIMSELF-- HE'S GONNA CRASH DOWN THOSE STAIRS --WITH ME GOING ALONG FOR THE RIDE!
15

CAN'T WIGGLE OFF IN TIME!
THIS IS A NUTTY WAY FOR A SUPER-HERO TO MEET HIS END!

THWAP!
JUST ONE SLIM CHANCE-- IF MY SPIDER WEB IS STRONG ENOUGH TO HOLD US BOTH!

CRASH!
GERONIMO!!!

IT HELD! THE WEB HELD! WE'RE SWINGING BACK IN AGAIN! I STOPPED HIM!

THEN, WHEN THE NOW-DEACTIVATED LIVING BRAIN FINALLY SWINGS TO A HALT, THE TRIUMPHANT TEEN-AGER READJUSTS HIS CONTROLS, LOWERING THE MACHINE'S ARMS SO THAT HE CAN GET FREE!
IT WAS A GREAT RIDE, PAL... BUT I'M NOT SORRY IT'S OVER!

JUST THEN, AT THE OTHER END OF THE HALL...
SOMEBODY STOP THOSE TWO! THEY'RE RESPONSIBLE FOR WHAT HAPPENED!
DOWN THE STAIRS, QUICK! WE'LL LOSE 'EM IN THE LOCKER ROOM!

BUT, AT THAT MOMENT, IN THE LOCKER ROOM, FLASH THOMPSON REGAINS CONSCIOUSNESS...
OH, MY HEAD! PARKER MUST HAVE HAD A BRICK IN HIS GLOVE WHEN HE HIT ME!

MIGHT AS WELL GET DRESSED! I'LL HAVE TO FIND SOME EXCUSE FOR NOT BEATING PUNY PARKER!
DRAT THIS KNOTTED SHOE-LACE!

FOOTSTEPS--RUNNING TOWARDS ME! WHAT'S UP? WHO CAN-- HEY!
LOOK OUT! I THOUGHT THIS PLACE WAS EMPTY! OOF!
16

WELL, I'LL BE--! THEY PLUMB KNOCKED THEMSELVES OUT!

WOW! LOOK AT THAT! FLASH CAUGHT BOTH OF THOSE GUYS!
GREAT WORK, FLASH! HOW'D YOU DO IT?

YOU KNOW ME! I JUST UP AND LET 'EM HAVE IT!
MEANTIME, HAVING CHANGED BACK TO HIS NORMAL IDENTITY, PETER PARKER GETS AN IDEA...
THIS IS TOO GOOD AN OPPORTUNITY TO PASS UP!

I JUST REALIZED, FLASH--YOU'RE THE ONLY ONE WHO WASN'T AROUND WHILE SPIDER-MAN WAS FIGHTING THE LIVING BRAIN!
AND YOU KNOCKED THESE TWO BURLY GUYS OUT AS EASY AS PIE! AND YOU'RE JUST ABOUT SPIDER-MAN'S SIZE!
SAY! PARKER'S RIGHT, FOR ONCE! I NEVER THOUGHT OF THAT!

AND YOU TRIED TO GET THE BRAIN'S ANSWER TO SPIDER-MAN'S IDENTITY AWAY FROM ME! IT ALL TIES IN, DOESN'T IT?
KNOCK IT OFF, BOOKWORM! YOU'RE IMAGINING THINGS! I'M NOT SPIDER-MAN!
BUT EVEN IF YOU WERE, YOU'D STILL DENY IT, WOULDN'T YOU?

THAT COULD BE WHY YOU LOST THE FIGHT TO PARKER! SO NOBODY WOULD SUSPECT WHO YOU REALLY ARE!
SURE! EVERYONE KNOWS YOU COULD BEAT PUNY PARKER IN YOUR SLEEP!
BUT--I CAN'T--THAT IS, I MEAN--I'M NOT--
HA! IF THEY KEEP IT UP, FLASH'LL START BELIEVING IT HIMSELF!
17

LATER, A LIGHT-HEARTED PETER PARKER BLITHLY WALKS HOME FROM SCHOOL, HAPPILY LOST IN HIS OWN THOUGHTS...
TOMORROW, I'LL SAY I LOST THE PAPER WITH SPIDER-MAN'S IDENTITY ON IT DURING ALL THE EXCITEMENT, SO THAT'S THAT!
AS FOR FLASH, I MANAGED TO WALLOP HIM WITHOUT GIVING MYSELF AWAY! ALL IN ALL, IT'S BEEN A MIGHTY PLEASANT DAY!
DON'T GO AWAY, FRIENDS! MORE TEEN-AGE FUN FOLLOWS, AS SPIDER-MAN MIXES IT UP WITH THAT OTHER YOUTHFUL SENSATION, THE HUMAN TORCH!

the END

SPIDER-MAN TACKLES THE TORCH!
SPIDER-MAN
A SPIDER-MAN SURPRISE EXTRA!
THIS IS WHERE DORIS EVANS, THE TORCH'S GIRL FRIEND, LIVES! WHILE I'M IN THE NEIGHBORHOOD, I'LL PAY HER A VISIT AND SHOW HER WHAT SHE'S MISSING BY NOT DATING SPIDER-MAN!
WELL, HIT MY HEAD AND CALL ME SHORTY! LOOKS LIKE I'M JUST IN TIME FOR A PARTY!
LOOK! THERE'S THE HUMAN TORCH! HI, JOHNNY... WE'VE BEEN WAITING FOR YOU!
JOHNNY STORM! YOU DIDN'T TELL ME YOU HAD A NEW STING-RAY! IT'S GORGEOUS!
TRAVELIN' IN STYLE THESE DAYS, EH, TORCH?
WELL, IT'S NO FANTASTI-CAR, BUT IT TAKES ME WHERE I'M GOIN'!
WRITTEN BY: STAN LEE
DRAWN BY: JACK KIRBY
INKED BY: STEVE DITKO
LETTERED BY: S. ROSEN
LAST WEEK HE WAS DRIVING AN XK JAG! AND NOW THIS! OH, IF ONLY DORIS HADN'T FOUND HIM FIRST!
X-529

A FEW MINUTES LATER...
HMMPH! IT DIDN'T TAKE LONG FOR THAT FLAMING PHONY TO START SHOWING OFF!

WELL, NOW I'LL SHOW THEM WHAT SPIDER-MAN CAN DO!
I'LL JUST WEAVE A LITTLE WEB-BAT OUT HERE! IT'LL KEEP THE PARTY FROM GETTING DULL!

WHILE INSIDE, THE TORCH USES HIS INFRA-RED GLOWING POWER TO DAZZLE HIS TEEN-AGE FRIENDS!
HERE, SALLY! I'LL PUT AN INFRA-RED SPOTLIGHT ON YOU WHILE YOU DANCE!
MMM! WAIT, TILL ACTORS' UNION HEARS ABOUT YOU, JOHNNY!

EEK! A BAT!
OHH! GET IT AWAY! IT'S SO DREADFUL-LOOKING!
HOLD IT, KIDS! THERE'S SOMETHING FUNNY ABOUT IT! IT ISN'T REAL!

I'LL JUST SWAT AT IT WITH THIS PILLOW, AND...
HEY! IT CAME APART! IT'S JUST A MASS OF SOME KIND OF THREADS!

NOT THREADS, SONNY BOY! ...WEBS! GEN-U-WINE SPIDER-MAN WEBS!...THE KIND YOUR FRIENDLY NEIGHBORHOOD GROCER DOESN'T SELL!
SPIDER-MAN!! I MIGHT HAVE KNOWN!!

STOP BRAGGING! YOU MIGHTN'T HAVE KNOWN! YOU'RE NOT SMART ENOUGH!
HOW DID SPIDER-MAN GET HERE??
HE'S GOT SOME NERVE CRASHING A PRIVATE PARTY!
JOHNNY, CAN'T YOU GET RID OF HIM??
2.

THANK YOU, KIND FRIENDS, FOR YOUR WARM WELCOME!
BEING YOU INSIST, I'LL BE GLAD TO JOIN YOUR LITTLE PARTY!
LISTEN, WEB-HEAD, I'VE GOT NEWS FOR YOU! YOU'RE AS FUNNY AS A RUSTY CRUTCH! SO GO CRAWL BACK UNDER YOUR STONE!
SAY! YOU DON'T HAPPEN TO BE RELATED TO ANOTHER SUNSHINE BOY NAMED J. JONAH JAMESON, DO YOU?
I'LL JUST DO THAT LITTLE THING, WISE GUY!
AND AWAAAAY WE GO!
HERE! THIS'LL BRING YOU DOWN TO EARTH, LAUGHING BOY!
WATCH THAT FLAME, CORN-BALL! THESE WEBS COST MONEY!

OKAY, BIG MOUTH! YOU HAD YOUR CHANCE! IF YOU WON'T LEAVE PEACEFULLY, I'M GONNA TOSS YOU OUT ON YOUR POINTY EAR!
WHO WRITES YOUR DIALOGUE, SQUIRT?... FRANK MERRIWELL?
FLAME ON!
IF IT'S A FIGHT YOU WANT, C'MON OUTSIDE!
HE FLOATS THROUGH THE AIR WITH THE GREATEST OF EASE!

I GUESS THAT'LL TEACH YOU NOT TO MESS AROUND WITH THE HUMAN TORCH!
YOU KIDDIN'?? I JUST WANTED TO SEE WHAT YOU CAN DO! AND NOW IT'S MY TURN! DON'T GO 'WAY, JOHNNY BOY!

OKAY, YOU ANIMATED INSECT! YOU ASKED FOR IT! HERE I COME!
MERCY ME! I'D BETTER PREPARE A LITTLE WELCOME FOR SUCH A BIG, BAD BLAZING BIRDBRAIN!
COME 'N GET IT, TORCHY! THIS'LL COOL YOU OFF, BUT GOOD!!
3.

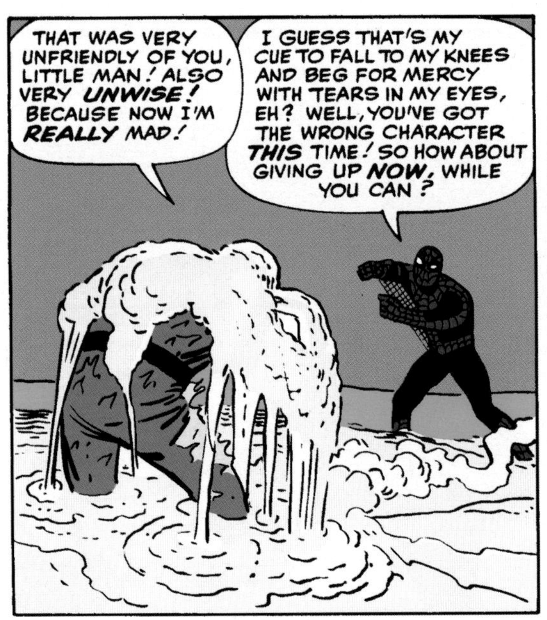
THAT WAS VERY UNFRIENDLY OF YOU, LITTLE MAN! ALSO VERY UNWISE! BECAUSE NOW I'M REALLY MAD!
I GUESS THAT'S MY CUE TO FALL TO MY KNEES AND BEG FOR MERCY WITH TEARS IN MY EYES, EH? WELL, YOU'VE GOT THE WRONG CHARACTER THIS TIME! SO HOW ABOUT GIVING UP NOW, WHILE YOU CAN?

BUT, DRYING OFF WITHIN SECONDS, DUE TO THE INNER HEAT GENERATED BY HIS INTENSE ANGER, THE TORCH TRIES ANOTHER MANEUVER!
HERE'S A LITTLE STUNT YOU HADN'T COUNTED ON, MEAT-HEAD!
I CAN FOCUS MY FLAME ON A SMALL PLOT OF GROUND, MAKING IT ERUPT... LIKE THIS!
WATCH IT, FELLA! A THING LIKE THIS CAN GIVE A GUY A HEADACHE!

VER-RY FUNNY! NOW LET'S SEE HOW THESE FLAMIN' BUZZ-SAWS AMUSE YOU!
I'LL MAKE YOU WISH YOU'D NEVER HEARD OF THE HUMAN TORCH BY THE TIME I'M THROUGH WITH YOU!

I NOTICE YOU'RE NOT MAKIN' WITH THE WISE-CRACKS NOW, BIG MAN!
THOSE THINGS ARE COMING TOO CLOSE FOR COMFORT ...BUT I'M NOT GONNA TELL HIM THAT! MAYBE I SHOULDA JUST QUIT WHEN I WAS AHEAD!

MAYBE IT'S NOT FAIR TO USE SO MUCH FLAME AGAINST HIM, BUT I CAN'T HELP IT!
THAT GUY REALLY GETS UNDER MY SKIN!

COME BACK, SLIPPERY SAM! I'M NOT THROUGH WITH YOU YET! HERE, THIS FIREBALL WILL SPREAD INTO A NET, TRAPPING YOU TILL YOU SAY "UNCLE"!
4.

But with his super-human agility, Spider-Man easily darts through the spaces in the Torch's flame net...
WHEW! I GUESS I'D BETTER JUST CALL IT A DRAW AND CUT OUT OF HERE! I DIDN'T EXPECT THAT HUMAN MATCH-STICK TO GET SO ANGRY!!

SUDDENLY, BEFORE SPIDER-MAN CAN REGAIN HIS FEET, HE SEES...
CAN I GIVE YOU A HAND, SON?
OL' TORCHY AIN'T AS EASY TO HANDLE AS YA THOUGHT, HUH?
MISTER FANTASTIC!! INVISIBLE GIRL!! AND THE MUSCLE-BOUND THING!!

WAIT! WHAT ARE YOU DOING? KNOCK IT OFF, BOY!
THINK I'M GONNA LET YOU SIT THERE AND LAUGH AT ME?? WELL, YOU'VE GOT ANOTHER THINK COMING... ALL OF YOU!

NO ONE'S LAUGHING AT YOU, YOU FOOL! STOP!! DON'T FORCE US TO GET ROUGH!
CLAM UP, SKINNY! WHAT'S WRONG WITH GETTIN' ROUGH?! I'M ITCHIN' TO TANGLE WITH THAT CLOWN!
I'M REALLY MAD NOW! I DON'T CARE HOW MANY OF YOU THERE ARE! I'LL CLOBBER YOU ALL! AND THEN I'LL GO BACK AND SETTLE UP WITH THAT FLAMING FREAK!!

STAND BACK, BOYS AND GIRLS! OL' BENJAMIN J. GRIMM IS GONNA KNOCK A LITTLE SENSE INTO THAT CREEP'S FAT HEAD!

FOR THE LUVVA PETE! WHERE'D HE GO?
I'LL GIVE YOU THREE GUESSES, GARGOYLE!

WELL, AIN'T YOU THE LITTLE FUN BOY!! I HOPE YOUR INSURANCE IS ALL PAID UP, BRIGHT EYES!
YOUR CONCERN FOR MY WELFARE TOUCHES ME DEEPLY, HANDSOME! WHEN DID YOU JOIN THE SALVATION ARMY?
5.

PHOOEY! EVERYBODY'S A COMEDIAN NOWADAYS!!
NOT EVERY-BODY! YOU'RE A BORE, THING!

AND NOW, I'LL MAKE A PAIR OF WINGS OUT OF MY WEB FLUID, AND CRASH-DIVE DOWN AND PULVERIZE YOU!

KNOW SOMETHIN', FATHEAD?? I WAS HOPIN' YOU'D TRY THAT!!
EASY, BEN! HE'S ONLY A LAD!
YEAH? WELL, THIS "LAD" IS GONNA DEMOLISH THAT BIG APE!

BUT, BEFORE SPIDER-MAN AND THE THING CAN TANGLE...
HEY!! LEGGO! WHAT'S GOIN' ON HERE??
NICE WORK, SUE!
THIS NONSENSE HAS GONE FAR ENOUGH! NOW YOU JUST STOP IT!!

YOU'RE ENTIRELY TOO CLEVER, AND ADORABLE, TO BE FIGHTING WITH US! I'LL BET YOU'RE AS HANDSOME AS YOU ARE MUSCU-LAR UNDER THAT MASK!
AW, CUT IT OUT, SUE! I JUST ATE!

NOW, WHY DON'T YOU BOYS JUST SHAKE HANDS LIKE GENTLEMEN AND BURY THE HATCHET!?
I'D LIKE TO BURY IT, ALL RIGHT... AND I'LL GIVE YOU THREE GUESSES WHERE!
WELL, WELL, LOOK WHO JUST MADE A FUNNY!

GO ON BACK TO YOUR DULL PARTY, TORCH! I WOULDN'T JOIN YA ON A BET!
IT'S A GOOD THING YOU'VE GOT MR. FANTASTIC AND THE THING TO WET-NURSE YOU! AND AS FOR YOUR SISTER SUE...

...SHE'S THE ONLY GOOD THING ABOUT THE OVER-RATED FANTASTIC FOUR!!
FOR GOODNESS SAKE! LOOK WHAT HE LEFT! HE SPUN IT OUT OF HIS WEB FLUID... FOR ME!
LIKE WE ALWAYS SAY... SPIDER-MAN'S NOT SO DUMB! HE PICKS HIS ENEMIES VERY CAREFULLY! MORE THRILLS, FUN, AND FAST-MOVING FANTASY NEXT ISSUE! SEE YOU THEN!
6.

the AMAZING
SPIDER-MAN
APPROVED BY THE COMICS CODE AUTHORITY
IND.
MARVEL COMICS GROUP 12¢
9 FEB.
THE MOST ORIGINAL SUPER-HERO OF ALL TIME!
IN THIS GREAT ISSUE YOU WILL MEET...
ELECTRO!
A MENACE SO POWERFUL THAT SPIDER-MAN'S STRENGTH IS USELESS AGAINST HIM!
A BOOK-LENGTH COMIC COLOSSAL, PROVING AGAIN THAT THIS IS INDEED THE MARVEL AGE OF COMICS!
S DITKO

A SCENE YOU WILL NEVER FORGET! SEE... THE DEFEAT OF SPIDER-MAN!

SPIDER-MAN
"THE MAN CALLED ELECTRO!"
A BOOK-LENGTH TRIUMPH FROM THE NEW MARVEL AGE OF COMICS!
PD
WRITTEN BY: STAN LEE
ILLUSTRATED BY: STEVE DITKO
LETTERED BY: ART SIMEK
KNOW SOMETHING, LITTLE FRIEND? IF YOU'RE JUST STARTING TO READ THIS STORY, WE ENVY YOU! BECAUSE YOU'RE GONNA HAVE A BALL! THIS BOOK-LENGTH THRILLER FEATURES A REALLY FASCINATING SUPER-VILLAIN; IT'S CHOCK-FULL OF HUMAN INTEREST AND DRAMA; AND IT SHOWS SPIDER-MAN, WITH ALL HIS HUMAN PROBLEMS AND FRAILTIES, GREATER THAN YOU'VE EVER SEEN HIM BEFORE! BUT DON'T TAKE OUR WORD FOR IT-- AFTER ALL, WE'RE SPIDEY'S BEST BOOSTERS! SEE WHAT YOU THINK...
X-561
1

As our tale begins, a startled group of pedestrians in New York see one of the most colorful characters of all time dash past them at dazzling speed...
Look! It's Spider-Man!!
Wow! Wonder where he's rushing to??
Must be a matter of life or death!

Ignoring the crowds as if they don't exist, the amazing masked adventurer hurtles from rooftop to rooftop until he is virtually lost from sight!!
Have to hurry! Not a minute to lose!

Meanwhile, a short distance away...
Keep firing, Joe! Don't let them get away!
The odds are against us unless help arrives!

What a break!! Here comes Spider-Man!
With his help, those gunmen are as good as finished!

We're sunk! It's Spider-Man!
Might as well give up now, while we still can!
Yeah! We sure can't fight him, too!

H-he's swingin' right past us! He didn't even notice us!
What nuts we were to give up-- Spider-Man wasn't gonna butt in anyway!

A few minutes later...
I'm close to home now! Might as well start chang-ing to Peter Parker!
It's too dark for anyone to see me, and it'll save me time later!
2

HOME AT LAST! NOW TO RUSH UPSTAIRS!

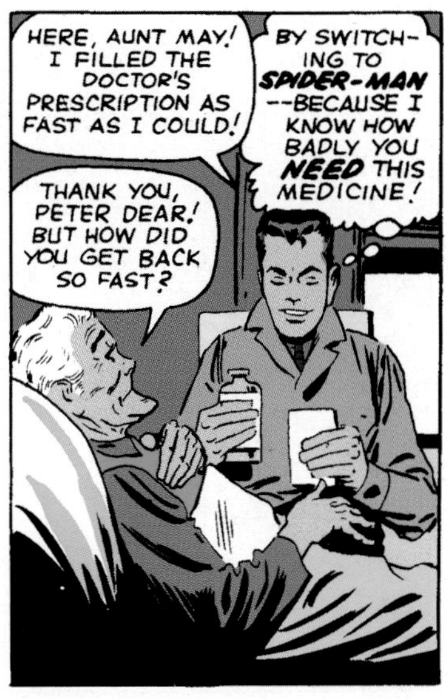
HERE, AUNT MAY! I FILLED THE DOCTOR'S PRESCRIPTION AS FAST AS I COULD!
BY SWITCH-ING TO SPIDER-MAN --BECAUSE I KNOW HOW BADLY YOU NEED THIS MEDICINE!
THANK YOU, PETER DEAR! BUT HOW DID YOU GET BACK SO FAST?

YOU'RE SUCH A DEAR BOY, PETER! I-I'M TIRED NOW-- I THINK I'LL GO TO SLEEP!
THAT'S GOOD, AUNT MAY! THE DOCTOR SAID YOU SHOULD GET A LOT OF REST!

I HAVEN'T THE HEART TO TELL HER WHAT ELSE THE DOCTOR SAID--ABOUT HOW ILL SHE REALLY IS!

SHE'S ASLEEP NOW! BUT I'D BETTER SIT HERE IN CASE SHE NEEDS ME!
POOR AUNT MAY! SHE'S ALWAYS BEEN SO GOOD TO ME-- JUST LIKE A MOTHER! IF ONLY I COULD DO SOMETHING

AND SO, PETER PARKER KEEPS THE LONG VIGIL, NOT DREAMING THAT A STRANGE FIGURE ON THE OTHER SIDE OF TOWN IS GOING TO PLAY A VERY IMPORTANT PART IN HIS LIFE VERY SOON...
I'M ALL WIRED UP FOR WHAT I MUST DO!

I'LL GIVE MYSELF A FULL CHARGE OF ELECTRICITY TONIGHT--FOR THERE'S NO TELLING WHAT I MAY RUN INTO!

THERE! NOW I'M READY TO TRY OUT MY NEW POWER-- AND THE WORLD IS ABOUT TO MEET-- ELECTRO!!

I MIGHT AS WELL START WITH SOMETHING DIFFICULT--LIKE THAT ARMORED CAR WHICH IS CARRYING A SHIPMENT OF GOLD!
3

DON'T BOTHER PUTTING THAT GOLD IN THE CAR! I'LL JUST TAKE IT NOW!
FOR THE LUVVA, PETE! WHAT'S THAT?
THIS TOWN IS FULL OF CRACK-POTS! SEARCH ME!

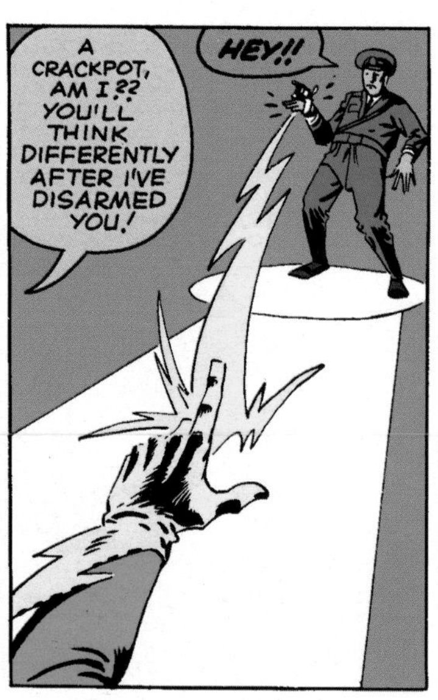
HEY!!
A CRACKPOT, AM I?? YOU'LL THINK DIFFERENTLY AFTER I'VE DISARMED YOU!

I TOLD YOU I'D TAKE THOSE BAGS!
OWW! HE'S TOSSING ELECTRIC SHOCKS!!

NATURALLY! THAT'S WHY I CALL MYSELF ELECTRO! ALL THE POWER OF ELECTRICITY IS MINE!
AND, IF YOU ARE STILL NOT CONVINCED...

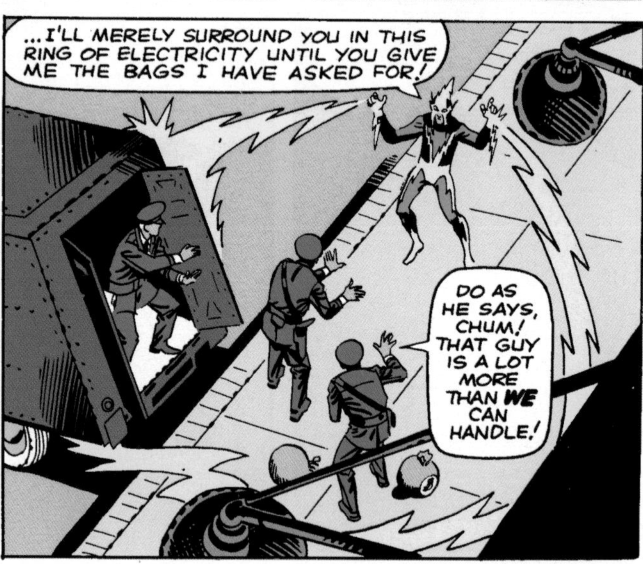
...I'LL MERELY SURROUND YOU IN THIS RING OF ELECTRICITY UNTIL YOU GIVE ME THE BAGS I HAVE ASKED FOR!
DO AS HE SAYS, CHUM! THAT GUY IS A LOT MORE THAN WE CAN HANDLE!

AND, THE NEXT MORNING, BACK AT PETER PARKER'S...
GOOD THING YOU CALLED ME, PETER! YOUR AUNT IS WORSE! WE'VE GOT TO SEND HER TO THE HOSPITAL!
THE HOSPITAL?!?!

BUT, PETER DEAR-- IF I GO TO THE HOSPITAL, WHO'LL LOOK AFTER YOU? WHO'LL GET YOU YOUR MEALS --TAKE CARE OF YOU--??
PLEASE, AUNT MAY, DON'T WORRY ABOUT ME! THE IMPOR-TANT THING IS FOR YOU TO GET WELL! I CAN TAKE CARE OF MYSELF-- HONEST!

LATER, AT SCHOOL, PETER IS OBLIVIOUS TO THE USUAL TAUNTS OF HIS CLASSMATES...
HI, BOOKWORM! WHAT'S NEW IN DULLSVILLE?
S'MATTER, TEACHER'S PET? TOO BUSY TO ANSWER US COMMON FOLKS?
4

I DON'T KNOW--MAYBE I'VE BEEN TOO ROUGH ON PARKER! HE'S MORE OF A MAN THAN I THOUGHT! I STILL REMEMBER THAT LAST FIGHT WE HAD!*
HEY, PETER, WAIT UP! I WANNA TALK TO YOU!
*AMAZING SPIDER-MAN #8 -- THE CASE OF "THE LIVING BRAIN!" -EDITOR

WOW! DID PETER PARKER GIVE YOU THE COLD SHOULDER, FLASH OLD BOY?
YEAH! THAT'S WHAT I GET FOR STARTIN' TO SOFTEN UP! PUNY PARKER ALWAYS WAS A BIG ZERO, AND HE ALWAYS WILL BE!

BUT THIS IS ONE TIME WHEN PETER PARKER COULDN'T CARE LESS FOR FLASH'S OPINION! A FEW MINUTES LATER WE FIND HIM AT THE HOSPITAL...
YOUR AUNT IS ALRIGHT AT THE MOMENT, SON! WE'RE NOT QUITE READY TO OPERATE YET! WOULD YOU LIKE TO SEE HER?
YES, DOC-- I SURE WOULD!

HELLO, AUNT MAY! I--OH, BETTY BRANT!!
ISN'T IT SWEET OF BETTY, PETER? SHE CAME TO VISIT!
WHEN I HEARD ABOUT YOUR AUNT, I CAME TO SEE IF THERE WAS ANYTHING I COULD DO! HOPE YOU DON'T MIND?

MIND? GOSH NO, BETTY! I APPRECIATE IT!
PETER, YOU LOOK PALE! ARE YOU EATING ENOUGH, DEAR?
OF COURSE, AUNT MAY! NOW YOU JUST WORRY ABOUT YOURSELF!

LATER, WHEN VISITING HOURS ARE OVER...
DO YOU MIND IF I DON'T SEE YOU HOME, BETTY? I, EH, HAVE SOMETHING IMPORTANT TO ATTEND TO!
CERTAINLY, PETER! I KNOW YOU MUST HAVE A LOT ON YOUR MIND, WHAT WITH YOUR AUNT'S ILLNESS AND ALL...

BUT, AFTER PETER HAS LEFT...
IT'S STRANGE--ALTHOUGH PETER SEEMS SO CALM, AND EASY-GOING, I GET THE FEELING THAT HE'S LIKE A SMOLDERING VOLCANO INSIDE, JUST WAITING TO ERUPT!
IT'S AS THOUGH HE CARRIES A DEEP SECRET WITHIN HIM--ONE WHICH NO ONE CAN EVER SHARE!

AND, BETTY BRANT IS CLOSER TO THE TRUTH THAN SHE SUSPECTS!
I'VE GOT TO RAISE SOME MONEY FAST! AUNT MAY'S OPERATION WILL COST MORE THAN WE HAVE IN THE BANK!
I'LL SCOUR THE CITY UNTIL I FIND SOME SORT OF CRIME THAT I CAN PHOTOGRAPH! THEN I'LL SELL THE PIX TO J. JONAH JAMESON FOR AS MUCH AS HE'LL PAY!

OH NO! IT'S STARTING TO RAIN! I'M LICKED BEFORE I START!
MY CAMERA ISN'T GOOD ENOUGH TO TAKE CLEAR PICTURES IN THE RAIN!
5

SOME SUPER-HERO I AM! I CAN JUST SEE THE HEADLINES NOW! "SPIDER-MAN CALLS OFF FIGHT AGAINST CRIME DUE TO RAIN!" PHOOEY!

WELL, NOW THAT I'M HOME, I'D BETTER RINSE OUT MY UNIFORM BEFORE IT SHRINKS!
WITH MY LUCK, I'LL PROBABLY WIND UP IN BED WITH A COLD! HMMM... WONDER IF THE HUMAN TORCH EVER HAS SINUS TROUBLE?

OH WELL, I'LL LEAVE MY DUDS TO DRY, AND-- HEY! I FORGOT!!
I LEFT THE SHADE UP! BOY, ALL I NEED IS TO HAVE THE NEIGHBORS SEE A SPIDER-MAN SUIT HANGING UP HERE!

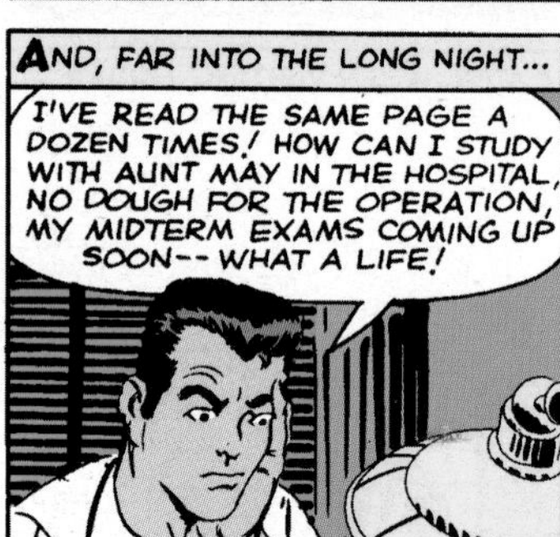
AND, FAR INTO THE LONG NIGHT...
I'VE READ THE SAME PAGE A DOZEN TIMES! HOW CAN I STUDY WITH AUNT MAY IN THE HOSPITAL, NO DOUGH FOR THE OPERATION, MY MIDTERM EXAMS COMING UP SOON-- WHAT A LIFE!

THE NEXT DAY, AT THE FOREST HILLS BANK...
BUT, MISTER JAMESON, IF YOU'LL WAIT TILL TOMORROW WE'LL HAVE ALL THOSE FIGURES FOR YOU!
NO! NOBODY KEEPS J. JONAH JAMESON WAITING! I WANT THOSE FIGURES, AND I WANT THEM NOW!

WELL, SIR, YOU'RE ONE OF OUR BIGGEST DEPOSITORS, SO OF COURSE WE'LL DO WHAT WE CAN!
THAT'S MORE LIKE IT! WHEN I GIVE AN ORDER, I EXPECT PEOPLE TO HOP!!

AT THAT VERY MOMENT, AT THE REAR ENTRANCE TO THE BANK...
SAY! WHAT WAS THAT-- LIGHTNING??

IT'S SOMEONE BREAKING IN-- TRYING TO ROB THE BANK! GOT TO GET TO THE ALARM AND-- OHHH!
ONE LOW-POWER BOLT, HITTING THE ALARM AS THE GUARD TOUCHES IT, WILL SHOCK HIM INTO UNCONSCIOUSNESS AND ALSO SILENCE THE ALARM! HOW EASY IT IS!

I AM ELECTRO! DO NOT RESIST ME AND PERHAPS YOU WILL LIVE TO SEE ANOTHER DAY!
GOOD HEAVENS!! WHO IS THAT??!
6

WHAT IS THE MEANING OF THIS? LOOK HERE, WHO-EVER YOU ARE! YOU CAN'T DO THIS--
WELL WELL! IF IT ISN'T J. JONAH JAMESON! SO YOU THINK I CAN'T, EH?
HIS ELECTRIC BOLTS ARE HIT-TING OUR TIE PINS--BELT BUCKLES--METAL TIPPED SHOE LACES!!! STOP IT! STOP!

STILL THINK I CAN'T DO THIS?? HA! YOU'RE NOT SO NOISY NOW!
HE KNEW WHO I WAS! THAT'S A CLUE! HE MUST BE SOMEONE I KNOW!!

SO! THE VAULT DOOR IS SECURED BY A TIME LOCK! WELL, THAT CAN'T STOP A MAN WITH MY POWERS!
I CAN CONTROL ANYTHING THAT OPERATES ELECTRI-CALLY!

MINUTES LATER...
DON'T ANYONE FOLLOW, OR TRY TO SOUND AN ALARM! MY BOLTS CAN REACH BACK A VERY GREAT DISTANCE!
HE'S ESCAP-ING WITH A FOR-TUNE!

LOOK!! THAT STRANGELY-GARBED MAN IS RACING UP THE SIDE OF THE BUILDING!
HE'S HOLDING ON TO THE IRON BEAMS IN THE BUILD-ING BY MEANS OF ELECTRIC RAYS--USING THEM LIKE A MAGNET!! INCREDIBLE!!

LATER, AFTER ELECTRO HAS REACHED THE ROOF OF THE BUILDING AND THEN VANISHED, THE POLICE BEGIN TO TAKE AND COMPARE NOTES...
HE WAS AVERAGE HEIGHT--VERY CONFIDENT! NEVER SEEMED TO DOUBT HIS POWER!
WHAT ELSE CAN YOU TELL US, SIR?

THERE'S ONLY ONE PERSON I CAN THINK OF WHO IS SO POWERFUL, SO CONFIDENT--WHO CAN CLIMB SHEER BUILDINGS--AND WHO KNOWS ME! AND THERE HE IS NOW, SWINGING UP ABOVE!!

THAT'S IT! IT HAS TO BE! ELECTRO IS SPIDER-MAN! HE HID THE MONEY, CHANGED HIS DISGUISE AND HE'S LEAVING NOW!
WHATEVER HAPPENED DOWN BELOW, IT'S OVER NOW! NO SENSE ME HANGING AROUND!
7

A FRANTIC MINUTE LATER...
I TELL YOU ELECTRO IS SPIDER-MAN! HE HAS TO BE-- THERE'S NO DOUBT ABOUT IT!
NOW CALM DOWN, MR. JAMESON! DO YOU HAVE ANY PROOF?? HOW DO YOU KNOW?

PROOF?!! IT CAN'T BE ANYONE BUT SPIDER-MAN! THAT'S PROOF ENOUGH!
EVEN THOUGH WE KNOW SO LITTLE ABOUT SPIDER-MAN, HE'S ALWAYS BEEN ON THE SIDE OF THE LAW! AND YET--
DON'T LET JAMESON INFLUENCE YOU! HE'D ACCUSE SPIDER-MAN OF ANYTHING!

AND, WHEN THE NEXT EDITIONS HIT THE STREET, THE CHIEF'S PREDICTION PROVES TO BE CORRECT...
HOLY SMOKE! DO YOU THINK THE BUGLE'S ACCUSATION IS TRUE??
IT MUST BE! HOW COULD THEY PRINT IT IF IT WEREN'T TRUE?!!
EXTRA DAILY BUGLE EXTRA
ELECTRO IS REALLY SPIDER-MAN!
SPIDER-MAN
ELECTRO
ON THE BASIS OF INDISPUTABLE EVIDENCE, THE BUGLE ACCUSES SPIDER-MAN OF LAUNCHING A CRIME WAVE DISGUISED AS

"IS SPIDER-MAN ELECTRO?" SUDDENLY, THAT ONE TOPIC IS ON EVERYONE'S LIPS!
SPIDER-MAN MUST BE ELECTRO!! WHY WOULD JAMESON'S PAPER PRINT IT IF IT ISN'T TRUE?
I'VE READ THE PAPER FROM FRONT TO BACK-- THEY STILL OFFER NO DEFINITE PROOF!
IF SPIDER-MAN ISN'T ELECTRO, WHY DOESN'T HE CATCH HIM??

AND, BACK AT THE HOSPITAL, WHERE PETER PARKER KEEPS THE LONG VIGIL...
AS IF I DON'T HAVE ENOUGH TROUBLE AS PETER PARKER, NOW JAMESON IS MAKING THINGS HOT FOR SPIDER-MAN!
THE DOCTOR WOULD LIKE TO SEE YOU NOW, PETER!

WE'RE ALMOST READY TO OPERATE ON YOUR AUNT, SON!
YOU REALIZE, OF COURSE, THAT THE SPECIALIST WE HAD TO ENGAGE CHARGES A FEE OF ONE THOUSAND DOLLARS?
Y-YES! BUT MY AUNT'S LIFE IS AT STAKE! DO WHAT HAS TO BE DONE! I'LL GET THE MONEY-- SOMEHOW!

MINUTES LATER, IN JAMESON'S PRIVATE OFFICE AT THE DAILY BUGLE...
A THOUSAND DOLLARS?? DO YOU REALIZE WHAT YOU'RE ASKING??! WHAT ON EARTH DO YOU NEED IT FOR??
IT'S A PERSONAL MATTER, MR. JAMESON! BUT IT'S VERY IMPORTANT!

SURE! SURE! YOU PROBABLY SAW A HOT-ROD YOU WANT TO BUY! I NEVER LEND MONEY, PARKER-- YOU SHOULD KNOW THAT! BUT, IF YOU CAN BRING ME PHOTOGRAPHIC PROOF THAT SPIDER-MAN IS ELECTRO, I'LL GLADLY GIVE YOU THE MONEY!
SAY! THAT GIVES ME AN IDEA!!

EXACTLY FIFTY SECONDS LATER...
WHAT A FOOL I AM! THERE'S A BIG REWARD FOR ELECTRO'S CAPTURE! IF I CAN NAB HIM, I WON'T HAVE TO BEG THE MONEY FROM ANYONE!
8

AND SO THE GRIM SEARCH BEGINS...
SOMEONE ON THAT ROOF BELOW... PROWLING IN THE DARK! WHAT A STROKE OF LUCK!

YEAH, JUST LIKE MY USUAL LUCK--ALL BAD! IT'S JUST A GUY WITH A TELESCOPE--STAR-GAZING!

HOUR AFTER HOUR, ALL THROUGH THE LONG NIGHT, SPIDER-MAN CONTINUES TO SEARCH--CONTINUES TO HOPE AGAINST HOPE, AS HIS CHANCES FOR SUCCESS NARROW WITH EACH TICK OF THE CLOCK!
I MUST FIND ELECTRO!! I MUST!!

THAT LIGHT--FLASHING FROM THAT DARKENED BUILDING!! PERHAPS--??

ANOTHER FALSE ALARM! JUST SOME WORKMEN MAKING EMERGENCY REPAIRS ON A POWER LINE!

AND STILL THE SEARCH CONTINUES, UNTIL AT LAST...
WAIT!! WHAT'S THAT TINGLING I SEEM TO FEEL??
IT'S MY SPIDER-SENSE! IT'S A WARNING! HE'S SOMEWHERE NEAR HERE! HE MUST BE!

I WAS RIGHT--AT LAST! THERE HE IS NOW!
HE'S USING HIS ELECTRIC POWER LIKE A MINE DETECTOR! HE JUST LOCATED A HIDDEN SAFE IN THAT DESERTED APARTMENT!

JEWELS! MONEY! NO MATTER HOW MUCH I TAKE, I WANT MORE--MUCH MORE! AND WITH MY GREAT POWER, NOTHING CAN STOP ME FROM GETTING IT!

MY TROUBLES ARE OVER AT LAST!! I'LL LET HIM LEAD ME TO HIS HIDEOUT, RECOVER HIS STOLEN LOOT, CAPTURE HIM, AND GET MY REWARD FROM THE POLICE!
MIGHT AS WELL TAKE A FEW PIX OF HIM WHILE I'M AT IT, TOO!
9

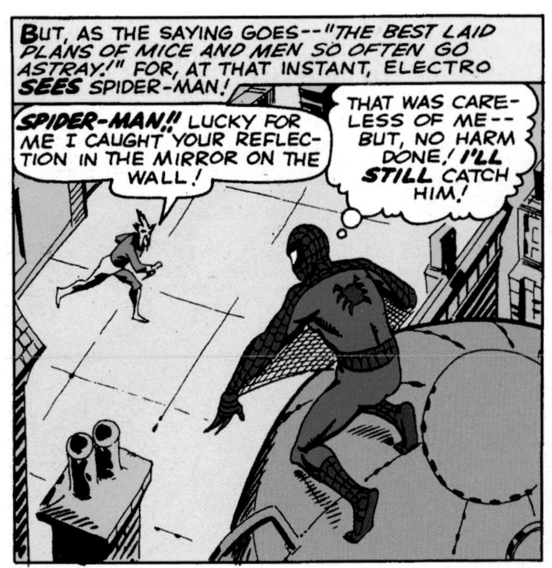
BUT, AS THE SAYING GOES--"THE BEST LAID PLANS OF MICE AND MEN SO OFTEN GO ASTRAY!" FOR, AT THAT INSTANT, ELECTRO SEES SPIDER-MAN!
SPIDER-MAN!! LUCKY FOR ME I CAUGHT YOUR REFLECTION IN THE MIRROR ON THE WALL!
THAT WAS CARELESS OF ME-- BUT, NO HARM DONE! I'LL STILL CATCH HIM!

I'VE BEEN HOPING WE'D MEET! I'VE BEEN ANXIOUS TO PROVE THAT MY POWER IS FAR GREATER THAN YOURS!
WHEW HE HURLED THAT LIGHTNING BOLT BEFORE I KNEW WHAT HAPPENED! I DUCKED IT ONLY BY SHEER DUMB LUCK!

NO TIME TO KID AROUND! I'LL HAVE TO USE MY WEB-- FAST!

AHH! GOT YOU!
THWAP!

STILL WANT TO BRAG ABOUT YOUR POWER, PLAYMATE? YOU'LL HAVE PLENTY OF CHANCE TO DO SO WHEN YOU'RE TELLIN' IT TO THE JUDGE!
THIS CORNY WEB OF YOURS WON'T STOP ME! MY ELECTRIC RAYS CAN BURN OUT OF ANYTHING!

AND ANYONE STUPID ENOUGH TO TOUCH ME WHILE MY BODY IS IN "ELECTRIC SHOCK CONDITION" HAS ONLY HIMSELF TO BLAME FOR THE CONSEQUENCES!
OHHHHH...!

I DIDN'T MEAN TO DO THAT-- BUT IT WAS HIS OWN FAULT! HE DIDN'T GIVE ME A CHANCE TO EXPLAIN THE DANGER OF TOUCHING ME! WELL, WITH HIM OUT OF THE WAY, NO SINGLE HUMAN IS STRONG ENOUGH TO CHALLENGE ME!
10

BUT, IF SPIDER-MAN UNDER-ESTIMATED ELECTRO'S POWER-- ELECTRO IS GUILTY OF THE SAME MISTAKE ABOUT SPIDER-MAN! THE MASTER CRIMINAL HAS FAILED TO TAKE INTO ACCOUNT THAT SPIDER-MAN'S SPIDER-INDUCED STRENGTH ENABLES HIM TO SURVIVE A SHOCK THAT CAN KILL AN ORDINARY HUMAN!

WHEW! MY HEAD! THAT ALMOST FINISHED ME!
NOT A TRACE OF ELECTRO! HE'S GONE!

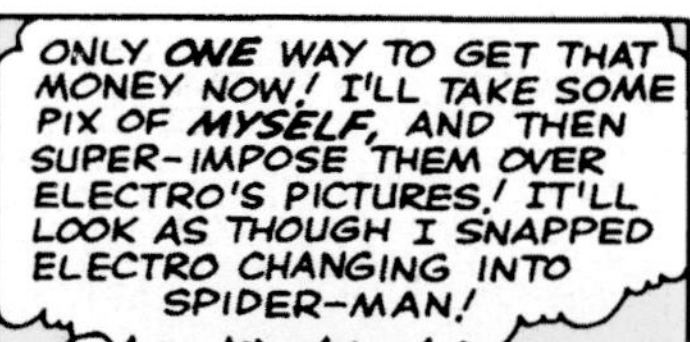

ONLY ONE WAY TO GET THAT MONEY NOW! I'LL TAKE SOME PIX OF MYSELF, AND THEN SUPER-IMPOSE THEM OVER ELECTRO'S PICTURES! IT'LL LOOK AS THOUGH I SNAPPED ELECTRO CHANGING INTO SPIDER-MAN!

THE NEXT DAY...

JUST WHAT I WANTED! PHOTO-GRAPHIC PROOF THAT SPIDER-MAN IS ELECTRO! DON'T KNOW HOW YOU DID IT, BUT HERE'S YOUR CHECK, PARKER!
I HATE TAKING MONEY UNDER FALSE PRE-TENSES--BUT I'LL MAKE UP FOR IT-- SOMEHOW!

I'VE NEVER CHEATED ANYONE BEFORE! IT FEELS TERRIBLE! IF IT WEREN'T SUCH AN EMERGENCY...

IS YOUR AUNT WORSE, PETER? YOU--YOU LOOK SO WORRIED!
NO, BETTY-- I'M NOT WORRIED--
JUST FEELING AWFULLY ASHAMED OF MYSELF!

THE NEXT EDITION OF J. JONAH JAMESON'S PAPER PLASTERS THE NEWS ALL OVER THE FRONT PAGE...

ILY BUGLE EXTRA

PROOF THAT SPIDER-MAN IS ELECTRO!

THESE PHOTOS, TAKEN BY A BUGLE STAFF PHOTOGRAPHER, SHOW SPIDER-MAN AND ELECTRO IN THE SAME AREA, WITHIN SECONDS OF EACH OTHER!... THE BUGLE DARES SPIDER-MAN TO DISPROVE OUR CLAIM!

AND, IN THE HOURS THAT FOLLOW, THE SENSATIONAL STORY IS ON EVERYONE'S LIPS...

JAMESON'S A NUT! WHY SHOULD SPIDER-MAN TAKE ANOTHER IDENTITY! NOBODY EVEN KNOWS WHO SPIDER-MAN IS!

MAYBE HE WANTS TO POSE AS ELECTRO AND THEN LATER PRETEND THAT HE KILLED ELECTRO, TO BECOME A HERO!

MR. JAMESON WOULDN'T PRINT IT IF IT WEREN'T TRUE!

BUT HE COULD MAKE A MIS-TAKE!

AND, IN A SECRET HIDEOUT, IN THE HEART OF THE CITY...

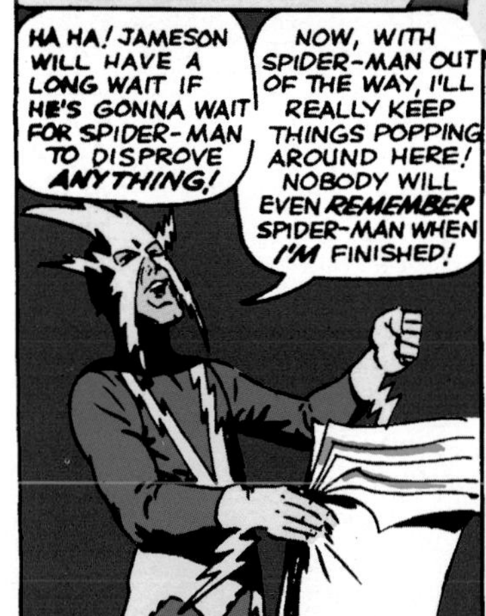

HA HA! JAMESON WILL HAVE A LONG WAIT IF HE'S GONNA WAIT FOR SPIDER-MAN TO DISPROVE ANYTHING!
NOW, WITH SPIDER-MAN OUT OF THE WAY, I'LL REALLY KEEP THINGS POPPING AROUND HERE! NOBODY WILL EVEN REMEMBER SPIDER-MAN WHEN I'M FINISHED!

AND NOBODY EVEN REMOTELY SUSPECTS WHO ELECTRO REALLY IS!! NOBODY KNOWS THAT I USED TO BE AN ORDINARY ELECTRIC LINEMAN NAMED MAX DILLON!

MAX, I NEED YOU! HARRIS IS IN TROUBLE ON A HIGH TENSION POLE! YOU'VE GOT TO HELP HIM DOWN!
FORGET IT! I DON'T DO ANYTHING FOR NOTHING! HOW MUCH BONUS WILL YOU GIVE ME?

BUT THE MAN'S LIFE IS IN DANGER! AND YOU'RE OUR BEST POLE MAN! OKAY-- YOU WIN! WE'LL PAY A HUNDRED BUCKS!

THAT'S MORE LIKE IT! NOW DON'T GET YOUR JAWS IN AN UPROAR! I'LL BRING 'IM DOWN!

11

DILLON IS A RAT! HE'D HAVE LEFT HARRIS UP THERE IF I DIDN'T OFFER TO PAY HIM! IF HE WASN'T OUR BEST POLE MAN I'D BOUNCE HIM IN A SECOND!

"BUT I DIDN'T CARE WHAT ANY-BODY THOUGHT OF ME--AND THEN, IT HAPPENED! A MILLION TO ONE CHANCE! I WAS WORK-ING ALONE ON A POLE, WHEN LIGHTNING STRUCK!"

ZZZZZZZZZ

"I SHOULD HAVE BEEN KILLED INSTANTLY, BUT BY A FANTASTIC FREAK OF FATE--DUE TO THE WAY I HAD BEEN GRASPING THE ELECTRIC WIRES--THE TWO BOLTS OF CURRENT CANCELLED EACH OTHER, AND..."
I-I'M STILL ALIVE!
IN FACT, I FEEL BETTER -- STRONGER THAN EVER!

"A SHORT TIME LATER, WHEN SOME WIRE CLOTHES HANGERS GOT TANGLED OVER MY ARM, I DIS-COVERED THE TRUTH ABOUT MYSELF--"
HEY! THERE'S CURRENT PASSING FROM MY BODY--THROUGH THE HANGERS--MAKING MY FINGERS SPARK!!

"I'M NO FOOL! I INSTANTLY REALIZED THE ACCIDENT HAD CHARGED MY BODY WITH ELEC-TRICITY! I RACED HOME AND BEGAN TO EXPERIMENT--TO SEE HOW POWERFUL I REALLY WAS..."
IT'S UNBELIEVABLE! MY BODY KEEPS RECHARGING IT-SELF! I'M LIKE A LIVING ELECTRICAL GENERATOR!!

THE MORE I PRACTICE, THE MORE SKILLED I BECOME! I CAN DO ANYTHING WITH MY ELECTRIC POWER! I CAN THROW IT--USE IT AS A WEAPON--

"TAKING EVERY CENT I HAD IN THE WORLD, I BOUGHT A RUN-DOWN HOUSE, AND EQUIPPED IT LIKE AN ELECTRICITY LAB!"
WITH THESE DEVICES, I CAN INCREASE MY POWER! THERE'S NOTHING I CANNOT DO!

"FINALLY, I RAN COMPLETELY OUT OF MONEY! BUT THAT DIDN'T WORRY ME!"
I'LL DISGUISE MYSELF--TAKE THE NAME ELECTRO--AND GET ALL THE DOUGH I WANT!

A FEW HOURS LATER, THE EXTRA-ORDINARY SUPERCHARGED CRIMINAL USES HIS GREAT POWER TO FORCE HIS WAY INTO A LOCKED DOWN-TOWN BUILDING...
THERE ARE OVER A DOZEN PRISONERS HERE, WAITING FOR TRANSFER TO THE FEDERAL PEN! I'LL SET THEM FREE--GET THEM TO JOIN ME--TO BE MY FLUNKIES!!
12

ONCE INSIDE, ELECTRO MOVES SWIFTLY...
I CAN'T FIGHT ALL THE POLICE WHO WILL BE COMING AFTER ME!
SO I'LL SET UP AN ELECTRIC BARRIER TO KEEP THEM BACK UNTIL I'VE FINISHED MY JOB!

AND, MINUTES LATER, AS PETER PARKER IS ON HIS WAY TO THE HOSPITAL, HE HEARS...
CALLING ALL CARS!! ELECTRO HAS BROKEN INTO THE WEST SIDE HOUSE OF DETENTION! ALL CARS PROCEED TO THE AREA!
ELECTRO AGAIN! AS SOON AS I SEE AUNT MAY AND MAKE SURE SHE'S OKAY, I'LL GO AFTER HIM--AS SPIDER-MAN!

BUT, AT THE HOSPITAL...
WE'RE READY TO OPERATE! YOUR AUNT HAS BEEN CALLING FOR YOU--SHE WANTS YOU TO BE HERE TILL IT'S OVER!
THEN I CAN'T TACKLE ELECTRO YET! NOT IF AUNT MAY WANTS ME-- NEEDS ME! I CAN'T RUN OUT ON HER!

DON'T WORRY, AUNT MAY! EVERYTHING WILL BE ALL RIGHT! I KNOW IT WILL!
YOU--YOU WON'T LEAVE ME, DEAR--??
I'LL BE RIGHT HERE ALL THE TIME-- I PROMISE!

PLEASE--PLEASE LET AUNT MAY COME THROUGH THIS ALL RIGHT!! SHE--SHE'S BEEN LIKE A MOTHER TO ME ALL THESE DIFFICULT YEARS--!

PETER--I CAME TO WAIT WITH YOU! I KNOW HOW DIFFICULT IT IS TO BE ALONE AT A TIME LIKE THIS!
BETTY!
MAYBE I HAVEN'T MANY FRIENDS--BUT ONE WONDERFUL ONE LIKE BETTY MAKES UP FOR ALL I HAVEN'T GOT!

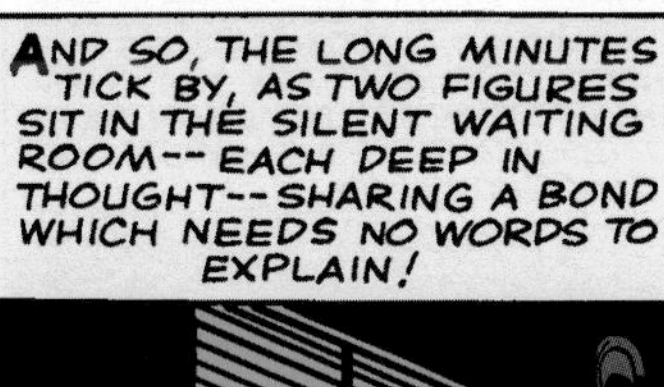
AND SO, THE LONG MINUTES TICK BY, AS TWO FIGURES SIT IN THE SILENT WAITING ROOM-- EACH DEEP IN THOUGHT--SHARING A BOND WHICH NEEDS NO WORDS TO EXPLAIN!

MEANWHILE, OUTSIDE THE HOUSE OF DETENTION...
HA! STILL NO SIGN OF SPIDER-MAN! THIS PROVES I'M RIGHT! HE CAN'T COME TO BATTLE ELECTRO BECAUSE HE HIMSELF IS ELECTRO!!
13

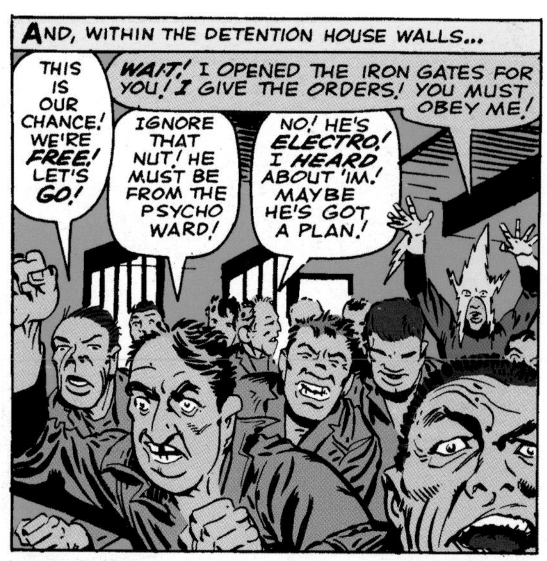
AND, WITHIN THE DETENTION HOUSE WALLS...
THIS IS OUR CHANCE! WE'RE FREE! LET'S GO!
WAIT! I OPENED THE IRON GATES FOR YOU! I GIVE THE ORDERS! YOU MUST OBEY ME!
IGNORE THAT NUT! HE MUST BE FROM THE PSYCHO WARD!
NO! HE'S ELECTRO! I HEARD ABOUT 'IM! MAYBE HE'S GOT A PLAN!

OUTSIDE THE BUILDING, THOSE ESCAPEES WHO DO TRY TO FLEE ARE QUICKLY ROUNDED UP BY THE VIGOROUS ACTION OF THE WAITING POLICE...
FUN TIME'S OVER, PAL! BACK INSIDE YOU GO!
WE SHOULD HAVE WAITED! SHOULD HAVE LISTENED TO ELECTRO! OHHH!
PD

AND, BACK AT THE HOSPITAL...
PARKER! COME IN! YOUR AUNT IS CALLING FOR YOU!
IS-- IS SHE--??
SHE'S ALL RIGHT, SON! THE OPERATION WAS A SUCCESS!

PETER-- PETER-- IS THAT YOU--? TAKE MY HAND, DEAR--
HERE I AM, AUNT MAY! YOU'RE GONNA BE WELL AGAIN! THE DOCTOR SAID SO!
THAT'S ENOUGH, BOY! SHE'S DOZING OFF NOW!

THE SEDATIVES WE GAVE HER WILL LET HER SLEEP TILL MORNING! THE DANGER IS OVER!
YOU LOOK LIKE YOU COULD USE SOME REST, TOO!
I GUESS SO! IT'S BEEN--QUITE A STRAIN!

BETTY, AUNT MAY IS GOING TO BE ALL RIGHT! THE OPERATION WAS SUCCESSFUL!
OH, I'M SO HAPPY FOR YOU, PETER!
AND NOW I'VE GOT TO GO! THEY NEED ME AT THE OFFICE! MR. JAMESON ISN'T THERE--HE WENT TO COVER THE DETENTION HOUSE RIOT!

PETER, PLEASE DON'T GO THERE TO TAKE ANY PICTURES! IT COULD BE DANGEROUS!
BUT, BETTY--THE DANGEROUS PIX ARE THE ONES JAMESON PAYS THE MOST FOR!

I WAS AFRAID OF THIS! YOU'RE BEGINNING TO ENJOY THE DANGER--THE EXCITEMENT! JUST LIKE--SOMEONE ELSE I ONCE KNEW--
I WISH I KNEW WHAT REALLY BOTHERS HER! IF ONLY SHE'D TELL ME SOME DAY!
14

MINUTES LATER, NO LONGER BURDENED BY WORRY OVER HIS AUNT, THE WORLD'S MOST DRAMATIC COSTUMED FIGURE STREAKS OVER THE ROOFTOPS OF NEW YORK--HIS HEART POUNDING WITH EXCITEMENT--HIS EVERY NERVE TINGLING WITH THE THRILL OF IMPENDING BATTLE!
AND NOW FOR--ELECTRO!

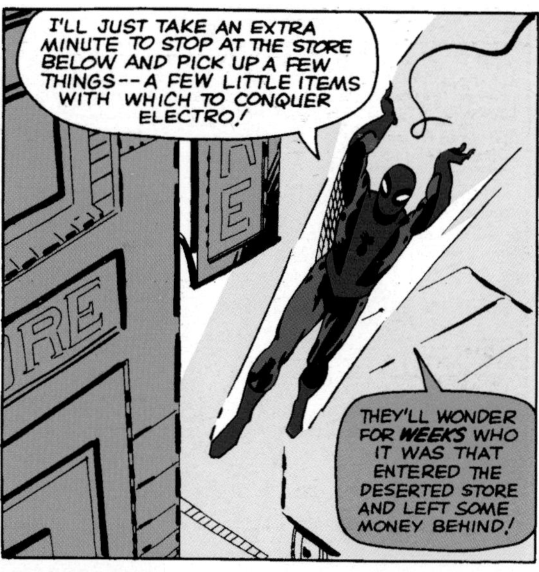
I'LL JUST TAKE AN EXTRA MINUTE TO STOP AT THE STORE BELOW AND PICK UP A FEW THINGS--A FEW LITTLE ITEMS WITH WHICH TO CONQUER ELECTRO!
THEY'LL WONDER FOR WEEKS WHO IT WAS THAT ENTERED THE DESERTED STORE AND LEFT SOME MONEY BEHIND!

AND, JUST A FEW MINUTES LATER...
NO SIGN OF SPIDER-MAN! THIS PROVES HE'S REALLY ELECTRO! I'LL PROBABLY WIN THE PULITZER PRIZE FOR MY SCOOP!!
THAT FOOL PARKER DOESN'T KNOW IT, BUT I'D HAVE PAID TWENTY THOUSAND DOLLARS FOR THOSE PICTURES!!
LOOK!! UP THERE --ON THE ROOF!!

HUH? UP WHERE??
OH NO!! NO!! IT CAN'T BE! IT CAN'T!!

THIS RUINS EVERYTHING! SPIDER-MAN ISN'T ELECTRO! ELECTRO IS STILL INSIDE!! I WAS WRONG!! WRONG!!
I'LL BE A LAUGHING STOCK! AND ALL BECAUSE OF PETER PARKER!

I HOPE ELECTRO HASN'T FLED YET! I'M LOOKING FORWARD TO THIS!

BETTER PUT ON THESE RUBBERS--AND THE RUBBER GLOVES I GOT AT THE STORE, TO HELP INSULATE MYSELF AGAINST HIM!

AND I'LL POSITION MY AUTOMATIC CAMERA TO GET SOME PICTURES OF WHAT-EVER TAKES PLACE!
15

AND, JUST A FEW FEET AWAY...
YOU MEN SAW WHAT HAPPENED TO THE FOOLS WHO TRIED TO ESCAPE WITHOUT OBEYING MY ORDERS!! THEY WERE ALL RECAPTURED!
BUT, IF YOU DO EXACTLY AS I SAY--AND PROMISE TO WORK FOR ME--I'LL FREE YOU ALL!
WE'RE WITH YOU, ELECTRO! JUST GET US OUTTA HERE!

GOOD! NOW HERE'S WHAT WE'LL--
WHAT'S THAT??? NO--IT CAN'T BE! H-HE'S DEAD!
IT'S THE SIGN OF THE SPIDER!! SPIDER-MAN IS HERE!!

I KNOW IT'S BAD MANNERS TO DROP IN WITHOUT AN INVITATION, BUT I'M SURE YOU'LL FORGIVE ME JUST THIS ONCE!

YOU SURVIVED MY ATTACK ONCE, SPIDER-MAN--BUT I WON'T BE SO CARELESS A SECOND TIME!
JUST STAY THERE AND KEEP TALKING, MISTER! I'LL GET TO YOU IN A MINUTE!

OKAY--THAT'LL STOP YOUR PLAYMATES FOR A WHILE! AND NOW--
LET'S SEE YOU DODGE THIS ELECTRIC BOLT, YOU OVER-CONFIDENT BRAGGART!
HE'S TOSSING METAL BEARINGS IN FRONT OF HIM! THEY'LL DEFLECT THE POWER OF THE BOLT!

ANYONE WITH ANY KNOWLEDGE OF SCIENCE KNOWS THAT ANYTHING METAL CAN ACT LIKE A LIGHTNING ROD--AS THIS STEEL CHAIR IS DOING!
YOU'RE WASTING YOUR TIME! MY CURRENT IS INEXHAUSTIBLE--AND YOU'LL SOON RUN OUT OF THINGS TO THROW!
16

YOU KIDDIN'?? I'M NOT GONNA SPEND ALL DAY TOSSING THINGS AT YOU!
THESE RUBBER GLOVES I'M WEARING WILL GIVE ME A CHANCE TO MASSAGE YOUR CHIN WHISKERS A WHILE--LIKE THIS!
THUD!

BUT, AS ELECTRO REELS BACK, BRUSHING AGAINST THE METAL CELL BARS, THE FLASH OF INTENSE CURRENT TEMPORARILY BLINDS SPIDER-MAN!
MY EYES-- CAN'T SEE!
HAH! ELECTRIC CURRENT REVITALIZES ME! NOW I'LL BE STRONGER THAN EVER!

I'VE GOT TO KEEP HIM AWAY TILL MY EYES CLEAR! THESE STEEL BEARINGS --THEY'LL DO THE TRICK!
HERE, SPARKY! KICK THESE AROUND FOR A WHILE!
BAH! IT'S THOSE BLASTED BEARINGS AGAIN!!!

I'LL STOP 'IM FOR YA, ELECTRO!! HEY--! WHA--??
DIDN'T THINK ANYONE WOULD BE DUMB ENOUGH TO TRY TO SNEAK UP BEHIND A FELLA WITH A SPIDER SENSE!!

IF IT'S ANY CONSOLATION TO YOU, CHUM-- I'M PULLING MY PUNCH ALL I CAN! I ONLY WANT TO KNOCK YOU OUT--NOT DEMOLISH YOU!
WHAM!

WONDER WHERE ELECTRO DISAPPEARED TO?
UH OH! THE OTHER PRISONERS ARE TRYING TO ESCAPE VIA THE ROOF! I BETTER HEAD 'EM OFF--FAST! HAVEN'T PLAYED LEAP-FROG SINCE I WAS A KID!
17

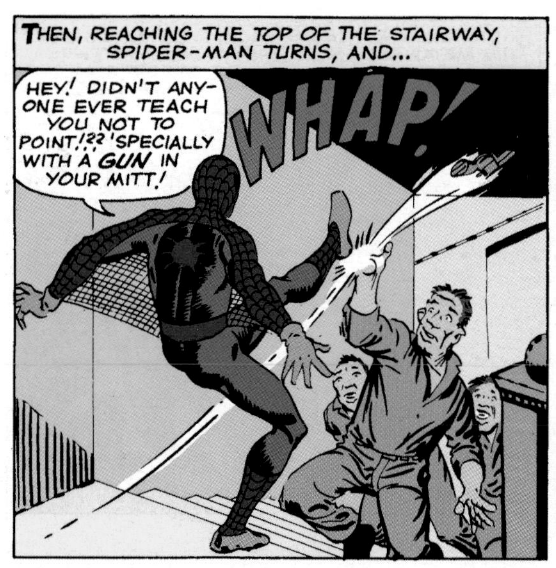

THEN, REACHING THE TOP OF THE STAIRWAY, SPIDER-MAN TURNS, AND...
HEY! DIDN'T ANYONE EVER TEACH YOU NOT TO POINT!?? 'SPECIALLY WITH A GUN IN YOUR MITT!
WHAP!

LET'S GET DOWN AGAIN! WE CAN'T TACKLE SPIDER-MAN!
ANYTHING'S BETTER THAN FACIN' HIM!
WE DIDN'T REALIZE HOW SOFT WE HAD IT IN OUR NICE, QUIET CELLS!

LOOK OUT! THE POLICE ARE DOWN HERE!!
YOU WERE EXPECTING MAYBE THE PONY EXPRESS??
I THINK WE'VE GOT 'EM ALL NOW--BUT ELECTRO'S STILL AT LARGE!

AND, SPEAKING OF ELECTRO--
WELL, WELL! LOOK WHO'S HERE! SO YOU WERE GONE BUT NOT FORGOTTEN, EH?

YOU MOVE PRETTY FAST, SPIDER-MAN! BUT HOW LONG DO YOU THINK YOU CAN KEEP DODGING ELECTRIC BOLTS BEFORE YOU COLLAPSE FROM SHEER EXHAUSTION??
LONG ENOUGH TO WRAP YOU UP, BIG MOUTH!

WELL, LITTLE MAN, I HAVE ANOTHER SURPRISE FOR YOU! I CAUGHT THE GUN THAT YOU KICKED DOWNSTAIRS! AND NOW WE'LL FIND OUT WHETHER A BULLET, OR AN ELECTRIC BOLT, CAN GET YOU FIRST!
AND WHAT DO YOU THINK I'LL BE DOING? STANDING AROUND AND WAITING FOR YOU?
18

HERE'S A BUCKET OF SAND FOR YOU TO CHEW ON WHILE YOU'RE MAKING UP THAT SLOW-WITTED MIND OF YOURS!
FIRE

IS THAT THE BEST YOU CAN DO? DON'T YOU KNOW THAT ELECTRIC CURRENT CAN TURN SAND TO GLASS?

SURE I KNOW IT! BUT WHILE YOU'RE BUSY SHOWING OFF, IT GIVES ME TIME TO SHOOT MY WEB AT YOUR GUN-- JAMMING IT SO YOU CAN'T FIRE! DO I MAKE MYSELF CLEAR??

LIVID WITH RAGE AND FRUSTRATION, ELECTRO SUDDENLY RIPS SOME HIGHLY CHARGED POWER WIRES FROM THE WALL, WHIRLING THEM MENACINGLY AROUND HIS HEAD!
YOU'VE MOCKED ME FOR THE LAST TIME! ANY ONE OF THESE WIRES, IF IT TOUCHES YOUR BODY, WILL RID THE EARTH OF SPIDER-MAN--FOREVER!

THIS IS SERIOUS! I CAN DEFLECT SOME OF THEM WITH MY RUBBER GLOVES-- BUT IF ONE TOUCHES MY BODY, IT'S CURTAINS FOR ME!

HE'S GETTING CLOSER! CAN'T BACK UP ANY FURTHER! WHAT HAVE I BUMPED INTO BEHIND ME???
19

IT'S A WATER MAIN--WITH A FIRE HOSE ATTACHED!!
SAY!! WHAT KIND OF SCIENCE MAJOR AM I, ANYWAY?? WHY DIDN'T I THINK OF THIS RIGHT AWAY??

WATER AND ELECTRICITY JUST DON'T MIX!!! NOW, IF I CAN JUST HIT THE MARK IN TIME!!

I DID IT!! IT'S A REAL SHORT-CIRCUIT! IT STOPPED HIM COLD!

LIFE SURE IS FUNNY! HERE'S ONE OF THE MOST POWERFUL CRIMINALS OF ALL TIME! AND WHAT FINALLY BEAT HIM?? JUST A DOUSING FROM A PLAIN, ORDINARY WATER HOSE!
MIGHT AS WELL REMOVE HIS MASK AND SEE WHO HE IS!

IF THIS WAS A MOVIE, I'D GASP IN SHOCK AND THEN I'D SAY: "GOOD HEAVENS! THE BUTLER!"
BUT THIS GUY I NEVER SAW BEFORE!
OH WELL, IT WON'T TAKE THE POLICE LONG TO FIND OUT WHO HE IS!

IN FACT, I CAN HEAR THEM COMING NOW! BETTER GET MY CAMERA AND GET OUT OF HERE!
HOPE THE PIX CAME OUT OKAY! IT'LL BE THE SCOOP OF THE YEAR!
20

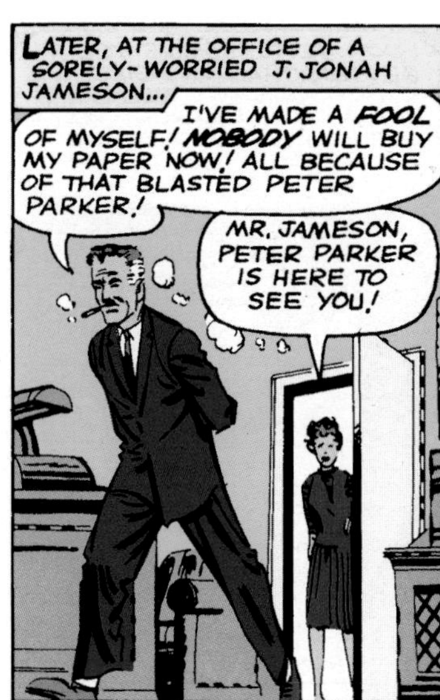
LATER, AT THE OFFICE OF A SORELY-WORRIED J. JONAH JAMESON...
I'VE MADE A FOOL OF MYSELF! NOBODY WILL BUY MY PAPER NOW! ALL BECAUSE OF THAT BLASTED PETER PARKER!
MR. JAMESON, PETER PARKER IS HERE TO SEE YOU!

PARKER!! YOU MEAN HE DARES TO SHOW HIS MISERABLE FACE AROUND HERE! SHOW THAT BLANKETTY-BLANK ★!?✱-×!? IN HERE! I'LL MAKE MINCE MEAT OF HIM!! WELL--DON'T JUST STAND THERE!!
Y-YES, SIR!! N-NO, SIR! YES SIR!

PARKER, BEFORE I FIRE YOU, I'M GONNA TELL YOU SOMETHING! I'M SUING YOU FOR FAKE PICTURES--FOR FRAUD--FOR--FOR--ANYTHING I CAN THINK OF!
RELAX, J.J.J.! YOU'RE NOT FIRING ME --AND YOU'RE NOT SUING ME!
WHAT??!!! WHO DO YOU THINK YOU'RE TALKING TO??

I'M TALKING TO A MAN WHO CAN'T FIRE ME BECAUSE I'M ONLY A FREE-LANCER! WE HAVEN'T GOT A CONTRACT! AND I'M ALSO TALKING TO A MAN WHO'S GONNA WHISTLE A DIFFERENT TUNE WHEN HE SEES THE PICTURES I HAVE FOR HIM!
MORE PICTURES? WH-WHAT KIND?

SEE FOR YOURSELF, MR. JAMESON! STILL WANNA SUE ME??
ACTION SHOTS OF ELECTRO FIGHTING SPIDER-MAN!! THEY'RE THE REAL THING! THEY'RE WORTH A FORTUNE!!

PARKER, YOU LITTLE OL' SON OF A GUN! YOU DIDN'T THINK I WAS REALLY ANGRY, -HEH HEH- DID YOU?
OF COURSE NOT, J.J.J.! EVERYONE KNOWS YOU NEVER LOSE YOUR TEMPER! YOU'RE THE MOST KIND-HEARTED, LOVEABLE PUBLISHER IN THE BUSINESS!

YEAH! -HEH HEH!- IT'S WRITTEN ALL OVER ME, ISN'T IT! NOW, JUST BECAUSE I'M ALL HEART, I'LL TELL YOU WHAT I'LL DO--I'LL TAKE THESE PICTURES FROM YOU AND I'LL FORGIVE YOU FOR THE OTHER PICTURES! FAIR ENOUGH??

PERFECT! NOW I'LL FEEL I'VE MADE UP FOR SELLING HIM THOSE FAKED PHOTOS BEFORE!
OKAY, MR. JAMESON --IT'S A DEAL!
I'M ROBBING HIM! I'LL MAKE A FORTUNE WITH HIS PICTURES! BUT I DESERVE IT--'CAUSE HE'S A FOOL!
21

AND, THE INSTANT PETER PARKER WALKS OUT OF HIS OFFICE...
STOP THE PRESSES!! PREPARE TO REPRINT PAGE ONE!! SEND ALL DEPARTMENT HEADS IN HERE ON THE DOUBLE!
WE'RE GOING TO PUT OUT AN EXTRA!!

SO--YOU DIDN'T PAY ANY ATTENTION TO ME! YOU WENT TO THE HOUSE OF DETENTION TO TAKE PICTURES AFTER ALL!
AW, DON'T BE ANGRY, BETTY! IT'S MY JOB!

LOOK, BETTY--I LIKE YOU BETTER THAN ANY GIRL I'VE EVER KNOWN! I WOULDN'T DO ANYTHING TO HURT YOU! BUT YOU CAN'T STOP ME FROM DOING WHAT I HAVE TO!

PETER, I NEVER TOLD YOU WHY I LEFT HIGH SCHOOL LAST YEAR AND TOOK A JOB! I NEVER TOLD YOU ABOUT SOMEONE I ONCE KNEW WHO--WHO REMINDED ME OF YOU! BUT I DON'T WANT TO BE HURT AGAIN!

OKAY, BETTY! I GET THE MESSAGE! SO I'M NOT MR. PERFECT! SORRY TO HAVE BOTHERED YOU!
NO! PETER--WAIT! YOU DON'T UNDERSTAND!

MINUTES LATER...
THE DOCTOR SAID I CAN GO HOME IN A FEW DAYS, PETER DEAR! BUT WHERE IS THAT NICE BETTY BRANT? SHE'S SUCH A SWEET GIRL!
HUH? OH, HER--SHE WAS KIND OF BUSY TODAY! ASKED ME TO GIVE YOU HER REGARDS!

FATE CAN SURE HAND A GUY SOME HARD KNOCKS!
I GOT MORE OF A SHOCK OUT OF BETTY FLARING UP, THAN I DID OUT OF ELECTRO! BUT I DIDN'T MEAN TO WALK OUT ON HER! WHAT GOT INTO ME?
22

I'LL HAVE TO APOLOGIZE TO HER! IF SHE EVER GOT MAD AT ME, I COULDN'T TAKE IT! NEVER REALIZED HOW MUCH I LIKE HER--NEED HER--HUH--WHO'S THAT?
PETER! WAIT--I-I'M SORRY FOR WHAT I SAID! PLEASE DON'T BE ANGRY!

AND SO, TWO THOUGHTFUL, SLIGHTLY CONFUSED YOUNG PEOPLE WALK OFF INTO THE DUSK... EACH GROPING FOR THE RIGHT WORDS TO SAY... EACH FEELING THE FIRST PANGS OF THAT EMOTION WE CALL--LOVE!
NEXT ISSUE: MORE FASCINATING DETAILS ABOUT THE LIFE AND ADVENTURES OF THE WORLD'S MOST AMAZING TEEN-AGER--SPIDER-MAN--THE SUPER-HERO WHO COULD BE--YOU!
THE END

the AMAZING SPIDER-MAN
IND.
APPROVED BY THE COMICS CODE AUTHORITY
MARVEL COMICS GROUP 12¢
10 MAR.
NEVER HAS ANYONE FOUGHT SUCH MERCILESS FOES AS...
"THE ENFORCERS!"
IN THIS ISSUE:
LEARN WHY J. JONAH JAMESON REALLY HATES SPIDER-MAN!

HOW CAN ONE LONE CRIME-FIGHTER, THOUGH POSSESSING THE POWER OF COUNTLESS SPIDERS, HOPE TO DEFEAT

"THE ENFORCERS!"

CAUTION! THINK TWICE BEFORE STARTING THIS MOVIE-LENGTH TALE! WE FEEL IT ONLY FAIR TO WARN YOU... ONCE YOU HAVE READ IT... ONCE YOU HAVE SAVORED THE THRILLS AND SURPRISES WHICH ONLY SPIDER-MAN CAN PROVIDE... YOU MAY FIND IT DIFFICULT TO EVER AGAIN BE SATISFIED BY LESSER MAGAZINES!

who is THE BIG MAN?
WITH THIS CLASSIC TALE, THE MARVEL AGE OF COMICS REACHES A NEW PLATEAU OF GREATNESS!!
WRITTEN BY: SMILING STAN LEE
ILLUSTRATED BY: SWINGING STEVE DITKO
LETTERED BY: SPARKLING SAM ROSEN

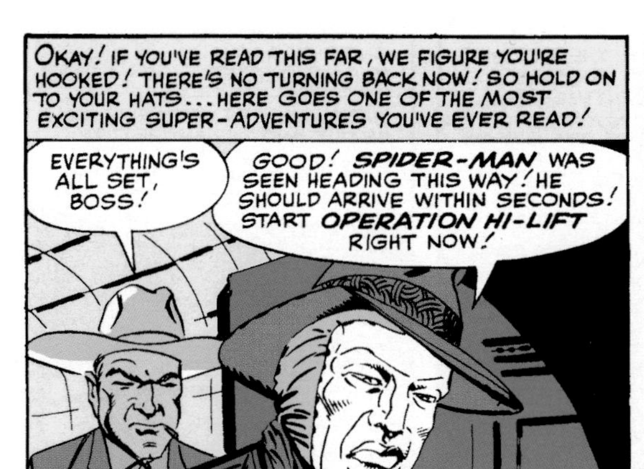
OKAY! IF YOU'VE READ THIS FAR, WE FIGURE YOU'RE HOOKED! THERE'S NO TURNING BACK NOW! SO HOLD ON TO YOUR HATS... HERE GOES ONE OF THE MOST EXCITING SUPER-ADVENTURES YOU'VE EVER READ!
EVERYTHING'S ALL SET, BOSS!
GOOD! SPIDER-MAN WAS SEEN HEADING THIS WAY! HE SHOULD ARRIVE WITHIN SECONDS! START OPERATION HI-LIFT RIGHT NOW!

AT A SIGNAL FROM THE MYSTERIOUS MASKED MAN, A PROFESSIONAL BURGLAR CAUTIOUSLY CLIMBS TOWARD THE END OF A LONG FLAGPOLE ...
COME BACK WITH THOSE JEWELS! YOU HAVEN'T A CHANCE OUT THERE!
I WOULDN'T MAKE BOOK ON THAT IF I WERE YOU! THE BIG MAN PLANNED THIS CAPER, AND HE NEVER FAILS!

AT THAT MOMENT, THE WORLD'S MOST DRAMATIC SUPER-HERO WITNESSES THE STRANGE SCENE, AND THEN...
IF THAT JOKER'S TRYING TO ESCAPE FROM THE POLICE, HE'S DOING IT THE HARD WAY!

I'D BETTER GRAB HIM BEFORE HE FALLS AND...
HEY! WHAT'S GOING ON?!!
IT WORKED! SPIDER-MAN NEVER SUSPECTED I HAD A CABLE WRAPPED AROUND ME!!

WE CAUGHT SPIDER-MAN FLAT-FOOTED, BOSS, JUST LIKE YOU SAID!
NATURALLY! THAT'S WHY I'M THE BIG MAN! HAUL HIM IN... FAST!

DON'T KNOW WHAT IT'S ALL ABOUT, BUT NOBODY MAKES A SAP OUT OF ME!
I'LL SWING AROUND THIS FLAGPOLE ON MY WEB, TO GET UP SOME STEAM, AND THEN...

I'LL GET HIM BEFORE HE CAN ESCAPE IN THAT HIDDEN WHIRLEY-BIRD!

BUT BEFORE SPIDER-MAN CAN ATTACH HIMSELF TO THE HOVERING HELICOPTER, AN UNEXPECTED BLAST OF BLINDING CHEMICAL FOAM MEETS HIM HEAD ON!
OOF! TH-THEY WERE PREPARED FOR MY CLUMSY ATTACK!
2.

THE CHAGRINED CRUSADER BREAKS HIS FALL BY QUICKLY FASHIONING A CRUDE PARACHUTE OUT OF HIS AMAZING WEB, AS HE BITTERLY THINKS...
I SURE WON'T WIN ANY MEDALS FOR THE DUMB-HEAD WAY I MUFFED THAT JOB!

AND DOWN BELOW, THE WATCHING CROWD SEEMS TO SHARE SPIDER-MAN'S SENTIMENTS...
BOY! HE SURE GOOFED THAT ONE!
SOME SUPER-HERO HE IS! HE'S JUST A BIG CLOWN!
THE GUY ON THE FLAG-POLE GOT AWAY SCOT FREE!

AND, HIGH ABOVE, IN THE HELICOPTER...
WITHIN MINUTES, THE NEWS WILL BE OUT AND THE ENTIRE CITY WILL KNOW HOW WE MADE A FOOL OF SPIDER-MAN! NOW HEAD FOR THE HIDEOUT!

A SHORT TIME LATER, THE BIG MAN ENTERS A SMOKE-FILLED ROOM...
IT'S ABOUT TIME YOU GOT HERE!
WE'VE GOT OUR OWN GANGS TO TAKE CARE OF! WE'RE NOT USED TO WAITIN' FOR ANYONE!
SILENCE! I CALLED THIS MEETING TO INFORM YOU THAT I'M TAKING OVER ALL THE RACKETS IN THE CITY! FROM NOW ON, THE BIG MAN IS HEAD OF THE CRIME SYNDICATE!

I'M GOING TO RUN THIS LITTLE ENTERPRISE LIKE A BIG BUSINESS!
AS BOSS OF OUR ORGANIZATION, I'LL GIVE ALL THE ORDERS!
...AND MY ENFORCERS HERE WILL MAKE SURE THAT MY ORDERS ARE CARRIED OUT! ANY QUESTIONS?

LOOK, BIG MAN, YOU'RE NOT TALKING TO KIDS!
NOBODY IS GONNA TELL ME WHAT TO DO! I'M CUTTIN' OUT!
THAT GOES FOR ME, TOO!
I BEG TO DIFFER, GENTLEMEN! ENFORCERS! CHANGE THEIR MINDS!

FIRST, LET ME PRESENT FANCY DAN! THOUGH SMALL, HIS FOOTWORK IS SO FAST AND DAZZLING, THAT NO ONE CAN LAY A HAND ON HIM WHILE HE PERFORMS LITTLE ODD JOBS FOR ME... SUCH AS THIS!

IF YOU ARE WONDERING HOW SUCH A LITTLE MAN CAN BE SO DANGEROUS, YOU MAY BE INTERESTED IN KNOWING THAT FANCY DAN IS A MASTER OF JUDO, AND ENTITLED TO WEAR THE COVETED BLACK BELT!
3.

NEXT, I'D LIKE YOU TO MEET THE OX! THOUGH HE IS SLOW AND PONDEROUS, YOUR PUNY BLOWS HAVE NO EFFECT ON HIM!

AND ANYONE WHO DARES TO INCUR HIS WRATH RARELY REMAINS CONSCIOUS LONG ENOUGH TO WORRY ABOUT IT!

FINALLY, MY THIRD ENFORCER HAS HIS OWN METHOD OF DEALING WITH OUR ENEMIES! SHOW THEM, MONTANA!

IN THE HANDS OF AN EXPERT LIKE MONTANA, HIS LASSO RESEMBLES A LIVING THING, COMPLETELY OBEDIENT TO ITS MASTER'S WILL!

YOU ALL KNOW HOW I OUT-SMARTED SPIDER-MAN EARLIER TODAY! AND YOU HAVE SEEN WHAT HAPPENS TO ANYONE FOOLISH ENOUGH TO RESIST ME...OR MY ENFORCERS!
OUR MEETING IS NOW ADJOURNED! YOU WILL RECEIVE FURTHER ORDERS FROM ME VERY SOON! UNDER MY LEADERSHIP, AIDED BY MY ENFORCERS, WE HAVE A GLORIOUS FUTURE AHEAD OF US!

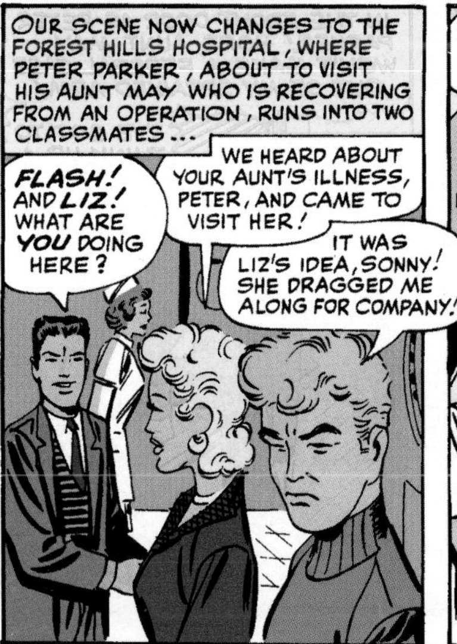
OUR SCENE NOW CHANGES TO THE FOREST HILLS HOSPITAL, WHERE PETER PARKER, ABOUT TO VISIT HIS AUNT MAY WHO IS RECOVERING FROM AN OPERATION, RUNS INTO TWO CLASSMATES...
FLASH! AND LIZ! WHAT ARE YOU DOING HERE?
WE HEARD ABOUT YOUR AUNT'S ILLNESS, PETER, AND CAME TO VISIT HER!
IT WAS LIZ'S IDEA, SONNY! SHE DRAGGED ME ALONG FOR COMPANY!

POOR FLASH! HE'S SO AFRAID I MIGHT FIND OUT HE'S REALLY GOT A HEART SOMEWHERE UNDER THAT THICK SKIN!
YOUR AUNT IS DOING AS WELL AS CAN BE EXPECTED, SON, AFTER HER OPERATION... BUT SHE DOES NEED A BLOOD TRANSFUSION! WHAT IS YOUR BLOOD TYPE?
A TRANSFUSION! I DON'T DARE GIVE MY BLOOD!

I GAINED MY SPIDER-STRENGTH BECAUSE OF THE BITE FROM A RADIOACTIVE SPIDER! IT AFFECTED MY BLOOD! BUT NO ONE MUST EVER KNOW!
I..I DON'T THINK I CAN DO IT, DOC!
PETER! IT'S YOUR OWN AUNT!
'S'MATTER? SCARED OF THE BIG BAD NEEDLE?
LIZ IS RIGHT! I MUST DO IT... NO MATTER WHAT! I CAN'T FAIL AUNT MAY!
4.

LUCKY FOR ME MY BLOOD CHECKED OUT OKAY! THE TESTS DIDN'T REVEAL MY SUPER QUALITIES!
JUST LIE THERE AND RELAX, SON! THIS WILL GIVE YOUR AUNT THE STRENGTH SHE NEEDS!

IF MY STRENGTH COMES FROM MY BLOOD, WHICH WAS AFFECTED BY THE SPIDER'S BITE, HOW WILL THIS TRANSFUSION AFFECT ME? I'LL PROBABLY BE SOME-WHAT WEAKENED FOR A WHILE, UNTIL THE BLOOD CELLS CAN REBUILD THEMSELVES!

AND THEN...
THAT'S IT, PETER! TAKE IT EASY FOR A FEW DAYS UNTIL YOU GET BACK TO NORMAL!
SURE, DOC! I WILL!
HOPE I WON'T BE NEEDED AS SPIDER-MAN FOR A WHILE! OH WELL, THE MAIN THING IS THAT AUNT MAY IS GETTING BETTER!

FINALLY...
THANKS TO YOU, PETER DEAR, THE DOCTOR SAYS I CAN LEAVE HERE, SHORTLY!
THAT'S GREAT, AUNT MAY! THE ABBOTTS, NEXT DOOR, WANT YOU TO JOIN THEM FOR A WEEK ON A TRIP TO FLORIDA! IT'LL BE JUST WHAT YOU NEED!

HOW WONDERFUL! THEY'RE SUCH WARM-HEARTED PEOPLE! BUT WHO'LL LOOK AFTER YOU, PETER?
I'LL BE OKAY, AUNT MAY! I'LL KEEP BUSY WITH MY SCHOOL WORK AND MY CHORES!

THUS, A SHORT TIME LATER...
TAKE CARE OF YOURSELF, PETER, DEAR! WEAR YOUR RUBBERS IN THE RAIN, AND BE SURE TO DRESS WARM ENOUGH! I PUT YOUR NOSE DROPS IN THE MEDICINE CHEST, AND...
SURE, AUNT MAY! JUST GET LOTS OF SUN AND DON'T WORRY ABOUT ME!
WE'LL TAKE GOOD CARE OF HER, PETE!

BUT, AS PETER'S AUNT HEADS SOUTH, A NEW CRIME WAVE BEGINS TO ERUPT IN THE CITY! UNDER THE LEADERSHIP OF THE MYSTERIOUS BIG MAN, A WELL-ORGANIZED AND POWERFUL NETWORK OF UNDERWORLD MOBS SEEM TO STRIKE EVERYWHERE AT ONCE!!
5.

POOLING THEIR FINANCIAL RESOURCES, THE CITY'S CRIMINALS SPARE NO EXPENSE IN BATTLING LAW AND ORDER...
IT'S UNBELIEVABLE!! THEY'RE LIFTING THE ENTIRE MAIL CAR INTO THE AIR BY MEANS OF THREE HELICOPTERS!
NO ONE SEEMS TO KNOW WHERE, OR HOW, THEY'LL STRIKE NEXT!

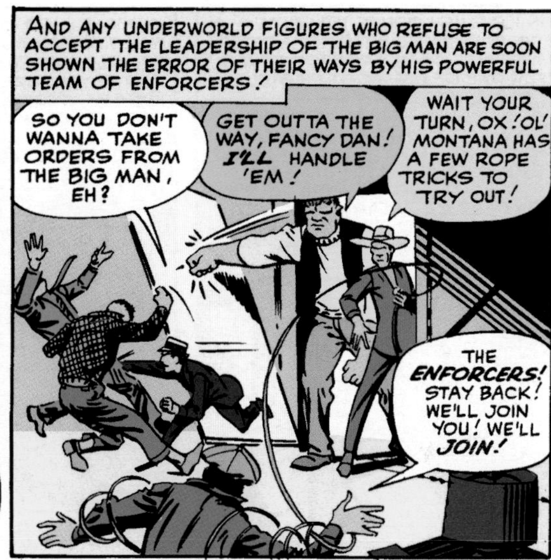
AND ANY UNDERWORLD FIGURES WHO REFUSE TO ACCEPT THE LEADERSHIP OF THE BIG MAN ARE SOON SHOWN THE ERROR OF THEIR WAYS BY HIS POWERFUL TEAM OF ENFORCERS!
SO YOU DON'T WANNA TAKE ORDERS FROM THE BIG MAN, EH?
GET OUTTA THE WAY, FANCY DAN! I'LL HANDLE 'EM!
WAIT YOUR TURN, OX! OL' MONTANA HAS A FEW ROPE TRICKS TO TRY OUT!
THE ENFORCERS! STAY BACK! WE'LL JOIN YOU! WE'LL JOIN!

PATIENTLY, SPIDER-MAN ROAMS THE CITY BY NIGHT, SEARCHING FOR SOME CLUE, SOME TRACE OF THE BIG MAN'S TRUE IDENTITY... BUT HIS QUEST SEEMS HOPELESS...
THE POLICE ARE DOING A GREAT JOB... WORKING NIGHT AND DAY!
THAT'S THE FIFTH BUNCH OF MOBSTERS THEY'VE GRABBED TODAY... BUT THEY'RE ALL AFRAID TO TALK! THEY'RE TERRIFIED OF THE BIG MAN AND HIS ENFORCERS!

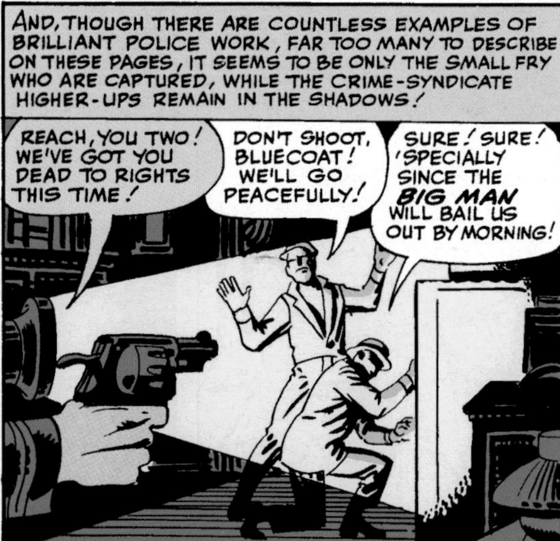
AND, THOUGH THERE ARE COUNTLESS EXAMPLES OF BRILLIANT POLICE WORK, FAR TOO MANY TO DESCRIBE ON THESE PAGES, IT SEEMS TO BE ONLY THE SMALL FRY WHO ARE CAPTURED, WHILE THE CRIME-SYNDICATE HIGHER-UPS REMAIN IN THE SHADOWS!
REACH, YOU TWO! WE'VE GOT YOU DEAD TO RIGHTS THIS TIME!
DON'T SHOOT, BLUECOAT! WE'LL GO PEACEFULLY!
SURE! SURE! 'SPECIALLY SINCE THE BIG MAN WILL BAIL US OUT BY MORNING!

AND THERE IS STILL ONE OTHER WHO ALSO ROAMS THE STREETS, SEARCHING ENDLESSLY FOR NEWS! IT IS J. JONAH JAMESON, THE HARD-HEADED PUBLISHER OF THE DAILY BUGLE AND NOW MAGAZINE...
ANOTHER ARREST, I SEE! BAH! IT'S A WASTE OF TIME BRINGING IN SUCH SMALL FISH! SPIDER-MAN IS THE ONE YOU SHOULD BE GOING AFTER! HE MUST BE MIXED UP IN ALL THIS SOMEHOW!

LOOK, MR. JAMESON... WHY DON'T YOU FORGET YOUR PERSONAL FEUD WITH SPIDER-MAN AND USE THE POWER OF YOUR PAPER TO HELP US NAB THE BIG MAN?! ASK YOUR READERS TO REPORT ANYTHING SUSPICIOUS!
NONSENSE! THERE IS NO BIG MAN! NOBODY'S EVER SEEN HIM AND TOLD ABOUT IT! SPIDER-MAN INVENTED SUCH A CHARACTER, TO THROW EVERYONE OFF THE TRACK!
6.

IN HIS PLUSH OFFICE THE NEXT DAY, IN THE DAILY BUGLE BUILDING, A DETERMINED J. JONAH JAMESON SENDS FOR ONE OF HIS MOST CAPABLE COLUMNISTS...

FOSWELL, I WANT YOU TO WRITE A SERIES OF ARTICLES WHICH WILL PROVE THAT THE BIG MAN IS NONE OTHER THAN SPIDER-MAN HIMSELF!
BUT WE HAVEN'T ANY PROOF, MR. JAMESON! THE POLICE DON'T YET KNOW WHO HE IS!

AND IF YOU GO OUT ON A LIMB THE WAY YOU DID LAST MONTH WHEN YOU CLAIMED HE WAS ELECTRO,* AND IF YOU TURN OUT WRONG AGAIN, PEOPLE WILL LOSE CONFIDENCE IN OUR PAPER!
QUIET!! I'LL DO THE TALKING!

* SPIDER-MAN #9 FEB. "THE WRATH OF ELECTRO!"...ED.

I'M STILL RUNNING THIS PAPER, FOSWELL! NOW, DO AS I SAY, OR I'LL FIRE YOU AND SEE TO IT, THAT NO PAPER EVER HIRES YOU AGAIN!
I'LL DO IT, MR. JAMESON! I'VE GOTTEN INTO THE HABIT OF EATING THREE SQUARES A DAY!

I GUESS YOU HEARD THAT, BETTY! BOY, DOES HE HATE SPIDER-MAN!
I KNOW! I HAVE TO LISTEN TO HIM ALL DAY LONG! I'M GLAD IT'S QUITTING TIME NOW, FOSWELL!

AND, AS BETTY BRANT LEAVES THE BUGLE BUILDING AND WAITS OUT FRONT...
I WONDER IF PETER WILL BE PASSING BY AS HE SOMETIMES DOES?
THAT'S HER, YOU GUYS! THAT'S BETTY BRANT!
WELL, WHAT ARE WE WAITIN' FOR!?

YOU KNOW WHO WE ARE, SISTER! WHERE'S THE REST OF THE MONEY YOU OWE?
BUT I'VE ALREADY PAID OFF THE WHOLE LOAN!
SURE, BUT YOU FORGOT THE INTEREST! THE BIG MAN DOUBLED IT SINCE YESTERDAY!
NO! HE CAN'T DO THAT! IT ISN'T FAIR!

LADY, WHEN THE BIG MAN TOOK OVER EVERY RACKET IN TOWN... INCLUDING THE LOAN SHARK RACKET, HE DIDN'T DO IT FOR HIS HEALTH! NOW, I WARN YOU!
HEY! WHAT'S GOIN' ON THERE?

PETER! KEEP OUT OF THIS! GO AWAY! THEY'RE DANGEROUS!
BETTY, YOU'RE SCARED! IF THEY'RE BOTHERING YOU...
WELL, WELL! SO THE GAL HAS A BOY FRIEND, EH? THAT'S REAL NICE.. FOR US!

WE'RE TOO GENTLEMANLY TO THREATEN A FEMALE, BUT THE OX IS GONNA SHOW YOU WHAT'LL HAPPEN TO THAT SQUIRT IF YOU DON'T PAY UP!
LEAN ON 'IM A LITTLE, OX!
NO! NO! DON'T HURT HIM! I'LL GET THE MONEY SOMEHOW!
7.

LUCKY FOR YOU SHE SAID THAT, SONNY!
IF ONLY I COULD TURN INTO SPIDER-MAN NOW!! BUT IT WOULD GIVE MY SECRET IDENTITY AWAY!
LET 'IM GO, OX!

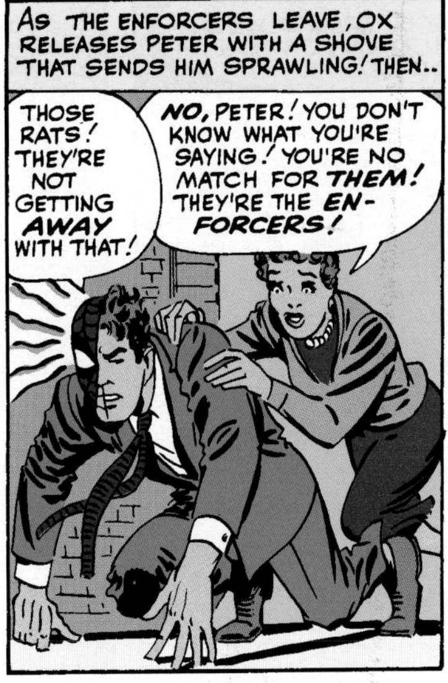
AS THE ENFORCERS LEAVE, OX RELEASES PETER WITH A SHOVE THAT SENDS HIM SPRAWLING! THEN..
THOSE RATS! THEY'RE NOT GETTING AWAY WITH THAT!
NO, PETER! YOU DON'T KNOW WHAT YOU'RE SAYING! YOU'RE NO MATCH FOR THEM! THEY'RE THE ENFORCERS!

THE ENFORCERS, EH? I'VE HEARD OF THEM! BUT HOW DID YOU GET INVOLVED?
I'M AFRAID TO TELL HIM THE TRUTH! IF HE KNOWS I FOOLISHLY BORROWED MONEY FROM A LOAN SHARK, HE'LL TRY TO HELP ME... AND HE'LL END UP GETTING HURT... OR WORSE!

I'M NOT INVOLVED, PETER! IT..IT WAS JUST A CASE OF MISTAKEN IDENTITY... THAT'S ALL!
BETTY!! YOU'RE NOT TELLING ME THE TRUTH! WAIT!! WHY WON'T YOU LEVEL WITH ME? BETTY!

I CAN'T DO IT! I CAN'T LET THE DEAREST, MOST WONDERFUL BOY I'VE EVER KNOWN GET MIXED UP WITH THE ENFORCERS BECAUSE OF ME!
I MUST HAVE BEEN WRONG ABOUT HER! SHE CAN'T CARE FOR ME IF SHE WON'T CONFIDE IN ME!

DEEPLY HURT... UNABLE TO UNDERSTAND THE MOTIVES OF THE GIRL HE LOVES, PETER PARKER CHANGES TO SPIDER-MAN WITHIN SECONDS, AS HIS LEAN, POWERFUL MUSCLES ACHE FOR BATTLE!!
AS PETER PARKER, I WAS JUST A HELPLESS, CONFUSED SCHOOL KID!
BUT AS SPIDER-MAN, THINGS ARE GONNA BE A LOT DIFFERENT... AS SOON AS I TRACK DOWN THE ENFORCERS!

THERE'S THE PUNK WHO POINTED OUT BETTY TO THEM!
HOLD IT, YOU WEASEL! I WANT TO TALK TO YOU!
HUH?!

IF YOU KNOW THE ENFORCERS, YOU PROBABLY KNOW WHERE I CAN FIND THEM! NOW TALK!
NO! NO! THEY'D KILL ME! YOU DON'T KNOW THEM... THEY FEAR NO ONE, BECAUSE THE BIG MAN IS BEHIND THEM!

HE'S TERRIFIED! HE TREMBLED AT THE VERY MENTION OF THE NAME OF THE ENFORCERS! ONLY ONE THING TO DO... I'VE GOT TO MAKE HIM FEAR SPIDER-MAN EVEN MORE!
I'LL JUST BLINDFOLD YOU WITH SOME WEBBING, AND THEN...
?
8.

MINUTES LATER, AFTER THE BLINDFOLD HAS BEEN REMOVED...
THIS WON'T DO YOU ANY GOOD, SPIDER-MAN! I DON'T SCARE EASY, AND... HEY!

YOU ARE IN MY SPIDER'S WEB! NOW, WILL YOU TALK, OR WON'T YOU ?
TH-THAT THING BEHIND YOU! D-DON'T LET IT COME ANY CLOSER... PLEASE...!!

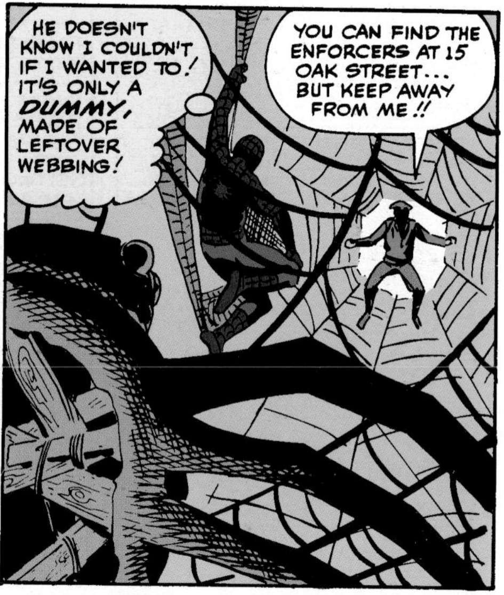
HE DOESN'T KNOW I COULDN'T IF I WANTED TO! IT'S ONLY A DUMMY, MADE OF LEFTOVER WEBBING!
YOU CAN FIND THE ENFORCERS AT 15 OAK STREET... BUT KEEP AWAY FROM ME !!

EXACTLY FIVE SECONDS LATER...
NOW TO GIVE THE ENFORCERS A LITTLE WORKOUT... AND HOPE THEY'LL LEAD ME TO THE BIG MAN HIMSELF!

THIS IS THE PLACE! I'LL JUST... HEY! WHA...??

I'VE BEEN LASSOED... LIKE A RUNAWAY STEER! ...BEING PULLED INTO THAT WINDOW!

GOOD WORK, MONTANA! AND NOW, GET RID OF SPIDER-MAN ONCE AND FOR ALL! I CAN'T HAVE HIM TRYING TO INTERFERE WITH MY PLANS!
THE BIG MAN! AND THE ENFORCERS! I'VE GOT YOU ALL TOGETHER!
CORRECTION, MY FRIEND! IT IS WE WHO HAVE YOU! GET HIM, OX!

EVEN A REAL OX COULDN'T "GET" ME, SO NO PHONY ONE IS GONNA DO IT!
AND YOU CAN'T CATCH SPIDER-MAN TWICE WITH THE SAME ROPE TRICK, MISTER!
WHUMPH!!
9.

A GUY YOUR SIZE MUST BE NUTS TO TRY TO TANGLE WITH ME!
HEY! I MISSED! NEVER SAW ANYONE MOVE SO FAST!
DON'T LET MY SIZE FOOL YOU, WISE-GUY! THEY DON'T CALL ME FANCY DAN FOR NOTHING!

AND THEY DON'T CALL ME SPIDER-MAN FOR NOTHING! FAST AS YOU ARE, MY SPIDER SENSE AND SPIDER REFLEXES WILL HELP ME TO NAIL YOU... LIKE THIS!
UH-OH! A LASSO ..!ROUND MY WRIST!

PULLING ME OFF BALANCE... CAN'T SHIFT MY WEIGHT IN TIME... CAN'T DUCK THIS --- OWW!
I BEEN WAITIN' TO LAND A HAY-MAKER ON SPIDER-MAN!

BUT, WHAT MIGHT BE A "HAYMAKER" TO ANYONE ELSE, JUST ANGERS SPIDER-MAN ENOUGH TO SPUR HIM TO STILL MORE DAZZLING FEATS, SUCH AS...
LOOK OUT! HE FLIPPED BACKWARDS.. THRU THE ROPE!

HE'S STRONG... AND SWIFT... BUT IT'S STILL THREE AGAINST ONE... AND WHEN A GUY AS FAST AS FANCY DAN IS ALSO A JUDO EXPERT, WHAT CHANCE CAN SPIDER-MAN HAVE?

STOP FLAPPIN' YOUR LIPS AND KEEP FIGHTIN'! HE'S A LONG WAY FROM BEIN' LICKED YET!

YOU SAID A MOUTHFUL, CUDDLES!
UNGHH!

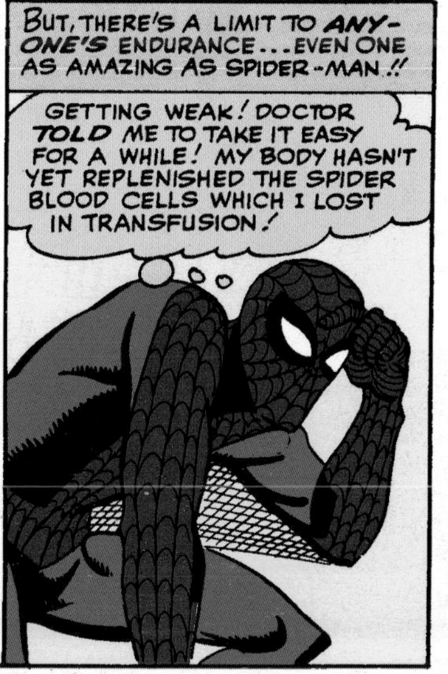
BUT, THERE'S A LIMIT TO ANY-ONE'S ENDURANCE... EVEN ONE AS AMAZING AS SPIDER-MAN!!
GETTING WEAK! DOCTOR TOLD ME TO TAKE IT EASY FOR A WHILE! MY BODY HASN'T YET REPLENISHED THE SPIDER BLOOD CELLS WHICH I LOST IN TRANSFUSION!

HATE TO HAVE 'EM THINK I'M RUNNING OUT ON A FIGHT, BUT I'VE GOT TO CUT OUT WHILE I STILL CAN!
10.

FIRST THING TO DO IS GET RID OF THE LIGHT!
WHERE'D HE GO?

WITH THE AID OF MY SPIDER-SENSE, IT'S A BREEZE FOR ME TO FIND MY WAY OUT IN THE DARK!
BUT I'D SURE LIKE TO KNOW WHERE THE BIG MAN DUCKED OUT TO DURING THE FIGHT!

MINUTES LATER, AS THE EXHAUSTED TEEN-AGER HIDES IN THE SHADOWS, CATCHING HIS BREATH, HE SEES...
IT'S JONAH JAMESON! WHAT'S HE DOING HERE? I WONDER...?!

THE BIG MAN WOULD HAVE TO BE SOME-ONE SMART, SOMEONE WITH MONEY... SOMEONE WHO KNOWS WHAT'S GOING ON! BUT I CAN'T BELIEVE THAT JONAH HIMSELF...

PUZZLED, SPIDER-MAN CHANGES TO PETER PARKER, RETURNS HOME, AND MAKES A PHONE CALL...
BETTY SHOULD BE HOME BY NOW! I'LL CALL AND ASK HER IF SHE KNOWS WHY JONAH WOULD HAVE BEEN IN THAT NEIGHBORHOOD!
HMM, SHE'S NOT ANSWERING THE PHONE! HOPE NOTHING'S WRONG!

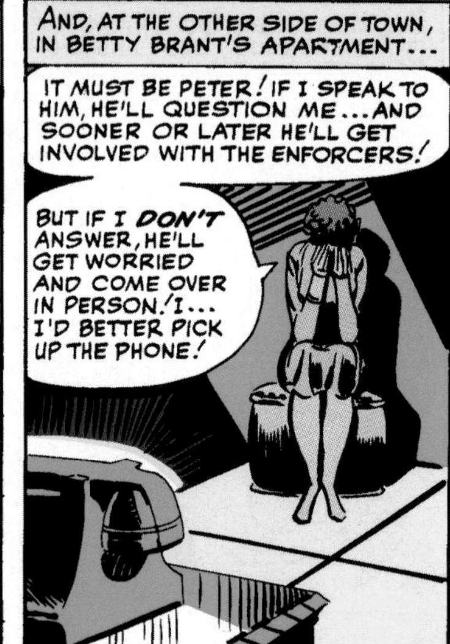
AND, AT THE OTHER SIDE OF TOWN, IN BETTY BRANT'S APARTMENT...
IT MUST BE PETER! IF I SPEAK TO HIM, HE'LL QUESTION ME...AND SOONER OR LATER HE'LL GET INVOLVED WITH THE ENFORCERS!
BUT IF I DON'T ANSWER, HE'LL GET WORRIED AND COME OVER IN PERSON! I... I'D BETTER PICK UP THE PHONE!

BETTY! ARE YOU ALL RIGHT? I WANT TO ASK YOU SOMETHING!
NO, PETER.. NOT NOW! I'LL SPEAK TO YOU TOMORROW! PLEASE!

I CAN'T LET HIM FALL INTO THE HANDS OF THE ENFORCERS BECAUSE OF ME!
THERE'S ONLY ONE THING TO DO...I'VE GOT TO LEAVE! NEVER SEE HIM AGAIN!

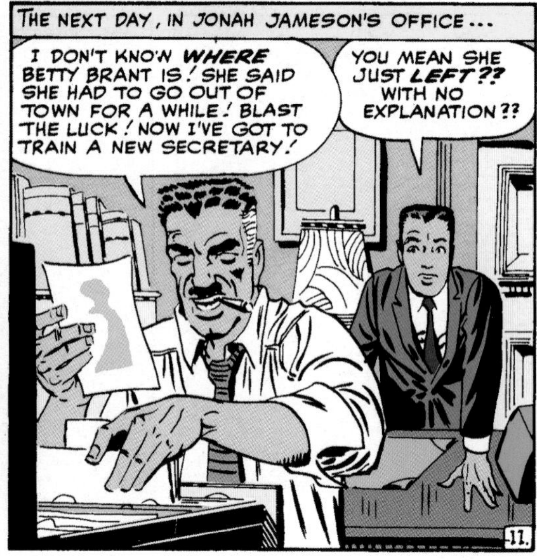
THE NEXT DAY, IN JONAH JAMESON'S OFFICE...
I DON'T KNOW WHERE BETTY BRANT IS! SHE SAID SHE HAD TO GO OUT OF TOWN FOR A WHILE! BLAST THE LUCK! NOW I'VE GOT TO TRAIN A NEW SECRETARY!
YOU MEAN SHE JUST LEFT?? WITH NO EXPLANATION??
11.

LOOK, KID, I'VE GOT MY OWN PROBLEMS! I'VE STILL GOT A NEWSPAPER TO GET OUT!
HIS HEART'S AS COLD AS AN ICE CUBE! HE DOESN'T CARE ABOUT ANY-ONE!

AS FOR YOU, I DON'T KEEP YOU AROUND BECAUSE I LIKE YOUR LOOKS! YOU'RE PAID TO GET PICTURES... SO GO GET SOME! AND TELL FOSWELL I'M WAITING FOR HIS NEW COLUMN ON SPIDER-MAN!

SECONDS LATER, IN FREDERICK FOSWELL'S OFFICE...
MR. FOSWELL, YOU DON'T REALLY BELIEVE THE JAZZ YOU WRITE ABOUT SPIDER-MAN BEING THE BIG MAN DO YOU?
LOOK, SON, I WRITE WHAT JAMESON TELLS ME TO! HE'S THE BOSS HERE!

I'D SAY THAT PETER RABBIT WAS THE BIG MAN IF HE TOLD ME TO! YOU DON'T WORK ON THIS NEWS-PAPER AND ARGUE WITH OL' PRUNE FACE!
I GUESS YOU'RE RIGHT... BUT IT SURE SEEMS UNFAIR!

WHY IS JAMESON SO ANXIOUS TO PUT SUSPICION ON SPIDER-MAN!? AND WHAT WAS HE DOING IN THE NEIGHBORHOOD WHERE THE ENFORCERS WERE?? CAN J.J.J. HIMSELF BE LEADING A DOUBLE LIFE??

BETTY'S RUN OUT ON ME!.. FOR SOME REASON I CAN'T FIGURE OUT!
AND THE BIG MAN IS GETTING A TIGHTER GRIP ON ALL THE RACKETS IN THE CITY, BECAUSE THE AVERAGE MAN IS TOO SCARED OF THE ENFORCERS TO REPORT THEM TO THE POLICE, OR TO DEFY THEM!
AND HERE I SIT WONDERING WHAT TO DO NEXT! SOME HOT SHOT SUPER-HERO I AM!

AS SPIDER-MAN, I MIGHT BE ABLE TO SMASH THE CRIME SYNDICATE... IF I COULD FIND THEIR MAIN HEADQUARTERS, AND LEARN WHO THE BIG MAN REALLY IS!
NUTS! THEY'RE NOT GOING TO SEND SPIDER-MAN AN INVITATION TO COME AND VISIT THEM... BUT PETER PARKER MAY BE ABLE TO GET HIMSELF CAPTURED BY THEM! IT'S DANGEROUS... BUT IT'S THE ONLY WAY!

AND SO, AT SCHOOL NEXT DAY, PETE PUTS HIS PERIL-OUS PLAN INTO OPERATION...
YOU MEAN TO SAY THAT YOU FIGURED OUT WHO THE BIG MAN IS, WHEN NOBODY ELSE HAS ANY IDEA?!! YOU'RE NUTS, PARKER!
YEAH? WELL, YOU'LL SING A DIFFERENT TUNE WHEN I TELL MY THEORY TO THE POLICE AND GET A BIG FAT REWARD FOR HELPING TO NAB HIM!
MAYBE OL' BOOKWARM PARKER DID FIGURE OUT THE BIG MAN'S IDENTITY! HE'S A WHIZ ON PUZZLES AND STUFF LIKE THAT!
12.

AWW, IF YOU ASK ME, PUNY PARKER IS JUST SHOWIN' OFF--LIKE HE ALWAYS TRIES TO DO!
PSSST! PETE--COME HERE! I WANNA TALK TO YOU!
FLASH! WHAT ARE YOU HIDIN' AROUND CORNERS FOR?

KEEP YOUR VOICE DOWN AND LISTEN, YOU NUT! HAVEN'T YOU MORE SENSE THAN TO GO AROUND YAPPIN' HOW YOU'RE GONNA BLOW THE WHISTLE ON THE BIG MAN? YOUR LIFE WON'T BE WORTH A NICKLE IF THE ENFORCERS FIND OUT!
THANKS FOR THE WARNING, FELLA! I DIDN'T KNOW YOU CARED!

BUT FLASH'S WARNING HAS COME TOO LATE! FOR NEWS TRAVELS FAST-- ESPECIALLY NEWS ABOUT THE BIG MAN...
SO! THAT KID PARKER KNOWS WHO THE BIG MAN IS, HUH? THE ENFORCERS OUGHTTA PAY PLENTY FOR THAT TIP!

AND, WITHIN MINUTES...
THAT'S RIGHT, BOSS! THIS KID PARKER IS TELLIN' EVERYONE HE KNOWS WHO YOU ARE! AND HE'S GOIN' TO THE POLICE WITH THE INFORMATION!
PETER PARKER? HOW DID HE FIND OUT?!
YOU MEAN YOU KNOW HIM, BOSS?

OF COURSE I KNOW HIM! DON'T STAND HERE ASKING FOOL QUESTIONS! GO GET HIM!

AND, AT POLICE HEADQUARTERS--
WE JUST GOT A CALL FROM SPIDER-MAN! SAYS WE SHOULD BE ON THE ALERT TONIGHT FOR A SIGNAL FROM HIM! HE'S GOING AFTER THE ENFORCERS!
BETTER ALERT ALL UNITS! THERE MUST BE SOMETHING COOKING!
POLIC

LATER, AS PETER WANDERS THROUGH THE LONELIEST PARTS OF THE CITY...
INTO THE CAR, BIG MOUTH! YOU'RE GOIN' FOR A LITTLE RIDE!
MY PLAN WORKED! I'VE JUST GOT TO HOPE THAT THEY TAKE ME TO THE BIG MAN BEFORE TRYING TO SILENCE ME!

SO YOU KNOW WHO THE BIG MAN IS, EH? WELL, WISE GUY--HE KNOWS YOU--AND HE WANTS TO HAVE A LITTLE VISIT WITH YOU!
THE BIG MAN KNOWS ME!! CAN IT BE THAT MY HUNCH WAS RIGHT--ABOUT J. JONAH JAMESON??

BUT IT CAN'T BE! I KNOW HE'S SELFISH-- STINGY--AND HOT-TEMPERED! HE'S JEALOUS OF SPIDER-MAN--AND OF ANYONE WHO'S MORE GLAMOROUS THAN HE IS! BUT WHY SHOULD HE TURN TO CRIME??
13

FINALLY, THE ENFORCERS' CAR REACHES A LARGE INDOOR AUTO PARKING BUILDING...
HERE WE ARE, BRIGHT EYES! NO HARM SHOWING YOU OUR HEAD-QUARTERS -- IT'S THE LAST THING YOU'RE EVER GONNA SEE!

INSIDE, JUNIOR-- UNTIL THE BIG MAN SENDS FOR YOU!
WELL, THIS IS WHAT I WANTED! I JUST HOPE I DIDN'T BITE OFF A LOT MORE THAN I CAN CHEW!

ALONE IN THE ROOM, PETER STRIPS OFF HIS OUTER CLOTHES, AND THEN...
PETER PARKER COULD NEVER REACH THAT AIR VENT IN THE CEILING -- BUT FOR SPIDER-MAN, IT'LL BE A BREEZE!

COME ON, SPIDER STRENGTH!! JUST A LITTLE MORE OOMPH NOW! AHH, I'M GETTING IT!

AND, JUST ON THE OTHER SIDE OF THE WALL...
ALL THE RACKET BOSSES IN THE CITY ARE HERE FOR THIS WEEK'S NEW ORDERS, BOSS!
GOOD! THE POLICE ARE BEGINNING TO CATCH TOO MANY OF OUR UNDERLINGS --SO I HAVE SOME PLANS FOR NEW PRECAUTIONS FOR US TO TAKE!

WOW! I'VE STUMBLED ONTO SOMETHING BIG! EVERY TOP MOBSTER IN THE CITY SEEMS TO BE DOWN THERE! TOO MANY FOR EVEN SPIDER-MAN TO HANDLE! I'D BETTER ALERT THE POLICE!

WHAT'S THE MATTER WITH ME! I WAS SO INTENT ON WHAT I SAW THAT I DIDN'T HEED THE SILENT TINGLE OF MY SPIDER SENSE!
BIG MAN! UP HERE--I JUST CAUGHT A SPY! SPIDER-MAN!

AFTER HIM-- ALL OF YOU! HE MUST NOT ESCAPE! GET HIM!
DON'T BE SUCH AN EAGER BEAVER, BIG MAN! I'M NOT GOIN' ANYWHERE!

NO NEED TO RUSH, BOYS! TAKE YOUR TIME! I'LL SEE THAT YOU ALL GET WHAT'S COMING TO YOU!
WHAM! SOK!
14

TOO MANY GATHERING AROUND ME! THEY'LL PULL ME DOWN BY SHEER WEIGHT OF NUMBERS!
I'M GETTING BORED, GROUP! HOW ABOUT A CHANGE OF SCENE! HERE WE GO!

SAY! I'VE ALWAYS WANTED TO DRIVE ONE OF THESE SPORTY JOBS!!
HOLD IT, BOYS! I'M MAKIN' THIS TRIP SOLO!
THUNK!
BOP!

ATTA BOY, OX! GRAB THE BUMPER! NOW LIFT! HIGHER-- GOOD!
THAT LITTLE MAN AIN'T GOIN' ANYWHERE IF I CAN HELP IT! NOBODY'S STRONGER THAN THE OX!
OH WELL-- I PREFER A FOUR-SPEED GEARBOX, ANYWAY!

NICE TRY, PLAYMATES! I'LL GIVE YOU AN "A" FOR EFFORT!
WISH I FELT AS CONFIDENT AS I'M TRYING TO SOUND! I'VE GOT TO FIND A WAY OUT OF THIS PLACE!

UH OH! THE BIG MAN'S TRYING TO SLOW ME DOWN BY ROLLING OIL DRUMS DOWN THE RAMP AT ME!
I STOPPED HIM FOR YOU, YOU CLUMSY OAFS! NOW GET HIM!

MUCH OBLIGED, BIG MAN! THESE DRUMS ARE JUST WHAT I NEEDED!
MY SPIDER ABILITY CAN KEEP ME BALANCED WELL ENOUGH TO "RIDE" ONE OF THEM RIGHT THRU YOUR BULLY BOYS!
15

YOUR OVERCONFIDENCE WILL BE YOUR UNDOING, SPIDER-MAN! LASSO HIM, MONTANA!
I HEAR YUH TALKIN', BOSS!
UH OH! I FORGOT ABOUT HIM!

I'VE GOT TO MOVE FAST! THIS OUGHTTA MAKE HIM DROP THAT LARIAT!
HE FLIPPED IN MID-AIR-- SHOVING THAT DRUM TOWARDS ME! IT'S GONNA HIT ME!

SO FAR, SO GOOD! BUT I'VE GOT TO USE MY WEB FLUID CAREFULLY! THEY'RE NOT GONNA STOP TO GIVE ME TIME TO RELOAD!
THWAP!

EACH OF YOU GRAB A TIRE! THROW IT!
WHEW! THEY DON'T LET UP FOR A SECOND!

GIVE ME THOSE TIRES! I'LL SHOW YA HOW TO STOP THAT LITTLE RUNT!

BUT EVEN THE POWERFUL OX IS THWARTED BY SPIDER-MAN'S AMAZING AGILITY!
MY REFLEXES HELP ME TO DODGE THESE THINGS WITH EASE! AND WHEN I CAN'T GET AROUND THEM, I CAN ALWAYS ZIP THRU 'EM!
16

PRETTY TRICKY, MASKED MAN! BUT NOW LET'S SEE HOW GOOD YOU ARE ON AN OILY, GREASED FLOOR!!

ACCORDING TO THE LATEST SUPER-HERO MANUAL, THE WELL-TRAINED COSTUMED CRIME FIGHTER TURNS EVERY OBSTACLE INTO AN ADVANTAGE! SEE WHAT I MEAN?
HE'S SLIDING ON THE FLOOR--LIKE AN ICE-SKATER! LOOK OUT!

YOU CAN'T DODGE US FOREVER!! RUSH 'IM FROM ALL SIDES, YOU GUYS!
HE'S RIGHT! I CAN'T DODGE THEM FOREVER! BUT I'M SURE GONNA GO DOWN TRYING!
WE'VE GOT HIM NOW!

YOU CHERUBS ARE MADE FOR EACH OTHER-- SO FAR BE IT FROM ME TO KEEP YOU APART!
WHUMP!

BUT, BEFORE SPIDER-MAN CAN REGAIN HIS FOOTING, THE FAST-MOVING FANCY DAN STRIKES AGAIN WITH A SKILLFUL JUDO ATTACK!
OOFF!
I FIGURE THEY WORE YOU DOWN ENOUGH! NOW I'LL FINISH YOU OFF!

A JUDO-TRAINED LITTLE MAN'S ALWAYS MORE THAN A MATCH FOR A GUY TWICE HIS SIZE! EVEN WHEN THE GUY IS SPIDER-MAN!
REMEMBER THOSE WORDS, LITTLE FRIEND! YOU'RE GONNA START REGRETTING THEM REAL SOON!
17

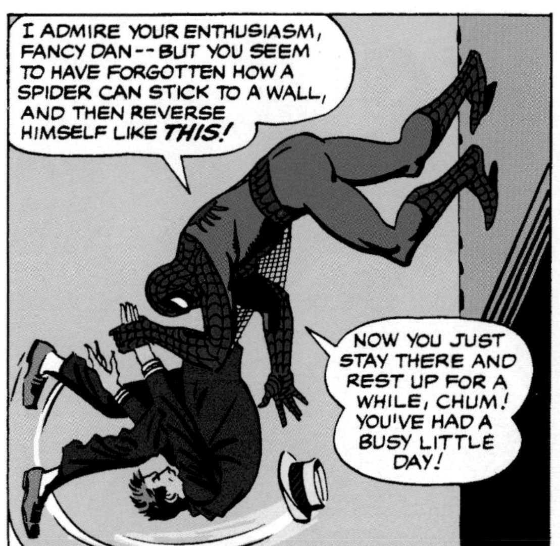
I ADMIRE YOUR ENTHUSIASM, FANCY DAN-- BUT YOU SEEM TO HAVE FORGOTTEN HOW A SPIDER CAN STICK TO A WALL, AND THEN REVERSE HIMSELF LIKE *THIS!*
NOW YOU JUST STAY THERE AND REST UP FOR A WHILE, CHUM! YOU'VE HAD A BUSY LITTLE DAY!

SAY! DON'T YOU GUYS EVER TAKE A LUNCH BREAK OR ANYTHING?? YOU'VE GOT ME WORKING OVERTIME!
MY HEART'S POUNDING LIKE A TRIP-HAMMER! I'VE *GOT* TO GET SOME REST SOON! IF ONLY I CAN THINK OF A WAY TO SIGNAL THE *POLICE!!*

THEN, AS HE SKILLFULLY KEEPS ONE STEP AHEAD OF HIS PURSUERS...
I'VE *GOT* IT! I'LL REMOVE MY SPIDER-LIGHT SIGNAL FROM MY BELT...

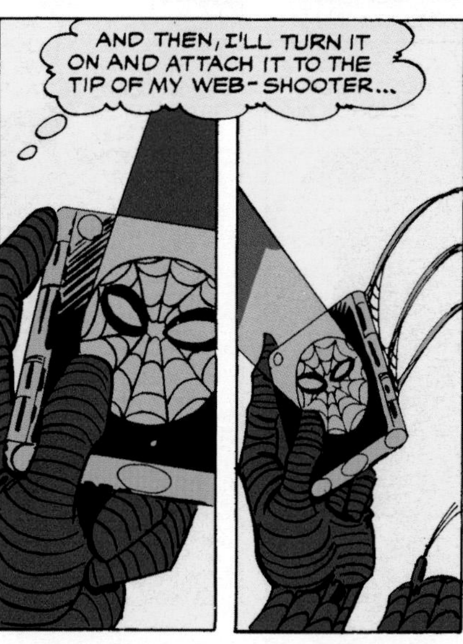
AND THEN, I'LL TURN IT ON AND ATTACH IT TO THE TIP OF MY WEB-SHOOTER...

AND AWAAAAAY WE GO!!

BULLS EYE!!

THE SPIDER SIGNAL!! I'VE GOT TO CALL HEADQUARTERS!!

THEN, WITHIN THIRTY SECONDS, THE SOUND OF BLARING SIRENS FILLS THE NIGHT AIR IN THE SLUMBERING CITY...
IT'S THE ACME GARAGE! GIVE 'ER THE GAS!
WHEEEEEEEEEEEE
POLICE
18

WHILE WITHIN THE STRUCTURE, THE FATEFUL BATTLE CONTINUES...
KEEP AFTER HIM! HE'S TIRING! HE'S ONLY HUMAN! YOU'RE WEARING HIM DOWN!
RELAX, BIG MAN--THEY'RE DOIN' OKAY WITHOUT A CHEER-LEADER!

BUT SUDDENLY, AN EAR-PIERCING WAIL IS HEARD FROM OUTSIDE...
WHEEE
THE POLICE!!
AND NOT A MINUTE TOO SOON!

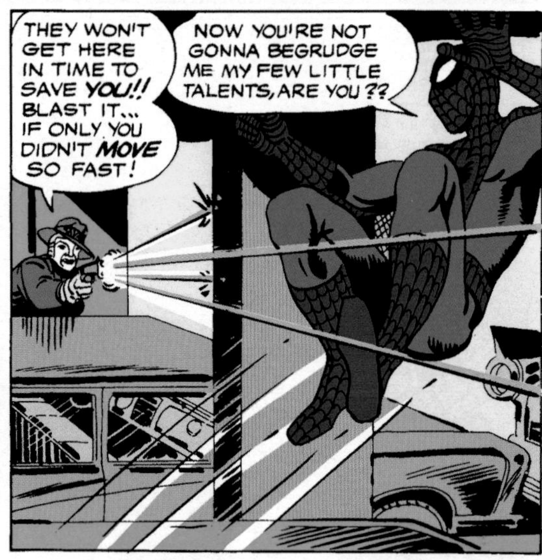
THEY WON'T GET HERE IN TIME TO SAVE YOU!! BLAST IT... IF ONLY YOU DIDN'T MOVE SO FAST!
NOW YOU'RE NOT GONNA BEGRUDGE ME MY FEW LITTLE TALENTS, ARE YOU??

OKAY NOW, BIG MAN... THE PARTY'S OVER!
I COUNTED THOSE SHOTS... AND YOUR GUN'S EMPTY! SO NOW IT'S MAN TO MAN!

SORRY, SPIDER-MAN! I DON'T FIGHT BY YOUR RULES! I KNOW WHEN TO MAKE MY EXIT!
19

NOW I KNOW I'M TIRED! ANY OTHER TIME I COULD HAVE CAUGHT HIM BEFORE HE GOT HALF-WAY TO THAT DOOR!
SLAM!

BOY, LEAVE IT TO THE POLICE! IT DOESN'T TAKE THEM LONG TO GO INTO ACTION! THEY'VE ROUNDED UP THE ENFORCERS, AND ALL THE OTHER HOODS!
TOO BAD THE BIG MAN SLIPPED THRU MY FINGERS! BUT MAYBE I CAN STILL TRACK HIM DOWN!

IF HE'S THE ONE I THINK HE IS--IT'S GONNA BE A REAL PLEASURE TO BRING HIM IN!!

A SHORT TIME LATER, A HARRASSED J. JONAH JAMESON RUSHES INTO THE DAILY BUGLE BUILDING...
WHAT A MISERABLE WEEK THIS HAS BEEN! EVERYTHING IS GOING WRONG!!

I STILL HAVEN'T BEEN ABLE TO DEFINITELY PROVE THAT SPIDER-MAN IS THE MASKED LEADER OF THE CITY'S CRIME SYNDICATE! BUT I'VE GOT TO! I'M TOO FAR OUT ON A LIMB TO TURN BACK!

LOOK HOW NERVOUS HE IS! I KNEW I WAS RIGHT! HE'S WORRIED SICK ABOUT HIS CRIME RING BEING BROKEN UP!

WELL, I'LL GIVE HIM STILL MORE TO WORRY ABOUT, AND--UH OH! SOMEONE'S COMING!
MR. JAMESON...
WHAT IS IT?

I'VE GOT THE PROOFS OF THE NEW COLUMN ABOUT SPIDER-MAN! THOUGHT YOU'D LIKE TO SEE IT!
TEAR IT UP!! I NEED MORE THAN A COLUMN NOW! I NEED PROOF THAT SPIDER-MAN IS THE BIG MAN!
20

WHY? WHAT'S HAPPENED?
YOU FOOL! HAVEN'T YOU HEARD THE RADIO NEWS BULLETINS?? THE ENFORCERS HAVE BEEN CAPTURED! THE CRIME SYNDICATE IS BROKEN UP! ONLY THE BIG MAN HAS ESCAPED! AND THE POLICE ARE APT TO FIND HIM BEFORE TOO LONG!
WE'VE FOUND HIM ALREADY, JAMESON!
HUH?

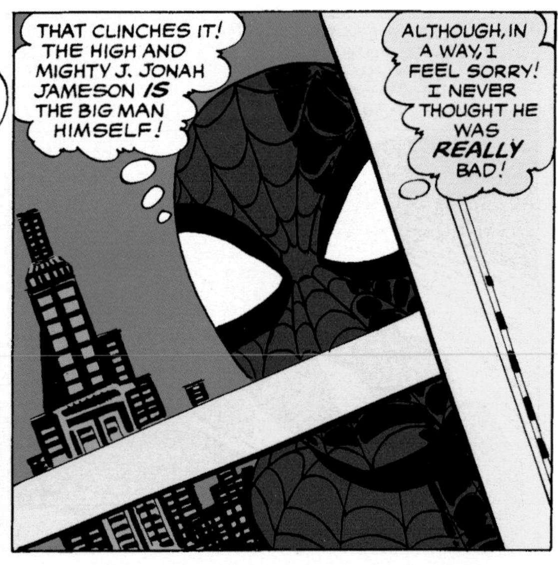
THAT CLINCHES IT! THE HIGH AND MIGHTY J. JONAH JAMESON IS THE BIG MAN HIMSELF!
ALTHOUGH, IN A WAY, I FEEL SORRY! I NEVER THOUGHT HE WAS REALLY BAD!

DON'T TRY TO SNEAK OUT OF HERE, FOSWELL! WE HAVE THE PLACE SURROUNDED! YOU MIGHT AS WELL COME ALONG PEACEFULLY!
FREDERICK FOSWELL?! BUT I THOUGHT IT WAS JONAH?? HOW CAN LITTLE FOSWELL BE THE BIG MAN?
FOSWELL?

WE FOUND ALL THE EVIDENCE WE NEEDED IN YOUR CAR, WHICH WE SAW SPEEDING AWAY FROM THE GARAGE!
PRETTY CLEVER, FOSWELL--USING SPECIAL BUILT-UP SHOES--AN OVER-SIZED PADDED JACKET, AND A SMALL AMPLIFIER TO DISGUISE YOUR VOICE!
I'D HAVE GOTTEN AWAY WITH IT, TOO... IF NOT FOR SOME CRUMMY LUCK!

HE ADMITS IT! IT IS FOSWELL! I NEVER EVEN SUSPECTED...
SOME BIG BRAIN I AM! I NOT ONLY HAVE THE PROPORTIONATE STRENGTH OF A SPIDER--I'M JUST ABOUT AS DUMB, TOO!

AS FOR J. JONAH JAMESON--THAT ESTIMABLE CITIZEN JUST NEVER GIVES UP!
EVEN THOUGH YOU'RE THE BIG MAN, SPIDER-MAN WAS IN LEAGUE WITH YOU, WASN'T HE? ADMIT IT! IF HE WASN'T, I'LL BE A LAUGHING-STOCK AGAIN!
BAH! I'LL WORRY ABOUT IT ALL THE WAY TO JAIL!
21

LATER, AFTER HIS OFFICE HAS EMPTIED OUT...
AM I ALWAYS TO BE THWARTED, EMBARRASSED, FRUSTRATED BY SPIDER-MAN??
I HATE THAT COSTUMED FREAK MORE THAN I'VE EVER HATED ANYONE BEFORE! I'LL NEVER BE CONTENTED WHILE HE'S FREE!

ALL MY LIFE I'VE BEEN INTERESTED IN ONLY ONE THING-- MAKING MONEY! AND YET, SPIDER-MAN RISKS HIS LIFE DAY AFTER DAY WITH NO THOUGHT OF REWARD! IF A MAN LIKE HIM IS GOOD--IS A HERO-- THEN WHAT AM I??
I CAN NEVER RESPECT MYSELF WHILE HE LIVES!

SPIDER-MAN REPRESENTS EVERYTHING THAT I'M NOT! HE'S BRAVE, POWERFUL AND UNSELFISH! THE TRUTH IS, I ENVY HIM! I, J. JONAH JAMESON--MILLIONAIRE, MAN OF THE WORLD, CIVIC LEADER--I'D GIVE EVERYTHING I OWN TO BE THE MAN THAT HE IS!
BUT I CAN NEVER CLIMB TO HIS LEVEL! SO ALL THAT REMAINS FOR ME IS--TO TRY TO TEAR HIM DOWN--BECAUSE, HEAVEN HELP ME--I'M JEALOUS OF HIM!

AND, AT THE OTHER SIDE OF TOWN, AS SPIDER-MAN REACHES HIS HOME...
HERE'S A LETTER FROM AUNT MAY! SHE'S HAVING A FINE TIME IN FLORIDA!
BUT NOTHING FROM BETTY! NOT EVEN A CARD!

WHAT IF SHE NEVER GETS IN TOUCH WITH ME?? IF I NEVER HEAR FROM HER AGAIN??
IT MAY BE WHAT SHE WANTS! PERHAPS SHE DOESN'T CARE FOR ME--AND SHE WANTS TO MAKE A CLEAN BREAK!

NO! I CAN'T BELIEVE IT! I WON'T! IT'S SOMETHING ELSE! SHE'S IN TROUBLE--WORRIED! IF ONLY I KNEW WHAT THE MATTER WAS! IF ONLY SHE'D LET ME HELP HER!!

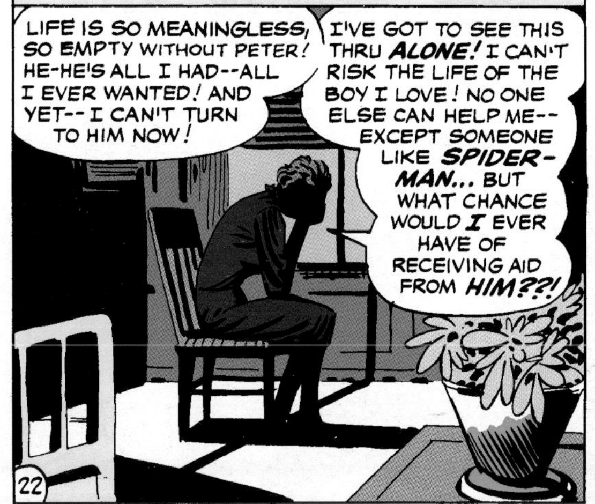
AT THAT MOMENT, IN A SMALL TOWN IN PENNSYLVANIA, BETTY BRANT SITS ALONE IN A LOCKED HOTEL ROOM, WEEPING SILENTLY TO HERSELF...
LIFE IS SO MEANINGLESS, SO EMPTY WITHOUT PETER! HE-HE'S ALL I HAD--ALL I EVER WANTED! AND YET-- I CAN'T TURN TO HIM NOW!
I'VE GOT TO SEE THIS THRU ALONE! I CAN'T RISK THE LIFE OF THE BOY I LOVE! NO ONE ELSE CAN HELP ME--EXCEPT SOMEONE LIKE SPIDER-MAN... BUT WHAT CHANCE WOULD I EVER HAVE OF RECEIVING AID FROM HIM??!
22

AND SO WE LEAVE OUR FRIENDS DANGLING IN A WEB FAR MORE POWERFUL THAN ANY WHICH SPIDER-MAN CAN WEAVE--THE MYSTERIOUS, DRAMATIC WEB OF FATE! NEXT ISSUE WE WILL MEET A GREAT NEW VILLAIN-- FIND MORE SPECTACULAR THRILLS--AS SPIDER-MAN DISCOVERS THE STRANGE SECRET OF BETTY BRANT!
THE END
...FOR NOW!

APPROVED BY THE COMICS CODE AUTHORITY
AMAZING FANTASY
12¢
MC
15
AUG.
INTRODUCING:
IN THIS EPIC, SURPRISE-FILLED ISSUE...
SPIDER-MAN!
THOUGH THE WORLD MAY MOCK PETER PARKER, THE TIMID TEEN-AGER...
...IT WILL SOON MARVEL AT THE AWESOME MIGHT OF... SPIDER-MAN!
ALSO IN THIS ISSUE:
AN IMPORTANT MESSAGE TO YOU, FROM THE EDITOR--ABOUT THE NEW AMAZING!